The SharePoint 2010 Handbook

A Collection of Short Chapters for Delivering Successful
SharePoint Projects

Paul Beck
Veronique Palmer
Jasper Oosterveld
Symon Garfield
Giles Hamson
Suzanne George
Rene Modery
Conrad Grobler
Ashraf Islam
John Stover
Justin Meadows
Mark Macrae
John Timney

Authors   Paul Beck, Veronique Palmer, Jasper Oosterveld, Symon Garfield, Giles

Hamson, Suzanne George, Rene Modery, Conrad Grobler, Ashraf Islam, John

Stover, Justin Meadows, Mark Macrae, John Timney

Title   The SharePoint 2010 Handbook

Copyright © 2011

paul.beck@sharepointsite.co.uk

Disclaimer – the book contains the views and opinions of the authors. Neither the authors nor the publisher accepts any liability for any direct or indirect losses arising from the use of information in this book. The information in this book is provided "as is" without any representations or warranties, express or implied. The authors make no representations or warranties in relation to the information or advice contained in this book.

ISBN-13: 978-1466486744

ISBN-10: 1466486740

Version 1.0

Foreword

Microsoft SharePoint 2010 is an extremely powerful software product with many applications, but few people really understand how to apply SharePoint to their business.

Although SharePoint has historically existed in the domain of big business, it has increasingly infiltrated organisations of all sizes. For example, SharePoint Online brings SharePoint to even the smallest of companies. Generally, large organisations are better at exploiting SharePoint's capabilities, since they can afford big project teams with many experts. Unfortunately, SME's and businesses new to SharePoint do not have such resources and therefore often do not realise the full value of SharePoint. Even in well-resourced businesses, the dissemination of information between experts and team members can be poor.

To address some of these issues, I have tried to put together a book that encourages the dissemination of expertise within the SharePoint community. The book aims to explain some of the key topics of SharePoint 2010 as well as to broaden the understanding of SharePoint so that its full business effectiveness might be better exploited. Each topic has been written as a separate chapter by different authors, each drawing on their own real world experience.

As editor, I personally discovered many invaluable tips from the contributing authors, which turned out to be of direct application to my own SharePoint projects. I hope you will derive the same benefits.

-    Paul Beck

Who should read this book

The book is aimed at a general SharePoint audience. It should be accessible by both technical and commercial people alike that are involved on SharePoint projects.

The book is not intended to be an implementation guide per se, but rather seeks to tackle some of the strategic issues that technical and business professionals face together.

The topics are sufficiently wide-ranging to give new users to SharePoint the confidence to avoid common hitches, while also complementing the knowledge of more experienced SharePoint consultants into areas outside of their field of expertise.

Acknowledgements

I would like to thank the authors of the book as well as Colin McGowan, Duncan Goodall, Desmond Russell, Michael Pretorius, Dave Coleman, Matthew Tucker Amardeep Bhogal and Ryan Barlow who provided valuable assistance in preparing this publication.

The following people acted as individual chapter editors:
Duncan Goodall - 3 chapters
Veronique Palmer
Giles Hamson
Mark Macrae
Justin Meadows
Matthew Tucker
Ashraf Islam
Paul Beck
Jasper Oosterveld
Rene Modery
Conrad Grobler

Contents

1.   Structuring a SharePoint 2010 Practice

Introduction

SharePoint 2010 is quite simply "nothing like SharePoint 2007"! It is vastly more scalable, significantly more complex, and hugely appealing as an information management hub. A consequence of the successful re-architecture of the product to such a strategic hub product and the core of the Microsoft tools strategy is that programmes and projects Employers and recruiters need to think carefully about the new range of planning roles and skill sets required to satisfy a successful "end-to-end" delivery of SharePoint 2010.

Demand and salaries for SharePoint 2010 Professionals across the board have increased dramatically as organisations perform a land grab on experienced staff. They have realised that those better placed will not only weather this skills storm but also grab a host of emerging new business opportunities.

Unfortunately, few recruiters understand the complexities of delivery and the demands SharePoint brings to staffing delivery programmes or emerging Practices. Typically, neither do internal Human Resource departments. One could argue that this problem is even evident in Microsoft literature as Technet and MSDN also have little information published on how to fill this void.

This chapter seeks to address that by explaining the range of roles and skill sets required to build a successful SharePoint 2010 Practice, to plan for internal career progression and assist with staff retention.

Getting your Terminology Correct

Understanding SharePoint 2010 does not necessarily mean that you understand the hierarchical grading of the staff that might be required to deliver it; or the relevant experience levels and profiles needed to cover service and strategy.

Most organisations understand that there are senior developers and developers, but few organisations classify or band that into a directly correlated grade. This correlation can help significantly in understanding the skill level and breadth of each individual in a Practice. This understanding can subsequently help with resource planning, training, career direction and critical staff retention. It is important that your staff understand their position, and understand what a career path might look like in your organisation.

It also helps a project planner to understand the cost difference between two members of staff with equal grades, but comparably different skill sets.

This does not seem important until you have a SharePoint project that is heavily dependent on specialist

SharePoint skills like Performance Point or Accessibility Compliance and suddenly you are paying twice as much for a comparable grade with specialist skills, directly affecting the profitability of your project.

There are two aspects of planning roles to be aware of which can be applied to staffing: S Grades and the concept of the "I" or "T Shaped" SharePoint professional. Understanding this creates for a stronger and more balanced SharePoint practice and more successful delivery projects.

S Grading

An "S Grade" is simply a means of identifying a Seniority Grade level, so an S3 for example would be someone fresh from university or training with little real world experience. An S8 would be someone who is very experienced and probably has quite a few years of IT behind them. They are likely to have worked on or led major programmes of work. The most appropriate career path would move an S3 through the S grades to S4, S5 etc. with deviations to their career normally driven by specialisms in the product stream. An example would be a gradual career move from a SharePoint Business Analyst to a SharePoint Information Architect.

You might ask why we do not start at S1 and what happens to the S1 and to S2 roles? Both of those roles should ideally be reserved for trainee or project office staff and while important to the practice or project are peripheral to the importance of getting the delivery stream organised and so are outside the consideration for direct practice roles, but you should not neglect them from project planning purposes.

You should bear in mind that the concept of S Grades may not apply to your organisation. Small Practices with few staff may not need this granularity of grading. It becomes more important as you begin to exploit the features of SharePoint 2010 Enterprise and your Practice grows in size.

I shaped and T Shaped Professionals

Not to be confused with S Grades, the "I" or "T Shaped" measuring stick is a way of calculating specific employee depth and breadth in a specific technology.

A developer for example would typically be very I shaped – deep skills with little breadth over and above the realm of development. They likely know the SharePoint API very well but have no idea how to manage a project and nor should they. Conversely, a Development Team Leader requires some degree of skills in people management and project planning and normally has code design skills commensurate with that role earned from experience. It is a narrower T shaped professional in that they have some breadth, not just depth. Thus, a Development Team leader may be T Shaped, and graded to S5 or S6 where the developer is I shaped and graded to S3 or S4.

Knowing how to meld the above two factors together allows you to not only assess the current skill and experience levels of staff in your practice or programme, but also helps you identify gaps and training opportunities. Add to this a need for appropriate security cleared personnel and you have an easy to use measuring stick on which to build a practice.

We look much more closely at the allocation of T/I Shapes and S Grades against specific roles later in the chapter.

Moving into the Enterprise Space

To understand the merits of planning roles for SharePoint 2010 staff you need to understand some of the background of the evolution of SharePoint as a product and the issues the industry has faced.

SharePoint 2007 was a relatively easy solution to deliver. There were only a few technical models to adopt and those projects trying to push the limit found some hard restrictions they had significant difficulty overcoming. The platform shape was "fairly" rigid and it was easy to size as there were hard limits that were very well publicised and sizing tools to assist. Historically, this led to most SharePoint 2007 projects delivered by group IT instead of delivered as an Enterprise level product set and owned by the business. Thus Enterprise level thinking around architecture and governance was (and sadly remains with 2010 projects), sorely lacking.

A consequence of that lack of holistic thinking was many failed projects; and many poor implementations mainly caused by project managers, architects and implementation staff without the correct experience; (thin T) levels and no Enterprise Architecture skills (short I). The much demanded "SharePoint Architect" was EVERYTHING in the 2007 world and his word was law; even though he typically had no experience in Service Management and/or Governance and was usually a very "I" Shaped person.

Microsoft has gone a considerable way in addressing many of those technical limitations with SharePoint 2010, specifically the issues of scale and redundancy, and now has many architectural patterns that we can exploit.

These advances have come at an architectural and governance cost to practices as 2010 is significantly more complex to design, implement and govern than its predecessor!

The Enterprise space for 2010 now includes design considerations around:

- Exploitation of the Service application
- Platform Devolvement across geographies
- Database mirroring and virtually unlimited database scale-out
- Huge scalability through devolved shared services such as FAST search
- Huge expansion of metadata use and social computing
- Significant Records Management capability

- Massive product integration potential, both Microsoft and third party
- Multi-tenanting
- Office online hosting opportunities
- Business Intelligence and Audit
- Service Management
- Adherence to Enterprise Frameworks

Far from an exhaustive list, much of what that listed above does not fall into the domain of the "typical" SharePoint Architect who deals with IT led projects, and instead stems right into the domain of the Enterprise Architect (EA) who deals with the concepts of Business Change and Enterprise Strategy. This is not something SharePoint can address, but it is something that is a *significant* risk to the success of any SharePoint project and as such is a concern for any SharePoint Practice.

The issue of Strategy and Clarity

If there is one thing SharePoint 2007 projects taught us, it is that many of them failed due to a lack of strategy, clarity and poor holistic thinking. Much of this comes down to the overuse of incorrect job titles and a poor understanding of skills breadth (S). Everyone wanted to be a "SharePoint Architect" or a "SharePoint Consultant", or even a "SharePoint Consultant Architect" and many people called themselves architect when they were developers (I) with a few projects behind them.

There is unfortunately still a huge skill-thinking gap evident across the industry, and specifically in recruitment but we are slowly beginning to see fewer job advertisements seeking a random "SharePoint Architect" who can write C# code, manipulate SQL server, create CAML and sweep floors. It is and continues to be an issue caused by a lack of understanding.

Any Architect doing development work is likely one of two things:

1. Being overpaid

2. Incorrectly titled

If you are paying any architect the market rates, they should not be writing code. They should be leading strategies, setting best practice, creating high or low level designs, generating business and responding to requests for new work.

Developers are a lot cheaper to employ, even at contract rate than an architect would be. If you are paying below market rates for an architect, you may not have an architect who can set strategy correctly. If the answer to everything is to write code, then you have a developer where you need an architect.

Professional Enterprise Architects should always seek guidance and push methods and practices from industrially recognised frameworks such as the Microsoft Operational Framework (MOF) as it sets common methods and benchmarks. Some additional frameworks we draw from are the Information Technology Infrastructure Library (ITIL) and The Open Group

Architecture Framework (TOGAF v9). The shifting nature of SharePoint 2010 from an IT or product-led implementation into one strongly driven by governance and strategy means your practice or delivery programme needs to be more in tune with these current frameworks, and so do your staff.

Frameworks help us understand what the SharePoint industry is lacking and set the grounding for a cohesive SharePoint maturity model. They describe approaches to governance, models for artefact management. More importantly, they describe clearly defined planning roles that can influence bottom line revenue and mitigate risk; for example, Account Manager, IT Policy Manager and Service Level Manager are in MOF.

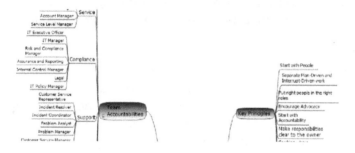

Figure 2 – Microsoft Operational Framework[1]

The ITIL Framework equally has clearly defined planning roles such as Capacity Managers, Operations Managers and Problem Managers.

---

[1]http://technet.microsoft.com/en-us/library/cc50604

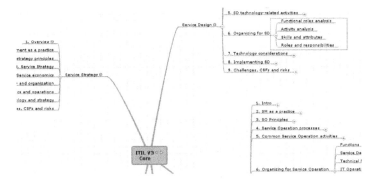

Figure 3 – ITIL v3.0 Mindmap[2]

TOGAF 9.0 is not only very clear on roles, it goes further by considering the requirements for those roles and on the difficulties caused by a lack of definition.

Roles	Architecture Board Member	Architecture Sponsor	Enterprise Architecture Manager	Enterprise Architecture Technology	Enterprise Architecture Data	Enterprise Architecture Applications	Enterprise Architecture Business	Program/ Project Manager	IT Designer
Generic Skills									
Leadership	4	4	4	3	3	3	3	4	1
Teamwork	3	3	4	4	4	4	4	4	2
Inter-personal	4	4	4	4	4	4	4	4	2
Oral Communications	3	3	4	4	4	4	4	4	2
Written Communications	3	3	4	4	4	4	4	3	3
Logical Analysis	2	2	4	4	4	4	4	3	3
Stakeholder Management	4	3	4	3	3	3	3	4	2
Risk Management	3	3	4	3	3	3	3	4	1

Figure 3 – TOGAF Enterprise Architecture Role and Skill Categories[3]

SharePoint is a product, it has no concept of planning roles and that is where we see difficulty. There is no definition and clear mapping of roles to skills - skills to

[2]http://www.mindmeister.com/5972018/itil-v3-core 9.aspx

[3]http://pubs.opengroup.org/architecture/togaf9-doc/arch/chap52.html "TOGAF is a registered trademark of The Open Group in the US and other countries." TOGAF® is best concisely described as an Open Group standard.

strategy - strategy to delivery. The industry needs more definition around planning roles for SharePoint 2010.

Definition will remain an issue until Practice Leads get better at this. There is such a shortage of resources, complimentary and diverse skills requirements within SharePoint 2010 and the changing enterprise that business finds it difficult to even identify the correct resources.

Reinforcing how valuable strategic frameworks can be to today's SharePoint professionals tends to be a lot wider than the product itself. TOGAF[4] recognises a major issue in the IT industry in that some of the terms used in our industry are poorly defined. For example "Enterprise Architecture" and "Enterprise Architect" are very widely used in industry but they are very poorly defined terms, as equally poorly defined as "SharePoint Architect" or "SharePoint Consultant", both of which are not granular enough roles for the 2010 world.

This issue is very evident in modern SharePoint recruitment drives. If the new roles required for your practice or project are ill defined, how can you plan your employee careers correctly, build a successful practice, or structure a project for delivery and be confident in those resource choices? You continue to run at risk, and risk is expensive. Best practice would always see us mitigate risk upfront but rarely is this seen in resource planning at practice level.

---

[4] Refer to TOGAF 9 Framework page 691

"People never have enough time to do work properly, but they always have enough time to do it over." (Patrick O'Beirne)[5]

However, this lack of definition in recruitment leads to some classic recruitment mistakes you need to learn how to avoid to ensure you are getting the best staff, into the correct strategic positions in the practice with enough clarity about the role they will perform.

Structuring the Perfect 2010 Job Advert

Below is a selection of real job adverts found in some of the leading job sites They are stripped of all identifiable references, but unfortunately still real!

The first shows some classic mistakes:

---

[5] Cross Reference ITIL V3 and MOF 4.0.
http://go.microsoft.com/fwlink/?LinkId=151991

Role: SharePoint Developer/ Architect
* Should have architected solutions based on SharePoint 2007
* Should be aware of most Microsoft technologies in a breadth fashion, and should have depth in at least two areas (for example, .Net 3.x, SQL Server, etc.)
* Should have 3 years of relevant experience in Architecting
Role Details
Architecture
* Should know how to approach SharePoint product fitment for a solution
* Should be aware of potential design considerations in SharePoint context
* Should have architected multiple enterprise class applications
* Should have knowledge of various architecture decisions, and non-functional requirement considerations, in general and specifically in the context of SharePoint
* Should have created architecture artifacts for engagements
* Will be responsible for architecting enterprise-class solutions, and for assessing architected solutions on SharePoint for Internet and Intranet scenarios
* Will be responsible for building architecture views and preparing solution architecture documents
Technology
* Should be aware of most Microsoft technologies in a breadth fashion, and should have depth in at least two areas (for example, .Net 3.x, SQL Server, etc.)
* Should know SharePoint capabilities and limitations well
* Must be aware of architectural paradigms and patterns and be able to apply them to definition and assessment exercises - should be aware of current architecture paradigms like SOA, S+S, etc.
SDLC
* Should be able to understand functional and non-functional requirements
* Should be able to estimate and validate efforts for proposed solutions on SharePoint
* Should be able to illustrate and document a solution architecture, and interact with the team to provide appropriate guidance
* Should be able to guide the team through development to Implementation
* Will be responsible for translating requirements to architecture
* Will be responsible for gathering non-functional requirements
Soft Skills
* High Integrity
* Status Reporting
* Team Management
* Problem solving skills and learning attitude
* Good communication, analytical and presentation skills
* Process oriented

The role is completely inappropriate and is a classic example of the "all encompassing" legacy "SharePoint Architect" problem.   Even   the   title   (SharePoint

Developer/ Architect) fails in describing what the company are seeking! They want a developer who can "architect" enterprise level solutions but no mention of any ability to integrate systems, and the range of "Should" skills need transferring to "Must". The correct role title would be better as "SharePoint Solutions Architect", or possibly "Development Team Leader". Consequently, it would have attracted the wrong candidates and the company would likely have ended up with systems that could not scale or integrate.

Title: **SharePoint Support Specialist**
Description: This is a phone support role. The support is from a user perspective. The right candidate will be able to solve problems for front end SharePoint users in 2007 (they are moving to 2010 soon).
Requirements: Requirements include: SharePoint 2007
Must be comfortable doing phone support

This role is entirely lacking in any real description of any actual responsibilities or depth of experience. It fails to request any 2010 skills even though it stipulates they are looking to step up the version. If you have ever staffed an IT helpdesk, you will understand that doing it well can be an art form! It is a major governance function and one of the critical places where SharePoint succeeds or fails in its ability to mature. Poor support sees end users lose faith and move away from the service. Millions of investment can be lost because the "Help Desk" has the wrong skill level, or a lack of proactive monitoring is apparent. The outcome is that user uptake drops resulting in a bad reputation for SharePoint.

Some recruiters however almost get it right:

Chief SharePoint Architect
Job Description:
* Provides overall guidance and direction to the evolution of the target platform
* Responsible for alignment of target platform design to support current and evolving business needs
* Responsible for reviewing and approving changes to the following
o Architecture
o Design guidelines
o Coding guidelines
o Information Architecture guidelines
o Migration guidelines
o New products/migration tools
o Infrastructure capacity changes
* Evangelize new capabilities for the platform as it evolves
* Regularly meet with key business/user representatives to understand key business needs
* Regularly meet with key product vendor/product managers (eg: SharePoint and Fast) to understand new releases, capabilities and align that with platform roadmap
* Regularly meet with Customer Architecture group to ensure alignment of platform to key architectural principles
* Regularly meet with Infrastructure leads to review infrastructure capacity and scalability needs

Person Specification:
* 12-15 years of experience as an Enterprise architect and evangelist
* Significant and deep knowledge of Portals, Collaboration, Content Management, Search, and Enterprise Security
* Significant experience with one or more leading ECM and Portal/Collaboration products, preferably on SharePoint
* Clear communication and consulting skills
* Experience working with various product vendors, technology leaders, evangelists, CTOs, infrastructure leaders
* Experience with prior responsibility to deliver tangible results in a senior or lead architect
* Excellent articulation and presentation skills

While the title (Chief SharePoint Architect) is not entirely relevant to SharePoint 2010's new more granular role demands, the context of the description is spot on for an Enterprise Architect who focuses on collaborative solutions. It has all the correct wording to match the skill level being sought (guidance, stakeholder representation, alignment of target platform design, capability evangelism etc.).

The lesson here is that it is critical that you correctly describe candidate descriptions and role expectations, especially if you are embracing the full potential of 2010 Enterprise. If the HR department and Practice Lead are struggling to do that, seek outside help. The return on investment of quickly finding the right staff and skills will offset the expense.

For employers:

- It helps you understand the role market, what are the competition seeking, it identifies trends in the market.
- Determine where T shape individuals are required when you have I shaped, and vice versa.
- It allows you to prepare clearer role descriptions, which attracts the right candidates and sets the correct salary expectations.
- It helps you establish career progression for your practice.
- It allows you to set clear goals and objectives for staff.
- It teaches you to handle agents better, and many of them are plain dishonest!
- The right staff will help you to grow your practice or govern over your 2010 investment.

For employees:

- Know your value within your business.
- Identify and pursue career paths within your organisation, rather than looking elsewhere for progression.
- Deliver on clearer goals and objectives.
- Know which jobs to chase to develop their careers to move from I to T, or vice versa!

Practice Roles

An easy way to think about structuring a Practice is to think of the areas of service we might work in and the skills matrix required.

- Strategy & Management
- Infrastructure
- Site Design
- Business Solutions
- Development
- Integration

By banding planning roles into a key role pillar, we can not only identify the roles and pillars necessary to structure our practice, we can ensure that the above skills matrix is entirely represented by our talent pool, coupled with ability to grow our practice or programme smoothly as market demands change and the measure of maturity[6] against 2010 increases.

We deliberately exclude direct sales roles and project office roles, both of which are a critical function of the practice but it is not a role we will factor into the delivery of the above service matrix against a direct SharePoint 2010 planning role.

Smaller practices or projects may merge roles if the demand for that role is not full time. Be careful not to allocate a role to an inappropriately skilled individual and *"hope"* they will do a good job.

The Six Pillars of a Practice

The rationale behind this pillar structuring and the granularity of the role breakdown requires the background of the previous sections, so please refer back should you need a reference point.

As the title describes planning roles within a practice can slot into one <u>and only one</u> of the Six Role Pillars:

Pillar 1: The Management Roles

These are the roles we might ultimately aim for in our SharePoint careers! They are the pinnacle of any Practice

---

[6]

http://amatterofdegree.typepad.com/a_matter_of_degree/2011/01/firstlookatsmmdata.html and for your staff occupying a planning role here could be an ultimate career objective or an aspiration for others.

Without management, there can be no strategy.

Pillar 2: Implementation Roles

Roles that build out the platform for us. They are a critical resource pool of diverse platform skills.

Without engineers and implementers, there can be no delivery.

Pillar 3: Support Roles

Roles that support the user community. They are a critical mix of administrative and personal skills.

Without support staff, there can be no service.

Pillar 4: Testing Roles

Roles ensuring we satisfy the requirement and deliver what we said we would! A move towards cost led agile projects is unfortunately seeing delivery getting sloppier with a noticeable lack of enterprise assurance in delivery so these roles are now critical to reduce programme risk.

Without testing, there can be no sign-off.

Pillar 5: Specialist Roles

The roles with skills we rarely require permanently. Cloud computing and remote or bespoke services are seeing a massively increased demand for specialist skills. Often this is a bought in skill.

Without specialist skills, there can be no consumption of essential services.

Pillar 6: Development Roles

These are the roles with the skills to code solutions for us. Creating webparts, WSP packages and manipulate the API!

Without developers, there can be no advanced augmentation.

All roles described in this chapter slot into only one of these pillars described above, and should never cross pillars, although you should expect staff to augment the S with new experience, broaden and deepen the T and move roles as they develop individually. You should therefore expect this selection of roles to be a starting point for refinement against your own practice, perhaps using it as a basis for correctly identifying planning role descriptions for recruitment. It must evolve with your organisation and change with each delivery programme, bringing roles on-board as the demand profile for skills and services changes and service maturity progresses.

Management Roles Pillar

SharePoint Programme Manager, SharePoint Design Authority, Enterprise Assurance and Strategy Consultant, Practice Lead.

This is the strongest pillar in your practice or project as it outlines and sets the strategies for success.

SharePoint Programme Manager

Role type: An essential and a rare senior consultancy skill

There will be some alignment to the Enterprise Assurance role but usually more able to plan in detail to align with business plans and business strategy for a multiple project and work stream perspective.

This role is active for the lifecycle of the programme. though often transitions back to an internal programme manager through cross skilling later. The Programme Manager works closely with the Design Authority to plan deliverables. He has I-Shape to T-Shape experience. The role relies upon the Design Authority and the Enterprise Assurance roles for technical steering. In a smaller business, we sometimes see this role performed by the Design Authority. It is one best devolved to a dedicated experienced resource, as it is not a technical role and can bog down the Design Authority with planning activity when they should focus on wider technical aspects. Other typical Programme manager skills apply (planning, finance etc.)

The planning S Grade would be S7, S8 or S9 depending on the complexity and size of the programme or project. Security Clearance is expected.

SharePoint Design Authority

Role type: An essential and a rare senior role strongly client focussed. The role often works alongside a Programme Manager or the clients Chief Information Officer. In the 2007 world, this is the role most akin to the more generic SharePoint Architect or perhaps Subject Matter Expert.

The Design Authority will be highly SharePoint literate on all versions, involved in the design workshops, coordinating all planning activities behind the server farm build, delivery and testing through to SharePoint service on boarding and solution delivery, any costing requests for additional work and post qualification questionnaire responses. The Design Authority should not be handling detailed low-level design elements but often does due to lack of SharePoint team resources or a misunderstanding of the scope of the role. They should never be installing or configuring software or writing code. A significant opportunity exists here to ensure good governance by ensuring this role exists in any practice for deployment to both programmes and projects. Do not mistake this for the legacy SharePoint Architect.

Deep T-Shape (product) experience is mandatory for this person and in today's climate it is a very difficult to find skill-set with experience! They work closely with both the

Assurance role and programme management. The role is indirectly involved or directly owns most aspects of the product implementation.

This role stays with the programme through the whole delivery lifecycle from concept to final sign-off! It is critical to have these skills in your practice.

The planning Grade would be at S8 or S9. Security Clearance is expected.

Enterprise Assurance & Strategy Architect

Role type: Essential but often mislabelled as "Chief Architect" when it is in fact now an Enterprise Architect role. Becoming a critical senior consultancy role as programmes grow in size and complexity, and thus inevitably drive forward business change, this is a very market scarce governance resource always working in the clients best interests.

The role has excellent knowledge and understanding of the strategy and evolution of SharePoint, its features and services, programme design, roadmap, narrative strategy, complementary product sets, best practises. They also have a fundamental understanding of logical SharePoint designs, information architecture and the business landscape for both 2007 and 2010. A key role in starting a deployment where no installation and configuration existed before, or assuring the implementation as an independent yet trusted external party. They will also be able to assist in integration strategies and international and global implementation and need to have a clear understanding of Virtualisation, Service Delivery, Disaster recovery (and Release Management as complimentary skill sets). This role is typically not a role involved in actual implementation and configuration but stays with the programme through the whole delivery lifecycle to assure design decisions and steer delivery.

Deep and broad T-Shape experience is required, with experience in more than one major sector such as telecoms, government or finance.

The role needs ITIL, TOGAF or MOF certification. A very difficult to find skill-set, more so in understanding the devolved architecture of 2010 which is mandatory! Works very closely with the design Authority roles and senior programme management and is indirectly involved in most aspects of the programme both client and project side!

Planning Grade: S8, S9 and Security Clearance or higher is a "must have" to best exploit this resource.

Practice Lead

Role type: Required but again often mistakenly occupied by someone entitled "SharePoint Architect" in many organisations.

Some SharePoint technical understanding coupled with strong business focused skills. They lead the team or practice of SharePoint Consultants. The Practice Lead has ownership of the SharePoint Practice including Project Management, Reporting, Resource and expertise Management, Practice growth, competency and training.

The role has a strong sales element, can talk limited architecture and usually leads on all bid responses with battlefield experience drawn from an earned background in Consulting or Project Management exposure in full lifecycle implementation, Presales and bid-support. Excellent communication skills are required for this coupled with strong business relationship development experience. Good networking skills are critical.

Planning Grade will be at S8, S9 and appropriate security clearance is a given.

Implementation Roles Pillar

Information Architect, Technical Architect, SharePoint Infrastructure Engineer, SharePoint Business Analyst, SharePoint Configuration Analyst, SharePoint Solutions Architect.

This pillar helps prop up the practice and has skills that the Management Pillar draws from to finalise designs, verify architecture and plan low-level design. It is to this pillar where we see the skills of the more traditional SharePoint Architect dispersed into granular roles better representing the enterprise nature of 2010:

Information Architect

Role type: An Essential role often ignored or side lined as an expensive luxury when in fact it is now critical to overall SharePoint success. This role helps establish policy for taxonomy, metadata, search, version control, archiving and data retention, logical information groupings, maps out information solutions into SharePoint and acts as a liaison point between the business and IT.

This role also manages interpretation of business integration requirements and assists in deciding where information best sits.   Often performed by the Design Authority historically the landscape for this role is changing to a very critical role in its own right with the adoption of 2010.

I to T-Shape depth of skill is required for this difficult to find and easy to sell skill-set but well suited to development of individuals and the most likely role for the majority of business related staff to adopt or for consultancy to pick up.

Planning Grade runs from S5, S6 to S7 and can be a specialised career path from S5 through S7. Security clearance would be typical.

Technical Architect

Role type: An essential role representing the designer and often the builder and configuration manager of the server farms dealing with IIS, SQL, SAN allocation, search configuration, operating system, patches and service packs, security, antivirus and backup restore services for SharePoint. This is not a Project Management role but may lead a team of engineers!

Very deep or growing I-Shape experience is required for this role. It is a very difficult to find skill-set and must be savvy enough to work closely with the Enterprise Assurance, Design Authority and Integration Engineer Roles.

Planning Grade is S6 and anyone above this grade assigned to this role should be diversifying their skills and adopting a wider remit. This is a critical, deep yet narrow skilled role. Security Clearance would be typical.

SharePoint Infrastructure Engineer

Role type: An essential role supplementing the technical architects of the practice, the person who actually builds the server farms and configures all necessary elements where the Technical Architect is consultative.

Deep I-Shape experience is required for what is a very hands-on role. It can be an expensive permanent resource as regular retraining is required (PowerShell skills for example are now mandatory) and therefore remains an intensely difficult to find skill-set!

The role works closely with the Assurance role and the Technical Architect and is a more critical role to 2010 implementations than it was to 2007 due to the diverse and devolved architecture and an increased need to for network, virtualisation and environment awareness!

Planning Grade should be S6 and grades assigned to this role should have extensive experience! Clearance or higher would be typical to cater for client side configuration work.

SharePoint Business Analyst

Role type: A highly desired role within a practice and one that carries a skilled understanding of the general SharePoint feature set but with business analysis skills to work with the business through workshops and focus groups to detail the requirements that will lead to eventual SharePoint solution delivery.

Primary activities would be to capture Business Requirements and act as a liaison with customers. To capture functional design requests and obtain sign-off with reference to non-functional requirements. To demonstrate solution during prototyping and customer demos.

This is fast becoming a critical role in all medium and large business driven SharePoint solutions. If the Business Analyst has extensive SharePoint Designer skills this role can often couple as a dual role of Business Analyst/Configuration Analyst but only if the individual has the correct experience. Typically they report to the Design Authority and the Development Team Lead collectively.

It is a difficult to find skill-set with any value of T, and planning Grade is through S4, S5 and S6 would provide a logical career planning route up to Solution Architect. Security clearance would be typical as client access to information is essential.

SharePoint Configuration Analyst

Role type: A highly desirable role often mistakenly disguised as a developer but in practice simply modifying existing web parts and other features of standard SharePoint services. It is often filled by the role of a highly skilled SharePoint administrator but they should have extensive SharePoint Designer skills and can often couple as a dual role of Business Analyst/Configuration Analyst if the individual has the correct experience.

The ability to translate business requirements into a functional solution and an ability to exploit and configure the SharePoint solution using the full range of office clients and browser tools is mandatory. They should be capable of creating, maintaining and reusing components in a service catalogue model (where applicable).

Previous experience in the following is essential: SharePoint 2007 (or SharePoint 2010) and SharePoint Designer, with web sites, workflow and InfoPath desirable.

An ability to work quickly and yet responsibly, choosing appropriate tools, within iterative/prototyping/SCRUM environments, self- contained environments, and shared Production services with growing I-Shaped experience.

Typically reports to the Design Authority and the Development Team Lead/Release Manager under a Change Approval Board.

Planning Grade would be S4, S5 to S6 and offers a specialised career path from S4 through S6 in this role! Given the data access requirements of this role, Security clearance would be typical.

SharePoint Solutions Architect

Role type: Highly Desirable based on a combined skill set taking the combined experience and skills of the Business Analyst and the SharePoint Configuration Analyst to create an individual that encompasses both roles under a somewhat parochial title, with a requirement to add to both skill-sets an ability to design team sites to meet business requirements.   This role is the natural progression for either the Business Analyst or SharePoint Configuration Analyst role as they gain significant experience in translating requirements into effective technical solutions delivered in SharePoint! It is by its very nature a strongly client facing role, as such specific business acumen, agreeing deadlines and deliverables and the ability to forge use cases, manage testing and understand elements of accessibility is a given.

Reporting directly to the Design Authority or to a sub-project manager to ensure consistency, the role is born from experience in the field. Works closely with the

Development Team Lead to manage the scope of work and subsequent deployments to agreed timelines.

Planning experience is essential as is the ability to manage the roles of SharePoint Configuration Analyst and Business Analyst!

It requires narrow-T shaped experience with deep I and a planning grade of S6 or S7. Offers a specialised career path only in S6 and S7 grades as the increase in business experience above this level implies anyone aiming for a higher S must diversify their career. Security clearance would be typical!

Support Roles Pillar

SharePoint Support Lead, SharePoint Administrator, SharePoint Database Analyst, Site Collection Administrator, SharePoint Trainer.

The pillar supports the user community. It has skills that the service needs to run and contains very granular roles that are not easily (and should not be) combined even in smaller organisations and practices. It is to this pillar where we see a breadth of ITIL services applied:

SharePoint Support Lead

Role Type: An essential role that is highly skilled in SharePoint technical management and the ITIL framework. They own the software implementation, configuration and release management acceptance, triage reporting, monitoring and service governance. It is a role often devolved to a senior administrator as a team leader role and occasionally devolved to client side staff. With the shortage of 2010 skills, this is difficult to find as an experienced skill-set but easily trained in through a training partner.

Moderate T shaped skill set with mandatory PowerShell skills and a planning grade of S6 to S7. It is not a role likely to be off-shored for government projects and suitable country specific clearance is typical.

SharePoint Administrator

Role Type: An essential and highly skilled SharePoint technical role looking after the software implementation and configuration once live, managing many elements of the day-to-day solution including site collection design and creation, feature management, search configuration etc.

They admin role is often used to cross train in house staff but that can be a mistake if not correctly targeted.

A senior administrator could be a SharePoint Support Team Leader and like the support lead role it can often be client side staff! It remains a very difficult to find experienced skill-set but easily trained in through a training partner. It should be a client side role or one devolved to support as soon as possible if delivered by a consultancy practice.

A small but rapidly expanding T shaped skill set with mandatory PowerShell skills! The growing technical depth as SharePoint is adopted demands more hands-on skill from this role directly correlated to the features employed. Thus, it is unique to each instance.

The planning grade can be S4, S5, S6, S7 and the role reports to the Support Lead. It can be a specialised career path from S4 through S7 as the experience level of the role alters and the assignment to it depends on the size of the project or programme requiring administrative support! It is not likely to be off-shored for government projects and appropriate geographical clearance would be typical.

SharePoint Database Analyst

Role type: Essential – not a general Database Analyst (DBA) role and many solutions now require dedicated DBA skills that have deep knowledge of the SharePoint database structure. They are the point of contact for SharePoint 2010 database designs.

The SharePoint DBA must be able to build and configure SQL 2005, SQL 2008 and later, and attach to SharePoint. Needs an in-depth and proven understanding of clustering and storage architecture mirroring options, log-shipping and Disaster Recovery options and be capable of performing due diligence on designs, assist in SharePoint Content database design and capacity planning, referring appropriately to the Security

Assessment, Disaster Recovery Planning and other non-functional requirements.

They must be capable of understanding the demands of SharePoint in relation to Disk IOP, SCSI and RAID setup, virtualisation concepts such as RDM and Thick Disk and best practice for LUN and DISK sizing and TEMP DB management.   The DBA is directly responsible for maintaining best practice in relation to SharePoint database configuration, maintenance plans, database monitoring and Integrity checking.

The role transitions into a production service role, they will be capable of responding to and resolving database related MOM and SCOM events, incidents and problems under   formalised   Change   Control,   hence   an understanding of formal Change Request processes and release procedures is essential, as is knowledge of ITIL.
The DBA is responsible for Database recovery from backup through to restoration of content services, pre-emptive preventative measures under control, evaluating risk assessments against any identification of business and application impact as a result of content database failure and upon restoration of service in line with defined SLA's.

They will work with the Enterprise Assurance and Test Manager to achieve SLA targets.

Planning Grade: S5, S6 could be a specialised career path from S4 through S6 depending on the complexity of the project, but most likely a strong S5, S6 position depending on the size of the project or programme and potentially shared responsibilities of this role residing within support. Security clearance would be typical.

Site Collection Administrator

Role type: Desired - Fast becoming a recognised role as we see organisation devolve management of their user community to team level. Often this is an internal role within the business or managed centrally by the SharePoint administrator.

There is opportunity to manage these positions from a support stance if you are providing resources or transition for a programme as part of your practice.

Shallow I shaped skills needed with strong customer facing skills and an ability to triage site collection access and structure issues.

Planning Grade is S5 or S6 if managing a small client support team.

SharePoint Trainers

Role type: Trainers need to be seen as an essential role for the business deployment of SharePoint, and therefore critical for any practice to have.

Trainers are the best way of succeeding in transforming the organisation, and so form an important part of program dynamics. The use of training staff must be part of a wider and pre-planned strategy and not an afterthought. As a practice, you need to build up your training staff depth of experience, as they are a useful on-sell skill.

Currently SharePoint Trainers with any in depth skills of SharePoint and a very good business understanding are extremely rare but there are specialist SharePoint Microsoft training partners in the meantime. This is a partnering opportunity to exploit while you grow your own internal skills.

Planning grade runs from S4 to S5. We see this climb to S6 if the role is purely a client side position and with good Internal Communications experience.

Testing Roles Pillar

SharePoint Test Manager, SharePoint Tester

This pillar supports the end-to-end delivery community. It has skills that the practice relies upon to prove legally that the programme of work did what it said it would do, to a state it agreed it would deliver, with a performance within acceptable tolerance. There are only two roles in this Pillar, but they are strong in their support of the Practice:

SharePoint Test Manager

Role Type: An Optional or Shared role within a Practice, but it is much more likely to be a dedicated role within a Programme. The role presumes an Independent Test function is required as part of the Delivery method or as a customer requirement, and that may not be the case, hence why the role may be optional or shared.

The Test Manager Defines the strategic approach to testing, including the overarching acceptance criteria, and approaches for manual and automated testing, as well as defining a regression test pack.

They define the testing cycles required for each release including specifying Functional and Non-Functional testing to be undertaken. This may include deciding whether Performance, Volumetric, Disaster Recovery, Accessibility, or Security testing are required. It may also include negotiating with the Customer over User Acceptance roles and test execution! Normally reporting into the Design Authority the Test Manager defines and approves test plans in accordance with deliverables.

They will work with the Configuration Manager and participate in Quality Gate Reviews, and Test scheduling with the Release Manager and Development Lead. They will define the programmes and tools used for testing, and ensure that they are within the strategic approved toolset, and at the right software versions.

When tied to a quality gate function, the Test Manager is responsible for ensuring that adequate and recorded developer testing has taken place prior to accepting releases into any Independent Testing environment.

Knowledge of the inner workings of SharePoint are less essential than an understanding of test metrics, how to match metrics to "Functional" and "Non-Functional Requirements" and valid test approaches for web based solutions.

Planning Grade is S6 and S7, so quite senior. This can be a specialised career path from S5 through S7 depending on the complexity of the project, but most likely a strong S6 position! Appropriate Security clearance is expected.

SharePoint Tester

Role type: An Essential role for Greenfield and Change programmes and reports directly to the Test Manager.

The Tester carries out the Functional, non-functional and security testing. They must be familiar with the full range of SharePoint Features and interaction with Client programmes for integration testing e.g. Office Client programmes (Word, Excel, PowerPoint, InfoPath, SharePoint Designer), Explorer views, Web browser(s), OOTB and Custom SharePoint Web Parts, Workflows, Versioning and Records Management.

The Tester has an ability to capture test evidence and record results including defects in all approved software and tools employed in the design. Experience of testing SharePoint is mandatory, as is an understanding of how to load test data against SharePoint to mimic Use Case inputs and outputs, and repeat the process as required.

Planning Grade is S5 or S6, with a deep and narrow T but could be a specialised career path from S4 through S6 depending on the complexity of the projects for the individual, but most likely a strong S5 position! It is an easy role to grow in the practice as it requires depth of experience. Security Clearance would be typical.

Specialist Roles Pillar

SharePoint Search Specialist, Accessibility Specialist, SharePoint Security Specialist, SharePoint Auditing Specialist, SharePoint Electronic Document and Records Management Specialist, SharePoint Integrator Specialist, SharePoint Release and Configuration Management Specialist, Workflow and Forms Specialist, Office 365 Consultant:

This pillar is not new to the 2010 world, but its eminence and importance in propping up any Practice should not be underestimated. The devolution of the Enterprise space to one of hosted service and devolved computing is seeing a significantly increased draw on specialist resources, and they tend to be an expensive commodity for any Practice to bear. This is the most fluid pillar in the Practice and carries the greatest range of roles.

SharePoint Search Specialist

Role type: Rapidly becoming essential for larger implementations and multi farm or international deployments, it is a very valuable Practice asset.

This specialist role works with the Information Architect, Enterprise Assurance and Technical Architect and other roles as well as the business and administrator to design, configure and establish strategy for the fundamental search engine solution.

With Fast in the 2010 version of SharePoint this role is become increasingly specialist for large organisations wishing to make great gains from their SharePoint search engines. This role is typically a temporary one and can transition to the SharePoint Administrator, so it is a good role for Practices to sell out temporarily.

It is currently a very difficult to find skill-set with a deeply technical skill set at the design level bordering on architecture!

Planning grade is S4, S5, S6 and S7 and is fast establishing itself a specialised career path from S4 through S7 as the experience level of the role alters the T Shape of the individual.

Accessibility Specialist

Role type: For larger implementations, multi farm deployments or international deployments this is an essential permanent Practice role. Local disability legislation is forcing an increase to the value of this role and a rapidly rising and unsatisfied demand for the skills base.

The role demands a thorough understanding of Web Content Accessibility Guidelines (WCAG), Web Accessibility Initiative (WAI) and Accessible Rich

Internet Applications (ARIA). The role works with specialist test agencies to own and define accessibility strategy and plan user acceptance testing in relation to SharePoint implementations.

It is likely that country specific legislation knowledge is necessary. For example:

- In the UK: a clear understanding of how to accomplish BS 8878 (British Standard for Digital Inclusion) is required - a mandatory aspect of the 2010 Disability Discrimination legislation.

- In France: knowledge of the R.G.A.A. (General Accessibility Referential for Administration) is required.

- In Germany: Knowledge of regulation on the creation of accessible information technology according to the Disability Discrimination Act is required.

Thus, the role demands a unique and evolving wide and deep T Shape. Do not underestimate its value as a highly lucrative Practice governance role.

Planning grade is S6, S7 to S8 and it can be a specialised career path from S6 through S7 as the T Shape changes depth. Local country security clearance is typical.

SharePoint Security Specialist

Role type: For larger implementations, multi farm deployments or international deployments this is an Optional permanent Practice role.

The push to Federation is seeing a rising demand for this role. Experience of Federated Identity Management (FIM), Security Assertion Mark-up Language (SAML), Token authentication and local government gateway access approaches, creation of Risk management accreditation document sets adds credibility and Practice value to this role, as does a deep or growing understanding of boundary security network architecture.

It is a very I shaped role and tends to carry country specific skills. It is an expensive role to keep on the books permanently.

Planning grade is S6, S7 or T8 and it could be a specialised career path from S6 through S7. Obviously local security clearance is a given.

SharePoint Auditing Specialist

Role type: For multi farm deployments or international deployments spanning more than one geographical region this is an Optional permanent Practice role, fast becoming Essential.

Currently a bought in skill the role specialises in local legal compliance and legal operations against the SharePoint stored data, reporting and ensuring critical data governance activities have occurred, like the destruction of data. It can be a shared role often combined with the client side role of Records Manager and implies a shallow to deep T shaped individual.

The role could involve recoverability testing and long term retention and storage strategies for SharePoint 2010 audit logs. As we see a growth in the uptake of SharePoint to encompass all things storage related, we will see the demand grow coupled with the emerging and strong need for e-discovery and reporting.

Planning grade should be S6, S7 or S8 and could be a specialised career path from S6 through S7. Local /regional clearance would be typical.

SharePoint Electronic Document and Records Management Specialist

Role type: For multi farm deployments or international deployments spanning more than one geographical region this is an Optional permanent Practice role, fast becoming Essential.

The Electronic Document and Records Management specialist role demands a deep understanding of E-Discovery, in-place and devolved Records Management approaches and architectures, establishing content routing opportunities, management and inheritance of content types and metadata, auditing processes, options and best practice, retention policies and how to apply them, and local compliance demands such Sarbanes Oxley, or The National Archives Compliance approaches

The role would involve recoverability testing and an ability to set and action long term retention and storage strategies for SharePoint 2010, Exchange 2010 and barcoded paper storage.

If coupled with the role of Auditing Specialist it also will consume that requisite skill set alongside the skills here.

Planning grade is S6, S7 or T8. It is a senior role policing the corporate records and information stores and offers a specialised career path from S6 through S7. As a Practice role it tends to be one that is lucratively sold out to clients and demands a broad brush T shape for any individual in this role.

SharePoint Integrator Specialist

Role type: Essential - this role is not currently recognised but often taken up by Partner companies providing integrated solutions or in house skilled staff for more dedicated Practices. They would be highly skilled SharePoint integration architects and would be handling SAP, PeopleSoft, Seibel and other platform integration projects interfacing with SharePoint.

This role may encompass some development skills as required. It can be off-shored to appropriately skilled teams or product specialists or picked up by the Infrastructure Engineer. It is typically a deep I shaped professional role.

Planning grade is S4, S5, S6 and S7 and could be a specialised career path from S4 through S7 as the experience level of the role and the assignment to it depends on the size of the project or programme requiring Integration support!

SharePoint Release and Configuration Manager

Role type: A highly essential role for all SharePoint programmes, therefore critical to a successful Practice.

The Configuration Manager defines the release strategy and supporting processes. They manage releases for a programme into and through the test environment(s) and through to Production. They are responsible for coordinating and ultimately approving the evaluation of releases with Development and Test leads, and with the client side and programme change board.

Working closely with Enterprise Assurance and delivery leads, the release manager will be expected to pick up Business and Technical issues and refer them back for review.

Currently a very difficult to find skill-set as there is no out-of the box all-encompassing release process that fits every SharePoint and 2010 project, so product experience and hands-on configuration management experience is critical to mould strategy for any programme and eventually hand this responsibility to support.

It tends not to be a full time project role, but always needs to be in any large programme. It is a very rare and potentially lucrative skill set for a deep I shaped professional.

Planning grade is S7! It can be a specialised career path from S6 up as the experience level of the role and the assignment to it depends on the size of the project or programme requiring configuration and release management approaches. It is a role born from experience in the field.

A lower level of security clearance would be typical.

Workflow and Forms Specialist

Role type: Rapidly emerging as an essential role skilled in asp.net forms, InfoPath forms design and creation and the design and application of workflow.

As such, it is a predominately deep I shaped role, usually wrapped with live implementation experience to add credibility!

The role must have a skilled knowledge of SharePoint from an integration and augmentation perspective. They need to understand the interactions with back end databases, and will often have associated skills in Visual Studio, Windows Workflow Foundation and/or Nintex/K2 or supporting third party tooling.

The role reports directly to the Development Team Lead but can equally report to a dedicated project manager if the design is heavily componentized! The role also works with the Enterprise Assurance as needed to strategies on small scale independent point solution.

Planning grade is S4, S5 to S6 and can be a specialised career path from S4 through S6 if the candidate is looking to deepen the I Shape and focus their career in this space!

Office 365 Consultant

Role type: Emerging Essential and currently a partnering management role with specialist suppliers that are emerging into the market.

Candidates must understand the market opportunities for selling 365 and Azure services and how to be successful as a BPOS or a 365 partner.

Critically, the role must understand the topology of 365 services for design (on premises, online, online dedicated, hybrid) and features of each, including continuity management! It is likely that the role holder understands quality standards such as ISO 27001, and has a grasp of cross geographical regulations, compliance and data privacy.

A very deep I shape understanding of BPOS/Office 365 software, services and licensing is required if preparing for dedicated practice roles. The skill set must be accompanied with a broad T shaped understanding of sales and marketing best practices with ability to articulate designs against the 365 roadmap.

This role can nicely fold into the Enterprise Assurance role but training is required and the role holder must pass the Microsoft Online Services Assessment!

Planning Grade would be around T7/T8 as a lot of Enterprise Architecture experience is required, thus a deep T.

Development Roles Pillar

Development Team Leader, SharePoint Developer, Specialist Application Architect, .NET Developer.

The last pillar to our Practice is the Development Pillar. It supports the delivery stream providing the augmentation to the service. As Practice roles, they are increasingly difficult to find as many developer opportunities were outsourced and the pay bracket dropped. This has resulted in a significant shortage of resource as people moved away from development coupled with a rising demand for developers, many of which are unfortunately very inexperienced in adopting patterns and best practices for 2010 and produce less than desirable code.

Development Team Leader

Role type: A highly desired management wrapper for SharePoint Developers, .NET developers, Configuration Management and Workflow Specialists.

The role promotes and enforces development best practice and acts as design authority for component implementation and package integration.

It is a difficult to find skill-set with real experience and the role works closely with the Technical architect, Design Authority and Enterprise Assurance roles.

They must be capable of client side consulting with man-management skills, even though it is a deeply I shaped skill set, with some complimentary T skills. They should understand traditional waterfall delivery mechanisms, and approaches based on Agile and Scrum.

Planning grade is a fairly low S5, S6 or perhaps S7 on very large programmes with significant customisations required but most Practice roles will be at the lower end of the S scale. It can be a specialised career path from S5 through S7 as the experience level of the role and the assignment to it depends on the size of the project or programmes development team and client interaction required.

SharePoint Developer

Role type: A very desired role for any Practice and should be a "well stocked" one. It is a widely advertised role but as varied as the day is long. Writing custom web parts, code and scripts for SharePoint to provide bespoke custom solutions for the SharePoint platform for bespoke business needs where out of the box services do not suffice.

The role reports directly to the Development Team Lead so management overhead is not an aspect of this role. Deep I shaped experience is required, but it can grow from small I so is a good Practice role to fill with novices, as long as the infrastructure is in place to bring them on and train them up well. It is not good practice to staff the development pillar with novices and hope they do well, so strong Development leadership is required if that's a strategy being adopted. Few T shaped skills are necessary for the role which means it has a narrow scope.

External development companies are also dedicated to writing custom SharePoint solutions, web parts and services so this role is often to integrate third party components.

Planning grade runs from S3, S4 to S5 and occasionally to S6 and offers a specialised career path from S3 through S6. It can be massively exploited with offshore skills if the Practice is setup to do this and is easily augmented with contract staff as demand shows!

Specialist Application Architect

Role type: A desired role, but not essential. Also, like the developer a widely advertised role but as varied as the day is long.

The role is typically involved in writing custom web parts, code and scripts for SharePoint to provide bespoke custom solutions for the SharePoint platform for niche bespoke application needs where out of the box services do not suffice. Specifically it is a role where SharePoint development skills need enhanced sector / product/ integration knowledge at the code level. The activities of the role can therefore be shared in the practice with the traditional SharePoint developer but the role is getting more and more sector specific with 2010 adoption.

Deep I shaped experience required, but can grow from small I. The role reports directly to the development Team Lead or to the Assurance and architecture roles given the sector specific skills!

Planning grade is S6 and can be well exploited with offshore skills!

.NET Developer

Role type: A non-essential role but again gaining in popularity for any Practice.

Like the Developer role it is a widely advertised role expected to write custom solutions using .NET often integrated into the SharePoint business solution.

This role is suitable for highly customised SharePoint environments. Often combined with C Sharp skills and other relevant skills!

It is not usually a role that occurs within a SharePoint development team as SharePoint specific skills are normally required however it can be a complimentary skill when integration is a core facet of the delivery or

PowerShell augmentation of the SharePoint administration activities is required.

This role is becoming more involved in build activities due to scripted installs and script based deployments and depending upon the placement in the Practice reports directly to the Development Team Leader but more likely report to the Technical Architect.

Deep I shaped experience is required and skilled individuals with advanced PowerShell are needed.

Planning grade S3, S4, S5 or S6 and can offer a specialised career path from S3 through S6 in the Practice. However, it can also be off-shored to cut costs!

Practice Hierarchy

If you were seeking a logical hierarchy to a SharePoint Practice it is a quite easy to identify the Pillar placement.

Management Hierarchy

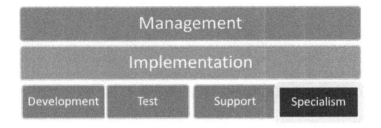

Figure 1 Practice Hierarchy

The Practice primarily draws from the Management Pillar Roles and they naturally sit at the top of the Practice, drawing from the Implementation Pillar for design and strategy reinforcement.

At the lower end of the Practice hierarchy are equally placed the Test, Development and Support Pillars which are not especially influential to the operation of the Practice.

Unusually it might seem the Specialist roles are also a low responsibility Pillar with little direct influence on the Practice unless it is a niche consultancy but given the transient nature of specialisms they should carry little managerial responsibility and do not directly influence the direction or management of the Practice.

Salary Hierarchy

When we flip this over to look at the cost of a Pillar to a Practice in relation how much individuals might cost:

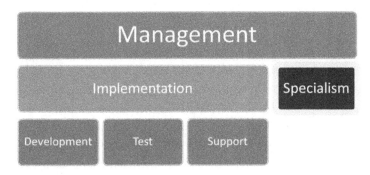

Figure 2 Salary Hierarchy

The specialism salaries tend to be higher, bordering or exceeding the cost of Implementation skills in the Practice.

The message from this of course is that the more your Practice seeks a niche, the more it needs to specialise and the more it will cost you to run your Practice.

This also directly correlates to Risk factors for your staff.

Risk Vs Reward

If, as an employee you did a salary analysis of the most lucrative planning roles then occupying a role in the Specialism Pillar is an attractive opportunity and at contract rates it could well outstrip the Management roles for salary. However, it is not a stepping stone to the

Management roles as a career route and specialising either as an individual or as a Practice carries a risk.

Just like being employed as a Bomb Disposal expert carries risk and might not be a good long term career choice, specialising in a 2010 specific activity as specialist career carries risk! Choosing third party workflow perhaps does not automatically imply that choice will give you career longevity as there is no guarantee that workflow as a specific feature of 2010 will be in the next version.

The same can be said for any niche practice as 2010 is an evolving beast, we do not know that a specific area of specialism will be there in the future. You are adding risk if you only focus on specialisms or niche add-ons to SharePoint but like everything else it's a balancing act. Specialism is always likely to earn more for the individual and for the Practice and you take the risk with the reward.

As a Practice, you need to be aware of the market and current geographical pay rates. Experienced staff continues to be in high demand. The grass is always greener on the other side if your Practice is not paying the correct rates. You can spend a small fortune getting a Practice established to see it stripped away and running at Risk because you didn't keep abreast of the market demand, and the rate curve.

Equally, a 2010 project can fail to deliver on time and within budget if it is not staffed by the right skills and experience levels so you need to balance that risk at every opportunity. Getting the correct planning roles into your Practice is one of those key opportunities and failing to realise it can cost your business dearly as you are not only risking the success of delivery, but the reputation of your Practice and the investment made in SharePoint 2010.

Summary

Hindsight gives us an excellent insight into the problems we might face in any SharePoint 2010 project. There are lessons to be a learned from the problems poor recruitment caused in SharePoint 2007 projects such as a lack of Enterprise level thinking. Knowing this can help us to identify and correctly staff a SharePoint 2010 Practice and not make the mistakes we have seen in the past repeat themselves.

As a Practice lead you need to be aware of the issues a lack of understanding around SharePoint 2010 planning roles can bring like a lack of holistic architecture and problems with staff retention. As a Practice employee you need to be aware of the opportunities that exist for you to advance your career.

The pillar model is an easy model for organising a SharePoint Practice. It is a model that encompasses the breadth of services across:

- Strategy
- Infrastructure
- Site Design
- Business Solutions
- Development
- Integration

The model helps your staff to know their responsibilities. It allows a Practice to evaluate the depth of skill required for any role required in delivering any project and the cost. The evaluation can help with planning gaps in individual skills portfolios. It helps with staff career progression and helps the Practice to identify and deal with resource shortfalls quickly, reducing risk and easing pressure on delivery.

SharePoint 2010 uptake has been dramatic. This has caused a significant draw on market availability of resources and Human Resources and recruitment are struggling to satisfy an increasing demand curve often caused by a poor understanding of the requirements for each role. Outside guidance is often a good way to address this in the short term.

Using the S Grading system (while entirely optional) allows you to grow staff into roles where shortfalls are occurring. It can help to identify where in your organisation planning roles can be merged, and where they need to be diversified. It can help you give breadth to the T Shape and depth to the I Shaped individual.

We simply have to get better at defining SharePoint planning roles and better understanding where to draw the correct skills from if we plan to reduce risks and grow as a Practice. If not, we will miss the business opportunities in exploiting what this fantastic product offers.

2.   SharePoint Test Environments

Introduction

Test environments for most information technology professionals are a no-brainer -- major system changes should be tested once, twice, even three times to provide the best possible experience to end users with little to no interruption in service. Recent virtualization technologies have made this easier than ever; one only needs to spin-up a new instance of a virtual machine and off they go with an entire SharePoint environment at their disposal.

SharePoint administrators will painfully learn, however, that this testing model does not adapt well to the componentized structure underlying a well-built SharePoint system. In this chapter we will review a few SharePoint system fundamentals, basic testing guidelines, and explore the case for building and maintaining a fully scaled test environment that is architecturally similar to an organization's production environment. We will also discuss the justification for why an organization might choose to build more than one test environment.

Using one or more fully-scaled test environments is the only way to understand the implications of a major system change. These environments also provide a mechanism for rehearsing system changes. With such a tool at their disposal, SharePoint administrators can maintain and administer their systems with confidence.

The Real SharePoint Administrator

Unless you are one of the lucky few, SharePoint is not the only enterprise system you are responsible for administering. This is good in some respects, and overwhelming in others.

For those fortunate enough to eat, sleep, and breathe SharePoint without concern for external systems, the reality is that you are most likely overwhelmed with the volume of support tasks that necessitated your single focus in the first place.

If one or more of your other responsibilities happens to be administering Active Directory, Exchange, or SQL, you're in luck when it comes to getting your new SharePoint farm up and running. There will be fewer meetings, less conflict over external system changes (i.e., delegation in Active Directory or SMTP Connectors in Exchange), and you can forgo the accusation of thinking in a "SharePoint bubble" in regards to organizational planning. Being the master of many domains has its drawbacks too. Your time and attention is in demand and build and implementation of your SharePoint farm is rarely going to occupy top priority status on your extensive list of deliverables.

The bottom line is: a real SharePoint administrator will rarely implement a perfect system. Whether it is project planning, infrastructure design and build, system architecture design and build, implementation, education and training, maintenance, or support, chances are that you are going to miss something! This means that at some point you will have to implement major system changes to fix an issue, repair an oversight, or implement a workaround for an unforeseen requirement.

If your SharePoint environment hosts custom or developed solutions (functionality that is not available out-of-the-box), your environment is more complex and perhaps even a little less stable. If you're the farm administrator and the developer, development is one more diversion from the plethora of administrative tasks that demand your time and attention. If you're simply an administrator that outsources development (internally or externally), you are at an even greater risk for problems and issues due to the inherit knowledge gap between understanding all the moving parts of your SharePoint farm and understanding which of those parts are affected by the developed solution(s).

Defining the realistic expectations and responsibilities of the *real SharePoint Administrator* is critical to making the case for not just a test environment, but also a test environment that simulates all the complexity of your production environment. Moreover, the real SharePoint administrator can continue to perform in a multi-threaded capacity (as will be organizationally expected) with reasonable assurance that major and minor system changes have been vetted to the best of the administrator's ability.

Understanding Your Environment's Architecture

I have already mentioned or made indirect reference to the complexity of a typical SharePoint environment. This complexity is a major contributor to the power and flexibility that SharePoint affords today's modern small business or enterprise.

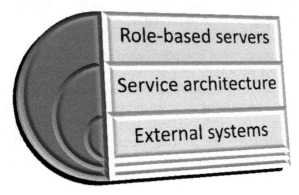

Figure 1 – Layers of complexity in a SharePoint farm

The architecture behind SharePoint itself is the first layer of complexity. The typical farm is likely to consist of various role-based servers: web front-ends that serve up content and respond to HTTP requests; application servers that perform the background jobs and tasks like user profile synchronization and search crawling and indexing; and SQL servers that house all of the databases that power the farm.

The second layer of complexity is less infrastructure-dependent and more of a logical arrangement of farm tasks and responsibilities. Again, it is worth stating that this very feature is what makes SharePoint 2010 not just powerful and flexible, but highly scalable. In this layer an administrator can, for example, designate that the web front ends have no application role whatsoever while the application server(s) host (or sub-divide) major system components such as user profile synchronization, search, business intelligence, or even Central Administration.

The third and final layer of complexity related to our discussion is external systems. SharePoint is most valuable to an organization because it can "reach out" and not only exploit the functionality of other systems, but pull back their data for further analysis or integration with other data sets. Some examples of external systems are Active Directory, Exchange, SQL (or other DBMSs), Project Server, and other business applications.

For an administrator to truly understand these three layers for a given SharePoint farm, the best tool at your disposal is a system diagram. Take the time to map out your system and translate it into a document that can serve not only your testing needs, but will be invaluable in discussing the environment with colleagues, internal or external teams, and leadership – not to mention its utility in a disaster recovery scenario.

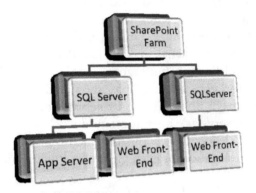

Figure 2 – Example system diagram

With a system diagram in-hand, building a production environment to match an existing test environment, or building one or more test environments to match production is less intimidating and much easier to accomplish. You should have a system diagram for each of your environments. A useful system diagram will contain the most important information to help you make quick decisions and easily determine the difference between environments.

Name and description of role-based servers

A thorough administrator might include infrastructure details such as whether the server is physical or virtualized, IP addressing, available memory and disk, etc.

Relationships

Is the SQL layer clustered? Are the web front-end servers network load balanced? Make sure the diagram communicates the relationships of the various servers in order to quickly determine bottlenecks or points of failure.

Services

Some services can run on more than one server while others retain affinity for a single server; make sure this is apparent in your diagram.

In order for these diagrams to serve their purpose, you must be sure to keep them up to date. The real SharePoint administrator has too much going on to remember that they moved the User Profile Service in the test environment yesterday to the second application server. It is probably best to incorporate the maintenance of these diagrams into your existing change control process. Then when you're testing new feature X in the test environment and issue Y comes up in production, you can quickly determine that the issue doesn't reproduce in the test environment because of your varying architecture.

Your time is valuable and understanding all of your environments' architecture is invaluable for day-to-day decision-making and hands-on build, maintenance, and support. Well maintained system diagrams will help build this understanding and provide vital information when testing.

Understanding Your Internal Level of Support

The level of support that you will maintain for your end users should really be part of your project planning for building out the SharePoint farm. However, being new to SharePoint altogether may leave you in a similar predicament in which I found myself with my team: a lack of understanding of what SharePoint can do translates into a doomed attempt to support everything.

Unless you have a fully staffed SharePoint team with unlimited resources and capital, supporting everything that SharePoint has to offer is unrealistic and impossible. While a formal service level agreement (SLA) may not be in order for your internal customers (your end users) as part of standard operating procedures, you're going to need its informal equivalent in order to properly test your system changes.

For example, many organizations may choose not to implement the social features included with SharePoint (MySites) as part of the initial roll-out. If you decide to reengineer the User Profile Service in such a farm, you won't need to worry about testing whether or not MySites might be affected.

Likewise, the assortment of site templates may prove overwhelming from not only a support perspective, but from your novice end users' point of view as well. If you deactivate the SharePoint Server Publishing Infrastructure feature for a site collection in which you've previously restricted the available site templates, not testing the scenario in which a new site is created means that you'll miss the fact that the restrictions are no longer in place.

Defining and understanding your internal level of support will help you to develop your use cases and any related testing to ensure those use cases are unaffected. It will also mean the difference between supporting a basic list versus supporting the unwieldy Assets Web Database that piqued a user's interest when it showed up spontaneously in their list of site templates.

Developing Testing "Scripts"

It is likely that the agile SharePoint administrator has an arsenal of scripts at their disposal for administering their SharePoint farm. However it is not these types of "scripts" to which I am referring.

A testing "script" in our discussion is more like a movie script that's handed to an actor. A good movie script will give the actor context for the emotion that they're expected to portray, cues for their physical placement, and text for their spoken lines.

A good testing script will give an administrator a quick rundown of what steps to perform in a test environment to make sure that the system is working correctly post-changes. The script may also serve as documentation that a particular system change is ready for production (should no issues present during testing).

A well-maintained testing script will be amended to include issues to look out for, expected behaviour, and perhaps even references to documentation that show what was done to fix a particular issue the last time.

To develop the ideal script, you must have an understanding of your environment's architecture and what level of support must be maintained for your users (see the previous two sections). As explained in earlier sections, your first test script is going to be neither perfect nor comprehensive. This is okay, as it will only get better as long as you commit to using the script when making changes to your system and updating the script based on your experience and expanding knowledge of the system.

Make sure that your script is detailed enough to be handed-off to an intern (wouldn't that be nice); describes expected behaviour; and includes clear markings to record pass/fail status. You'll also need to defend this script from your "good intentions". Don't let it fill up with useless activities or complex scenarios that will only impact a minority of your user population (unless that minority is high profile). If you're testing script is taking up so much of your time that you're avoiding or skipping it when implementing changes, it's time for you to re-work it and weed out the unnecessary clutter.

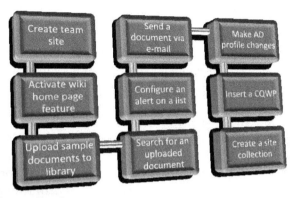

Figure 3 – An example testing script.

Your testing script should not include steps for testing the actual change that you're making but it should include the ability to record these steps and outcomes. The script should be able to be used for *any* system change and you shouldn't need to skip any portions of the script because they don't apply to the particular change scenario. If it doesn't apply, it probably shouldn't be part of the script.

A good testing script will uncover the disruption of a major functionality that is critical to your internal level of support. It's not going to reveal the weird stuff that only happens when the cow jumps over the moon, but it will save you from the embarrassment of not realizing that search has stopped working altogether.

Performing Testing in a Separate Environment

As mentioned in the introduction of this chapter, this should be a no-brainer for today's information technology professional. That being said, it's probably not uncommon for the *real SharePoint administrator* to attempt what they perceive as a minor system change in a production environment.

To be clear, **all system changes – major and minor – should be performed in a *separate* test environment**.

The script described in the previous section is useless in a production environment since by the time you finish testing everything your users are probably already calling and e-mailing so they can report the disruption in service.

In addition, some changes affect or involve the external systems mentioned in the *Understanding Your Environment's Architecture* section. Testing a change to SQL, Exchange, or a similar external system in your production environment can result in disaster. Isolating your first pass at changes to a non-production environment is the only way to ensure system stability, sustain end user confidence, and maintain your ability to be an effective administrator.

Fully Scaled and Contained Test Environments

Simulating the logical architecture of your SharePoint environment isn't going to be enough. If you are convinced (and I hope you are) that testing changes to your farm is an important and critical component of its administration, you must follow that to its logical conclusion. Take a look at your system diagrams and you'll begin to understand why.

The ideal test environment should be almost identical to your production environment. You'll have to make concessions due to cost and capacity (this is a test environment after all), but you should pursue as much of those resources as is feasible in your organization. After reading this chapter you should be able to present a rational argument to support and justify the additional expense and ongoing overhead.

With regards to SharePoint, if your production environment consists of a basic role-based architecture – a web front-end, an application server, and a SQL server – you should have the same three distinct servers in your test environment. You can extrapolate this to whatever complex arrangement of servers that you can build. The bottom line is: **the test environment should be as fully scaled as the production environment**.

Ideally, this environment should be contained in an entirely separate logical "container". In my experience, this means that I have an entire test domain of which my test farm is a member. This isolates my testing and changes **completely** from production. You can extend this same logic to Exchange or other external systems, however, this may pose more of an organizational and cultural challenge than you wish to take on.

A Lesson Learned

In the early stages of the small SharePoint farm that I administer, my team and I proudly sought the necessary licensing and infrastructure for our "test system" from our leadership. We were proud because we understood that SharePoint was complex enough for us to try things out somewhere other than production before introducing the changes to our users.

This test system was actually a standalone SharePoint farm whereas our production environment was semi-role-based (web front-ends, application server, and a SQL cluster). Things went great for a while as we rolled-out SharePoint to our users and we even tested some major changes.

But one particular thing kept nagging at us, whenever we took down one of our two web front-end servers in production, the whole farm would go down. We had no way of testing or even rehearsing system changes to our production environment and seeing the impact of these changes because there was only one server in the test environment. To make matters worse, troubleshooting by taking down servers and watching event and ULS logs was out of the question because it was production. After a few months and help from several teams, we finally pinpointed the issue to a known network load balancing limitation for virtualized servers.

The lesson learned is that had we maintained a fully scaled test environment (as opposed to a standalone farm) we could have quickly tested, diagnosed, and resolved the issue. A standalone farm will never reveal network load balancing issues nor will it allow an administrator to test or diagnose issues that arise via complications in a service architecture that consists of services appropriated to one or more servers.

If you can make a fully scaled and contained test environment a reality for your organization, great. If not, do the best you can and test carefully.

Maintaining Two or More Environments

Building out and using one test environment may not be adequate depending on the criticality of your SharePoint farm and the extent to which you are deploying custom and developed solutions. A solution under development may need to be built in one environment, certified in a second environment, and then implemented in the production environment.

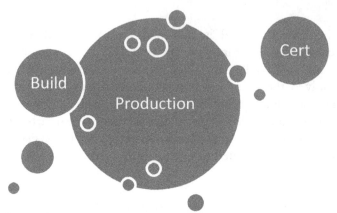

Figure 4 – Isolated test environments.

In the section *Understanding Your Environment's Architecture* I described the importance of developing and maintaining system diagrams. These diagrams are going to be critical when maintaining two or more environments.

The subject of change control is too complex and out of scope for this chapter, but there are plenty of resources out there that you can discover with little effort. A sound change control process is key to successfully maintaining two or more test environments.

No matter what process or methodology you choose, you must maintain these environments. Any deviations in patching, configuration, or architecture limit the effectiveness and accuracy of your testing. You'll need to make the maintenance of your environments as important as any other component of your farm administration duties.

Testing Major and Minor System Changes

Throughout this chapter I've repeatedly stated that all major and minor system changes should be tested in a test environment. This being said, you are an information technology professional and you are going to have to make some judgment calls about what needs to be tested and what does not. Customizing a list setting for a user does not warrant an all-hands-on-deck approach to testing like the addition of a SQL alias might.

A good rule of thumb in SharePoint is to analyze who is affected by the change (major or minor). If the proposed changes will affect a majority of users (51%), then it should probably be tested. If the proposed changes will cross site or site collection boundaries, then it should probably be tested.

Another rule of thumb is to analyze the potential that a change has to do harm to SharePoint or external systems. If the proposed changes involve any automation as part of the implementation, they should be tested. PowerShell is a very powerful tool and this power warrants caution and respect. Bad PowerShell code that wipes out all the sites in a site collection is acceptable in a test environment but detrimental in a production environment.

Anything that you don't understand should be done in a test environment first. The majority of us are learning as we go – SharePoint is too complex for any one person to be the end all be all expert. If you don't understand the change you're making you should probably test it out first. This is especially important for administrators like myself that rely on Internet searches or SharePoint community forums for support and solutions.

Another no-brainer candidate for testing are Microsoft patches. Most of us are all too familiar with this monthly ritual and they are no exception to our major/minor testing policy. They're also another justification for a fully scaled and contained testing environment (a SQL patch on a server with SQL express installed may impact the system differently than the corresponding patch for your clustered SQL servers).

We have established that testing is important, so don't render your test system useless by not using it. When in doubt, test it. The worst that can happen when testing properly is that you spend a little more time than you might have preferred on a system change. The worst that can happen should you not test, however, is that you disrupt the ability of many others in your organization to fulfil their roles and responsibilities.

Summary

The real SharePoint administrator is too busy, too overloaded, and too valuable to expend unnecessary energy, time, and resources on matters that could have been avoided. In addition, the SharePoint environment is too complex for any single administrator to understand the outcome of a change in two different environments with dissimilar infrastructure and architecture.

Through proper analysis and understanding of the architecture of all environments and the internal level of support that is expected from the SharePoint administrator, a basic testing script can be developed that offers a defense service disruptions that might otherwise go undetected during major system changes.

This script should be used in a separate test environment to surface issues or problems before the same changes are made in production. This has many benefits, not the least of which is the maintenance of confidence in the system on behalf of the user and the elimination of crisis management on behalf of the system administrator.

It is important that the test system(s) be as fully scaled as possible and as contained as possible. This can be accomplished by replicating the server infrastructure as well as ensuring that the external systems have similar testing counterparts so as not to disrupt service in systems other than SharePoint as part of testing. In addition to scale and boundaries, the various environments must be as consistent as possible since to do otherwise would be to invalidate the entire effort.

Major and minor system changes should be tested in a separate test environment and proper professional judgment should be exercised when deciding what should and should not be tested. It is better to have tested and found no issues than to have not tested and experience major issues.

3.   SharePoint Adoption

Introduction

There is a common misconception that merely installing SharePoint makes for a successful implementation. The true measure of success is how widely and effectively people in the company adopt the solution. Are they *actively* creating content? Have you asked yourself how you will get the business to use the service?

Anyone can cope when there is only one table booked in a restaurant; but what happens when you are booked to capacity with a waiting list - are you geared to cope with that demand. What if you get no bookings at all? Could you explain to your investors why no-one is visiting?

SharePoint user adoption is about how to get to a full house, how to be prepared for the rush, and how to manage it once it happens.

People will not 'magically' adopt SharePoint, there are measures you need to put into place to ensure that happens. Do this correctly and you will have a very high adoption rate; and consequently good return on investment for the capital outlay of the infrastructure.

This chapter is for anyone responsible for a SharePoint implementation, whether in business or IT.

So what's the problem?

Let's say you wanted to own a restaurant. You've decided there is a gap in the market for decent food in your town and you have found the answer. How do you go about this? Do you just open the classifieds, find the first restaurant you see on the market, pick up the phone and buy it? Unlikely.

It is feasible to assume one would first decide what type of food you would sell to fill that gap, look at locations, spend a lot of time evaluating different options, plan your budget, plan for staff. Once a location is purchased, you'd design the restaurant, brand it, make sure there's enough space for the number of clientele you plan on servicing, make sure the kitchen has all the latest equipment so that the chefs can prepare the best food in the quickest time possible. There would be menu planning, stock take, buying cutlery and crockery, hiring and training staff, testing dishes, advertising, laundering services, liaising with local suppliers for fresh produce, visiting local businesses to promote the opening, ongoing advertising, specials, constant revisiting of menus, expert front of house staff, wines, beverages, the list goes on and on.

All this would be in preparation for the first day you open your doors. Will you get a booking? If you have done everything right, yes you will. If your food and service are exemplary, you will get many bookings. If staff are properly trained, and you have planned enough supplies, you will handle it with ease.

Would you open your restaurant if you had no chefs and no waiters? Or if you did have staff, what if you had no menus or supplies in the cupboards? How successful do you think your restaurant would be?

If you are just the new manager in a restaurant with a bad reputation, you will be shouldered with all these responsibilities.

What does this have to do with SharePoint adoption?

Everything. In our SharePoint User Adoption Restaurant, there are eight main elements to ensure long term success.

1. **Ownership**
2. **Purpose**
3. **Planning**
4. **Team Work**
5. **Governance**
6. **Communication**
7. **Evangelism**
8. **Training**

1.1 Ownership

There is not a restaurant in the world that does not have an owner. Whether it be a once off or a franchise, someone owns it who is involved in day to day running of the business.

Without an owner / executive sponsor, it is going to be very difficult to get and maintain a direction, and manage SharePoint.

The owner needs signing powers and the authority to hire (or fire) staff. The owner needs to understand SharePoint and be able to make quick executive decisions on the maintenance and future of the solution. They need to head up the committee that will manage the solution.

A silent partner will not work in the SharePoint User Adoption Restaurant. It will take an active, interested, empowered owner to help drive and manage the success of it.

1.2 Purpose

What kind of restaurant are you planning to have? Noma – one of a kind in Denmark, voted the best restaurant in the world 2 years running, a seating costs $211 a head excluding drinks. Or McDonalds – on every street corner at $1 for a happy meal.

The SharePoint owner should have identified a business need, (gap in the market), that this service is going to address. It is however unfortunately often the case that SharePoint licenses are included free in the company's Enterprise Agreements, which makes it even *more* challenging to find a true purpose and positioning for SharePoint.

Decide why SharePoint is in your organisation from now on, regardless of its legacy. What are you trying to solve and how can SharePoint help you do that.   Every company will be unique in this regard.

Identify your top 3 – 5 business drivers and summarise how SharePoint can address those. For example:

"Our intranet strives to promote a productive, collaborative culture by providing all internal customers with an online service that will facilitate the accurate and timeous sharing of information across geographic locations".

The business drivers in this case included a problem with duplicated documents in the wrong versions that ended up in tenders that made the management team very unhappy. No one could find what they were looking for on the intranet. Finally, they need to become more social and communicative due to the mostly younger generation staff compliment in different regions.

With no purpose, there is no ROI (return on investment). How do you measure something if you don't know what you're measuring or why.

1.3 Planning

If you didn't do planning in your restaurant, how would you know how many table cloths to buy, knives and forks, plates, salt and pepper sets. There are the big-ticket items that need planning – bathrooms, cooking and scullery areas, parking, expanding the restaurant in future.

In your SharePoint implementation, planning is crucial. Some considerations:

- Hardware needs to be scalable.
- Software maintained.
- Teams trained.
- Communication planned.
- Operating model decided.
- Escalation procedures.
- Backups and disaster recovery.
- Information architecture and topology.
- Governance planning.
- Rollout planned.

The three operative words in SharePoint always: plan, plan, plan. Short-term pain, very long-term gain.

1.4 Team Work

Your restaurant could have the most beautiful décor in town, the finest linens, the biggest signage, the most delectable menu. However, if your 100-seater restaurant has one chef, no waiters, no manager and no front house staff; you are going to have a real problem serving all those people.

A waiter with no management experience can't be expected to run the restaurant. The manager with no culinary skills can't be expected to make a chocolate torte with a blueberry wine coulis. The Sous-chef can't be expected to direct traffic in the parking in the parking lot. The dishwasher can't be expected to draw up the shifts for the waiters and do a stock take. But you need all of these people with vastly different skills to make your restaurant a success.

There are many approaches to building the project team in SharePoint implementations and a common mistake is to rely on one individual.

Why do you expect one SharePoint developer to be able to install SharePoint, maintain the server, do custom development, brand the site, write a governance plan, give end user training, do site support for business, assign permissions, and develop the taxonomy structure? The only tasks he is qualified to do well, is the custom development. All the other tasks are specialised fields that require different people with different skills.

It is extremely rare to find one person who can do all those skills effectively. Having a jack-of-all-trades type person running your implementation is very risky. If that person leaves, all their knowledge leaves with them. They are impossible to find, constantly headhunted and justifiably very expensive. While they might handle the load in the beginning, before long they suffer from burn out and become ill from the stresses of the position.

You stand a good chance of losing that person because of all these reasons. It is prudent to take very good care of SharePoint Jack if you have one.

It takes a dedicated, full time team of people to run SharePoint in large companies. The biggest mistake companies make is not engaging business from day one. IT departments traditionally make the technology decisions for the organisation, but when it comes to SharePoint, a different approach needs to be followed.

SharePoint is not like other software, despite the perception that it is just another content management system. It really isn't. It is a business enabler designed to empower business professionals unlike any other software.

A quote by Marc Solomon, SharePoint Expert blogger on AIIM on 18 July 2011[7]:

"What these organizational capital guys didn't add to the mix is the fact that SharePoint changes the game completely. The habitual rigidity that comes with ECM planning is now a fluid, open, and potentially solvable series of incremental tweaks. We're no longer rulebound to legacy systems or hostage to outdated architectures."

Business needs to be engaged from the beginning because you need their buy-in. They will not "just" adopt SharePoint, you need to evangelise the benefits. They need to understand what the product is about and how it can address their ever-changing business needs. How SharePoint is managed directly affects the business professionals, they need a say in this.

For people to adopt a new technology it must be easy to use, it must make them feel good, and they need to see the point of using it. User adoption is about addressing these three drivers to gain a good adoption rate.

---

[7] http://www.aiim.org/community/blogs/expert/Speaking-Truth-to-SharePoint

Plan for redundancy – what will happen to your platform if SharePoint Jack leaves? All key SharePoint staff require a backup or succession plan.

Traditional IT helpdesks are very seldom effective in supporting SharePoint. It is not viable to give site owners a reference number and 2-day waiting period just to explain to them how to insert a new web part. For real success in supporting the platform, train up one or two (as a start), technology savvy business people to dedicate as SharePoint support.

There has to be transparent communication between the technical team (server admins, developers) and the business team (site collection administrators, evangelists, helpdesk, etc). Relationships of trust need to be built on both sides for the system to work. This takes time, but is an important success factor.

Your team needs to form a SharePoint Centre of Excellence with defined roles and responsibilities and mandate.

1.4 Governance

The waiters in the restaurant don't brush their hair and apply makeup in the middle of the restaurant. They don't just arrive whenever they feel like it to work a shift. The chefs don't just think up a recipe on the day and try cook 100 plates of it; there may not be any ingredients available for it. The owner decides when the restaurant will open and close, what will be served, and how staff may behave in front of customers.

Find the words that work in your organisation for SharePoint governance and the governance forum – administration, management, usage policy, acceptable use policy, instructions, regulations, operations, guidance, conduct, rules, steering committee, working group, management team, etc.

You *need* a governance plan – the sooner the better. WHEN you win the adoption challenge, measures need to be in place to ensure long-term stability, efficiency and support of the service.

There are two types of SharePoint governance, business and IT.

Business governance addresses the rules that directly impact the business professionals using the service. Areas include:

- What can people upload to SharePoint.
- Where can documents be uploaded to and why.
- How long documents must be kept.
- What type of re-usable information is there.
- How documentation must be classified.
- When does something become a record.
- What type of sites must be used for what purposes.
- How sites must be classified.
- How long can they keep a site.
- How is a site requested.
- How much space is assigned to each site.
- What if they need more space.
- What custom development is allowed, if any.

- What custom branding is allowed, if any.
- What are they allowed to change using SharePoint Designer.
- How often backups are run.
- Whether there is Disaster Recovery available.
- What are the escalation procedures.
- What features are available for use.
- The process involved to request new features.
- What type of tracking is compulsory to show ROI.
- What type of training may they attend.

The IT governance of SharePoint covers completely different areas, including:

- Creating the initial information architecture, (web apps and site collections), and assigning site collections to trained site collection administrators in business.
- Changing of service accounts passwords.
- What tools are used to effect backups and how often are they scheduled.
- Managing restores.
- Change management procedure for any custom development.
- Change management procedure for any changes to the server settings.
- Management and monitoring of content databases.
- Managing license usage.
- Managing trusted file locations.
- Establishing a Service Level Agreement for their internal clients.
- Upgrade management.

- Performance tuning.
- IIS Resets.
- Syncing between AD and SharePoint.

Take into account that the majority of governance rules affect the business professionals, so they shouldn't be so restrictive that it prevents people from using the service. Don't make rules for the sake of making rules. If you wouldn't fire someone over the specific rule, don't make it a rule in the first place.

The best success in governance management happens when it is run by a person from business, not IT. However, it is very important that the governance forum contains representatives from *both* business and IT.

Both parties will start to understand their respective challenges over time. For example, IT will understand that any changes to the settings could directly influence the usability on the front-end. Business will understand that if they require hourly backups it will cost a lot of money.

The governance plan and forum are designed to open communication channels and plan in advance for thousands of users consuming the SharePoint service.

When you have a full restaurant with a queue down the street, your planning and management will be invaluable to ensure happy customers regardless of the wait.

Having easy to follow governance and strong support teams in place will ensure your clients' needs are met with efficiency and professionalism. You need a plan to get to that point.

If you are in the position of having had SharePoint for a number of years with no governance in place, just start from today. Make sure you communicate constantly so you don't alienate your business professionals.

If your rollout hasn't happened yet, take the time to put some governance in place first. It will save you much pain later.

Six best practices to follow with governance:

a) Document and publish your plan, (use a wiki, not a Word document, it's easier to maintain and communicate – and then explain to people about the cool new technology being used).

b) Communicate it to everyone, (as well as every time it changes).

c) Enforce the policies by having consequence.

d) The governance forum should meet monthly at minimum and must be a compulsory meeting. All business areas to be represented.

e) Record all the decisions made in the meetings in minutes for transparency.

f) Maintain the plan by reviewing it every 6 months to ensure it is still aligned to business needs.

Tip : Add a compulsory field on any site request form that the requester has read, accepted and understood the terms conditions of the governance plan. Include a link to the plan for ease of access.

1.5 Communication

If the restaurant manager changes the menu and fails to communicate this to his chef, how will the chef know to prepare for a different selection? If a client is unhappy about the service or food, and the waiter fails to communicate this to the chef or owner to address it, the client is likely to walk out. What happens if that client was the New York Times food critic?

It is widely accepted that lack of planning and governance are major contributors to failed SharePoint implementations. Constant, clear communication is just as critical in order to succeed.

Communication needs to go to all site owners at least weekly. Impart tips and tricks, how to's, did you knows, rules, changes to the platform, great solutions configured by business professionals, new people on the team, what training to attend and where, events, etc etc. By communicating regularly to your user base, you establish a trust relationship with your team and your service.

This is important for two reasons. WHEN something goes wrong, (it's nature of the beast, technology is not always perfect); you will buy time to get it fixed. The last thing you want is to have the perception in business that SharePoint is unstable for whatever reason. People will not use that service if they don't trust it and they will spread the rumour like wildfire.

People are more likely to forgive a mishap when it occurs after having built up a trust relationship with consistent communication. If you don't, the perception of "typical IT, useless as usual" and "SharePoint is broken" will prevail. It is *extremely* difficult to turn perceptions like that around. It will take months if not years of constant evangelism to reverse and do irreparable damage to the project.

The second reason is to catch the transgressors who *will* test the system for weaknesses. Open and honest communication channels between the business and IT teams managing SharePoint will prevent people from phoning their buddy on the team to ask them to give them access to a site that they should not have access to. If the communication is working, the support teams will know about these people and block them accordingly.

There is quite an honour system at play in the SharePoint world. The access rights that the key resources are required to have for effective management is powerful. It needs to be part of the work ethic of the team not to undermine the governance rules in place for the sake of 'a buddy' who is trying to work the system.

The person who is allocated to take care of all communication on the service will soon be seen as the go-to person. Regardless of who the owner of SharePoint is, the person who does the communicating will be perceived as the person who can get things done. It is therefore very important that this person be a well-spoken, eloquent, empowered, knowledgeable, business professional who has a direct line to the platform owner, governance forum and IT team.   Business teams consuming the service will go to this person for all manner of reasons, and they need to be empowered to handle those queries.   For best practices, the communicator should also be the evangelist.

It is not always possible to reach every person in the organisation, especially in large organisations.   Make it part of the governance that all communications will be sent to the site owners only and it is their responsibility to communicate it to their respective teams.   Processes need to be put in place to maintain a list of all site owners.

Communication does not have to be via email.   It can be done via an Announcements web part or Discussion Forum using alerts to the relevant people.   It is best practices to follow this route so that all communications are stored on a site that should be open to everyone in the organisation.   If new people join the company and become site owners, they can view previous communication and get up to speed with the organisation.

Start communicating today.

1.7 Evangelism

To get your new restaurant well known in your area, you will need to do some advertising.   Sponsoring a taste faire or charity will help build credibility.   Going around to your local shops and businesses telling them about your specialities and offering free samples of your best dessert is a great way to get some customers.   Catering office parties as a sideline with your type of cuisine could help make you niche in your market.

How will you sell SharePoint to your business professionals? There needs to be a public face of SharePoint in the organisation to demo and evangelise SharePoint to effect good user adoption.

That person will provide specialized consulting services to business professionals regarding best practices, design ideas and information architecture. Their sole purpose is to encourage user adoption and embed a sense of excitement in the business regarding SharePoint.

This entails daily floor walking to meet the business and build rapport; demo'ing the technology, identifying new business opportunities where SharePoint can be leveraged, communicating with the site owners constantly, and most importantly; the liaison between business and IT on most SharePoint matters.

The evangelist also has a responsibility to manage expectation of what SharePoint can offer. Pitching a "silver bullet" when it is not is not the answer and will lead to disillusionment of the service.

It is important that the evangelist be a business person, not an IT person. Business professionals have a hard time identifying with an IT person and there is often mistrust between the two parties. The evangelist needs to have understanding and empathy for both camps and be able to maintain a neutral stance for the benefit of the larger project.

The long-term benefits of a full time evangelist shouldn't be under-estimated. People crave real relationships in all spheres of business and life. It's not about the technology, it's about people. It's about getting people excited about working again. It's about leaving people more energised than you found them. It's about giving a service that leaves your internal customers breathless! It's about building bridges, every moment in front of your customers is a moment of truth.

The evangelist will be building relationships across IT and business that when done right can create powerful new ideas, collaboration and a desire to share and learn from each other. It must be understood however, that this takes time.

In many instances, year 1 of a SharePoint project stays in the IT department because they believe business won't be able to handle it. Year 2 it is unleashed on business but with no governance, planning or training. Year 3 all parties realise it has gotten out of control and they need help. This is when the evangelists are invaluable, but it can take up to 2 years to rebuild what has been broken. Don't expect it to happen overnight, but it will happen.

Finding the right evangelist externally may be difficult because they are highly sought after. Alternatively, you can most certainly identify someone in-house and train him or her up to fulfil this role.

To assist the evangelism and adoption process, it is a good idea to create a site for all things SharePoint in the organisation. Hold a competition to name the site to create some excitement and get buy-in.

All staff should be directed to the site on any SharePoint related queries or issues. Use it to store information like:

- How to request a site, support or demo.
- Training options and materials.
- Tips, tricks and best practices.
- Governance plan and minutes of the governance forums.
- Core team's contact details as well as all the site collection administrators.
- All previous and current newsletters, articles and events.
- Stats on the platform and general information about what SharePoint is.
- Error repository and frequently asked questions.
- Surveys and a feedback section.

The benefit of a site of this nature is that all staff can do some self-service before logging a call; and refer other staff members to the site thereby cross skilling each other and promoting the service.

There are many roles required to make SharePoint a success in a large organisation, but an evangelist will make everyone else's jobs easier if they do *their* job well.

1.8 Training

An untrained chef is not going to be able to serve you much more than a toasted sandwich or a stew. They won't "just know" how to temper chocolate. Untrained waiters will end up trying to open a bottle of champagne at a customer's table using a corkscrew and wedging the bottle between their legs for leverage, (true story). It sounds obvious to someone who's had champagne that you twist the cork off, but to someone who has never done that, how would they know that is the procedure to get it open.

It is often assumed people will instinctively know how SharePoint works, but that is not the case. Maybe in the future release that might be a reality, but for SharePoint 2007 and 2010 that is not yet true for the majority of business professionals.

End user training costs can be some of the highest in all the costs associated with rolling out SharePoint in large organisations. Yet it is seldom budgeted for. It is also rare for IT departments to foot the training bill beyond a couple of key people in their own department. This has far-reaching consequences.

Once SharePoint has been released onto business without training, business eventually gets proactive and arranges their own training because they have their own budgets. Unfortunately, due to lack of communication, no guidance is given about what type of training to attend. So business does a search for SharePoint training and takes the first power course they come across – many a time this has been a SharePoint Designer course. While seasoned professionals will know that is not the right thing to do, business will be none the wiser and pay exorbitant fees for this training. They return to work completely overwhelmed and terrified of SharePoint.

One of two things happens. Either they attempt to use SharePoint but mess it up altogether; or they never touch it again and go back to file shares and email. Again, the relationship is broken and it takes time and the right person to rebuild it.

If people are not trained properly, they won't use SharePoint properly or effectively. They then innocently teach these bad habits to other business professionals. Before long, the service is a mess of subfolders, dormancy and bad practices.

In organisations with tens of thousands of people, it is not viable to train everybody. The core team needs specialised training in order to support the service on a long term basis. It is recommended that the server administrators and developers attend a one day end user course just so they can understand the challenges their clients have and what they interface with. This will make them better technical professionals which will assist with building those all-important trust relationships.

Identify the first group of core business professionals that will benefit from using SharePoint and get them trained first. It is impossible to go big bang with SharePoint adoption, so you have to stagger the expertise around the organisation. This will also allow for business professionals to cross skill each other.

There are pros and cons to internal and external training.

Internal is better if you have the *right* SharePoint trainer in-house, a dedicated training centre, system in place to manage the training, and decided who will pay for it all. The benefit is that it can work out cheaper; staff are trained on the organisation platform settings, training can be tailored to the governance rules and give one message.

The downside is that people don't always take it seriously because they can run out to do work and cancel at the last second because they don't see the billing. There are often network / facilities issues to be overcome in-house.

External training does allow for more concentration - but if you use more than one external training house, your staff will be given different messages by each one and tend to get confused about what to do when back at the office because of that.

External training is done on default settings and branding, if the company has a different look and feel, users won't know where to find settings they were taught at the training house. However, they have the infrastructure in place to facilitate classroom training, which most companies don't have.

Regardless of the strategy here, make sure the classes are small – ten people or less, so that specific attention may be given to each delegate. Putting 20 to 30 people in a class is not effective in getting the message across.

The timing of training is critical. If you train staff too soon and the rollout is delayed; the training will need to be redone as they will have forgotten what they were taught.

The level of training is just as important – you can't teach content types, permissions and Excel services to beginners. To be truly effective, the training needs to be customised and targeted to different audiences. Trying to pack every feature into one day or a 3 / 5 day power course is ineffective. It is too overwhelming and the majority of the time the delegates are scared off SharePoint altogether.

If you have SharePoint Enterprise licences in the organisation, understand that it will be a long process to get staff mature enough to be able to effectively leverage those features. You will need to contract external consultants to get those features working and maintained until your staff are in a position to understand them and take over.

It is a process that can be long and expensive. It is important to manage expectation in this arena.

A common question from business professionals is if there is an exam they can write to become qualified. There is a new certification called SharePoint 2010 Information Worker Exam 77-886[8], it requires experience on Enterprise Features of SharePoint. Should you not have this version of SharePoint in your organisation, design your own questionnaires in-house and automate them on your evangelism site so staff can measure their progress.

Training needs to be planned carefully. The number one complaint from business is that training is not supplied when SharePoint is rolled out. The biggest conflict with training is about who pays for it. Training is a long term, ongoing process over years in most cases. A central

---

[8] http://www.microsoft.com/learning/en/us/exam.aspx?ID=77-886#tab2

SharePoint budget will go a long way in preventing turf wars later.

Summary

If you follow all the adoption steps and use the right people in your SharePoint Centre of Excellence, there is *no way* you can fail the SharePoint adoption challenge. However, it is important to understand how interlinked all the aspects of user adoption are. You can't do one without the other and expect successful adoption and management. Just remember that it takes lots time. If it's a new implementation and SharePoint has never been used before, it will be easier if you follow these steps. If it's a legacy system that's just been upgraded to 2010, it will be more challenging – but it can be done. Take it one day at a time, start planning today. It's never too late.

1. Ownership – find an empowered, engaged owner.
2. Purpose – why are you here and where are you going.
3. Planning – short term pain, long term gain.
4. Team work – it takes a diverse, skilled, collaborative team to make it work.
5. Governance – start small and adapt as you grow and needs change.
6. Communication – share everything, transparency is king.
7. Evangelism – find the most empathetic person with a bubbly personality, who understands your business.
8. Training – ongoing costs and handholding that never go away.

4.   Social SharePoint

Introduction

The word 'Social has become a very popular term over the last couple of years. Everyone is familiar with Facebook, Twitter and YouTube. These so-called Social sites attract millions of visitors per day! So how does this translate to SharePoint 2010? What Social features are available?

Social features were also available (albeit limitedly) in the previous version Microsoft Office SharePoint Server 2007 (MOSS 2007). The main feature was the My Site. This site is a personal page for every user within a SharePoint Intranet portal. The user was able to share valuable information with colleagues, such as a mobile number, e-mail address, manager or skills. Other users were able to use the MOSS 2007 search engine to find a colleague with the skill *'Writing marketing material'*, for example. By using these features, users were able to connect and share information with each other.

SharePoint 2010 improves on this and now more new features are available. This chapter describes these features, and how they can improve collaboration within your organisation.

My Site

The My Site is the heart and soul of the SharePoint 2010 Social features. My Site allows users to create a personal profile, get an overview of tagged content and provide accurate and resourceful social search results.

My Site consists of three key components:

- My Profile
- My Content
- My Newsfeed

The following paragraphs provide an explanation, supported by screenshots, for these three modules.

My Profile

The following screenshot shows an example of the My Profile page:

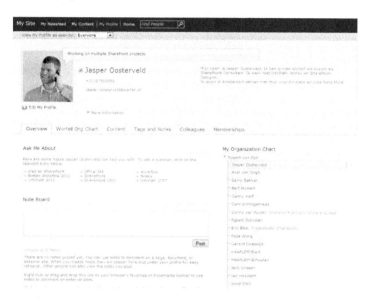

Multiple sections make up the top part of the profile page: a profile picture, employee information (e.g. name, e-mail and phone number) and a status update.

New to SharePoint 2010 is the possibility to leave a status update (recognize the Facebook aspect?). This tool allows the user to leave a short message for co-workers. This message will appear in the My Newsfeed section of the user's co-workers.

Note. The update only appears in the newsfeed of co-workers marked as a colleague of the user.

Not all the employee information is shown instantly. The visitor of the My Profile page needs to click on *More information*. Unsurprisingly, this results in the appearance of more information:

First name : Jasper

Last name : Oosterveld

Name : Jasper Oosterveld

Job Title : SharePoint Consultant

Manager : Robert van Son

About me :

Mijn naam is Jasper Oosterveld. Ik ben binnen Wortell
werkzaam als SharePoint Consultant. Ik werk met
InfoPath, Nintex en SharePoint Designer.

Ik woon in Amsterdam samen met mijn vriendin Katie
en onze hond Millie.

Ask Me About : InfoPath 2007, SharePoint 2010,
InfoPath 2010, Nintex, SharePoint, Nintex Workflow
2010, Workflow, Office 365, iPad en SharePoint

Department : SharePoint

The user can change most of this information by clicking on *Edit My Profile* under the profile picture. The user is now able to edit his or her profile:

In most cases, the user cannot change all fields. In this example, fields, such as *Name* and *Manager,* fill automatically because they are synchronized with Active Directory.

Note. A SharePoint Administrator with access to Central Administration (the administration hub of SharePoint) can decide which fields are synchronized with Active Directory.

I recommend automatically synchronizing certain profile fields. The management do not want employees changing their job title or department. This can create confusion within an organization and will result in wrong search results. I recommend connecting the following fields with Active Directory:

- Name
- E-mail address
- Job title
- Manager
- Department
- Work phone
- Mobile phone

The My Profile page comes with a standard set of profile fields. The SharePoint Administrator can configure (e.g. disable or rename) these fields or add new fields.

The My Profile page consists of multiple tabs:

- Overview
- Organizational Chart
- Content
- Tags and Notes
- Colleagues
- Memberships

In the following paragraphs, I will discuss the different tabs.

Overview

The overview tab contains several sections:

- Ask Me About
- Note Board
- Recent Activities
- My Organization Chart

Ask me About

The user can define topics, mostly skills, for co-workers to ask questions. The co-worker clicks on a topic and automatically, the note board contains a sentence with *'Question on Topic X'*. The co-worker can now leave a question and the user will receive an e-mail with the question. The two co-workers can now get in touch with each other and collaborate on the chosen topic.

Note. The user can decide if an e-mail needs to be sent after a co-worker leaves a message. This can be changed in the *Edit My Profile* screen.

Note Board

The note board speaks for itself. Co-workers can leave messages about work or non-work related topics. It is important to remember that these messages can be seen by every co-worker visiting the My Site. As such, I always advice customers to keep it business related.

Recent Activities
Recent activities by the user are shown here. This can vary from events like adding a new colleague or an upcoming birthday.

My Organization Chart
Co-workers with the same manager are shown in an organization chart. I will talk more about this in the next paragraph.

Organizational chart
This is one of the most interesting and useful new features in SharePoint 2010. The organizational chart shows each user's co-workers and managers. The following example is from our company portal:

The user can browse to the left and right to view co-workers. Every co-worker is shown by name and the introduction from the *'About Me field'* profile field. Presented above the user's profile picture is his/her manager. By clicking on the manager, the co-workers of the manager show up. The whole organisation, along with its organisation structure, is available to see by browsing through the organizational chart.

Note. The organizational chart can also function as a webpart in any part of the company portal.

Content
The content (e.g. documents or blog) of the user is displayed. I will explain this tab in detail in the My Content paragraph.

Tags and Notes
This tab shows the tags and notes created by the user. Read the Tags and Notes paragraph to learn more about this feature.

Colleagues
The user's co-workers, with the same manager, are automatically shown. The user can add more co-workers by clicking on *Add Colleagues*. After adding a co-worker, the newsfeed will show activities concerning the newly added colleague.

Membership
The membership tab shows SharePoint sites in which the user is a member (The user need to be in the Member SharePoint Group).

My Content

Users always love to use My Documents in Windows for storing documents, but they are never able to share these with others. What is the solution for this problem? Show your users how to use My Content.

This is best explained as being an online version of My Documents. Users can store documents in their shared documents library. These are automatically shared with all the other users. The user can also use their personal documents library for storing private documents.

My Content also comes with a blog. That means users can easily start blogging and share information with others. One of our customers is using this functionality by letting the management blog and publishing these articles on the home page of the Intranet Portal.

Note. I advise to start with a maximum storage limit on My Content. Otherwise, things can get out of control when users decide to upload all their vacation images.

Newsfeed

The newsfeed is another way for users to connect with each other. All the activities of the user's colleagues can be displayed. This includes everything from an upcoming birthday to an updated profile. The picture below shows an example of the newsfeed:

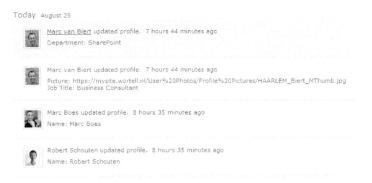

Let's say a user sees an update from a colleague about a newly gained expertise, such as InfoPath; the user can now click on the name of the colleague and leave a message on the My Profile page. The users are now able to easily collaborate and share knowledge about InfoPath.

The user can control the activities displayed by editing his or her profile:

Activities I am following:
- ☑ Note Board post
- ☑ Tagging with my interests
- ☑ Rating
- ☑ Status Message
- ☑ Sharing Interests
- ☑ Tagging by my colleague
- ☑ Job title change
- ☑ Manager change
- ☑ New blog post
- ☑ New membership
- ☑ Upcoming birthday
- ☑ Birthday
- ☑ Upcoming workplace anniversary
- ☑ Workplace anniversary
- ☑ New colleague
- ☑ Profile update

Check or uncheck boxes to set types of activities you want to see for your colleagues.

The user is now able to decide which activities to follow.

Tags and Notes

The ability to tag or leave a note for every type of content is another new function in SharePoint 2010. This tag or note can point to a document, a site or a Wiki page. The user can use the tag and note symbol at any time. It is always located at the top right part of the screen:

Note. I do not recommend using the *I Like It* option. Creating tags that are more specific is more useful in collaborating with co-workers.

After clicking on Tags & Notes, the user sees with the following screen:

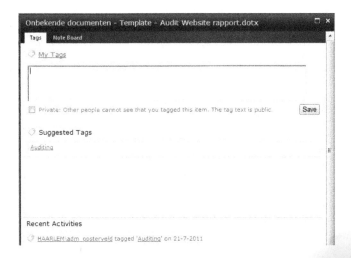

The Tags tab provides the user with the option, to add a tag. I recommend creating a tag no longer than one or two words. The header *Suggested Tags* gives the user an overview of tags created by other users. The *Recent Activities* function provides a summary of tags as well which summarizes all tagging activities of the selected content.

Note. The user can decide to mark the tag as private so it is not visible for other users.

To leave a description or message as seen below, the user can use the Notes tab:

This provides a summary of notes left from other users. Summaries include the user's name, profile picture and date created. By clicking on the name of a user, the My Profile page will load. The user can now contact the co-worker, for example by using the note board, and collaborate about auditing.

To make it easy for a user to remember all of the tags and notes used, the user can go to the My Profile page and click on the *Tags and Notes* tab. The user can click on a tag and all of selected tag's activities appear:

Activities for: SharePoint 2010

Tagged SP 2010 Wireframes.vsd with SharePoint 2010. 10/28/2010

View Related Activities   Make Private   Delete

Tagged Office 2010 en 2007 integ... with SharePoint 2010. 10/28/2010

View Related Activities   Make Private   Delete

Tagged Office Web Apps Multi Edi... with SharePoint 2010. 10/28/2010

View Related Activities   Make Private   Delete

The tagged content is clickable and opens automatically. It gets more interesting when the user clicks on the tag:

Every tag or note has its own profile page! The user gets a clear overview of **all** activities surrounding the tag. Each user can see the activity of every other user via this profile page.

The user has the following interesting options:

- Add the tag to the *'Interest'* employee field
- Add the tag to the *Ask Me About* section
- Leave a message for other users

By using the tag profile page, users can communicate and collaborate with each other resulting in the instant publication of interesting related content.

Rating

The rating system makes it possible to rate SharePoint content from 1 to 5 stars. Rating is useful for improving the quality of content, as people can see what others recommend and the SharePoint search algorithm will improve the contents ranking in search results. This feature requires activation before use. A user with full control permissions can go to library or list settings:

General Settings

Title, description and navigation

Versioning settings

Advanced settings

Validation settings

Column default value settings

Rating settings

Audience targeting settings

Metadata navigation settings

Per-location view settings

Form settings

Under *General Settings* the option *Rating settings* is available:

The user needs to select *Yes* and a new rating column is added to the list or library:

The user can rate the document from one to five stars. A timer job calculates the ratings from all users and runs by default once an hour, resulting in the display of the average score.

Presented as a column, the rating system can be used within list or library views.

Search results also allow the use of the ratings system. By changing the XSLT of the search results webpart. As seen in the following example:

http://o14/Documents/**Orange** Foods

A Clockwork **Orange** (1962) is a dystopian novel by Anthony Burgess.
A Clockwork **Orange** (1962) is a dystopian novel by Anthony Burgess. ... Cockney expression, "as queer as a clockwork **orange**".¹, and alludes to the prevention of the main ... The novel has been adapted for ...
☆ ☆ ☆ ☆
Authors: Windows User Date: 9/12/2009 Size: 32KB
http://o14/Documents/clockwork **orange**.docx

fall paint list.docx
Here are the new paint colors we'll be carrying this fall: ... **Orange** Marmalade .. Burnt **Orange**
☆ ☆ ☆
Authors: Windows User Date: 9/12/2009 Size: 30KB
http://o14/Documents/fall paint list.docx

Another interesting use of the rating system is adding the rating column in the refinement panel. This means users can filter search results by choosing a rating.

Social Search

Even the search engine from SharePoint was not able to escape the social virus! The social search provides multiple interesting features:

- Search for co-workers by name
- Search for co-workers by keyword such as an expertise 'SharePoint'
- Refinement panel
- Vanity search

It makes sense that it is possible to find a co-worker by name. A cool add-on to this feature 'Phonetic search'. This means that searching for Mike Smith, who is actually called Michael Smit, will still show Michael Smit in the search results.

One of my favourite features is searching by keyword. So, how does this work? Let us say a project manager is looking for a SharePoint Consultant and SharePoint Developer. The company has dozens of SharePoint Consultants and Developers and the project manager does not know all of them. The project manager can perform a search for a SharePoint Consultant:

The search results provide 11 possible SharePoint Consultants interesting for the project manager. The project manager can use the refinement panel on the left side of the screen to filter through the results.

The SharePoint Consultant the project manager is looking for needs to have InfoPath 2010 knowledge, so by clicking on *Show More* under Vakkennis (Skills) new filters appear:

Vakkennis

Any Vakkennis

SharePoint 2010

SharePoint 2007

SharePoint Designer...

BPOS

InfoPath 2010

SharePoint

InfoPath 2007

Information Worker ...

Prince2

SharePoint Designer...

SQL Server 2008

These metadata fields are extracted from all the My Profile pages for all the users. The project manager clicks on InfoPath 2010 and the search results are narrowed down further:

Only three SharePoint Consultants have this skill! It is now easier for the Project Manager to find the desired consultant. The project manager can perform the same actions for finding a SharePoint Developer.

The example above shows how important it is that all the users fill in the My Profile pages correctly.

Every user can improve his or her social find-ability by executing a search on his or her own name and understanding how they have been found in searches in the organisation. In SharePoint terms this is a called a vanity search. The result will look like this:

	Update My Profile	Update My Keywords
Help people find me	Number of searches that led to me: **2** time(s) in the last month **0** time(s) in the last week	Keyword searches that led to me: Jesper Jasper oosterveld lvnl oosterveld

I now understand how my colleagues found me while executing searches. In my case by my first name, full name, customer and last name. I see that only two searches led to my profile. To improve this, I can edit my profile.

Social features in the "real" world

RIBW Groep Overijssel is one of my employer's customers. It is a regional company specialized in guiding people, with psychiatric and psychological problems.

RIBW defined a couple of business goals:

- Improve the information flow to the employees
- Automating document and process management
- Connecting employees with each other

My company (Wortell) advised RIBW to build an internal collaboration portal based on the SharePoint 2010 platform. The platform provides team sites, a wiki knowledge base, a forum, a marketplace and the social features such as the My Site and social search.

RIBW had previous knowledge of the social features of SharePoint before the start of the project and they were interested in using the My Site and Social Search features. One of the goals was to replace their internal corporate directory by using the organizational chart of the My Site.

The social features are rapidly being adapted in the organisation. The board of directors use the blog functionality and employees enjoy the interactive way of connecting with each other by adding each other as colleagues and leaving messages through the note board.

This customer case shows how easy it can be for companies to achieve business goals by using out-of-the-box SharePoint (social) functionalities.

Summary

The features I described provide an overview of all the social possibilities of SharePoint 2010. I want to conclude my chapter with some tips for using and improving the social features.

Profile fields and Active Directory

Use Active Directory for synchronizing profile fields where possible. By using this method, the user guarantees the accuracy of his or her profile information. This results in better search results! Let the users add their own skillset and interests but make sure they cannot change their job title or e-mail address.

Tag cloud on the home page

Use the tags and notes cloud webpart on the home page of the Intranet. Configure it by showing the tags and notes from every user. I always advise customers to configure the Intranet portal as the home page of their browser. When the user loads a browser, he or she can see the tags used by co-workers, resulting in faster and more effective collaboration.

Train and inform your users

Out-of-the-box SharePoint comes with all of these great social features but that is not enough. Each SharePoint administrator (or other stakeholders) needs to systematically train and inform every user about taking advantage of these features. For example, tell them the advantage of tagging content by showing the tag user profile page.

Send out reminders (every two months) to your users to update their profile information. Highlight the project field out to your project managers. They can instruct project members to add a closed or current project.

5.   The Art of SharePoint Success

Introduction

Over the past five years, through engagements with hundreds of organisations, I've developed a framework for ensuring that investments in SharePoint deliver long term returns. This chapter is an introduction to the framework which consists of four key elements: Governance, Strategy, Transition and Architecture.

The rise and fall of SharePoint

SharePoint is a phenomenal success:

- it is Microsoft's fastest selling server based product ever

- it has generated in excess of one billion dollars in sales revenue for Microsoft. The only other Microsoft Server products to generate this level of revenue are SQL Server and Exchange Server, and SharePoint has reached this milestone more quickly than the others

- over one hundred million SharePoint licences have been sold worldwide

- IT industry analysts such as Forrester Research and Gartner rank SharePoint as a leader in a number of different technology markets including Search, Enterprise Content

Management, Social Computing, Collaboration, Information Access and Horizontal Portals

But many organisations struggle to realise the full value from investments in SharePoint. For example:

- at a large UK central government agency, an IT led project to a SharePoint Collaboration platform was halted by another group working on a Document Management project who felt that SharePoint was a threat. The £150,000 investment only delivered a pilot

- at an international insurance business the use of SharePoint was crippled by disagreement between different factions in the IT function

- the IT function within a global manufacturing organisation deployed a SharePoint based collaboration service. At first, the service was a huge success and enjoyed rapid adoption across the business and within months there were over 7,000 sites created. Users soon began to report difficulties in locating sites, multiple copies of documents began to appear, and the help desk was swamped with requests to recover deleted sites

- a marketing organisation reported that, "*SharePoint exists in our business but no one uses it…*"

Why SharePoint projects fail

The most common causes of SharePoint failure in my experience are:

1. Politics
2. Not knowing what SharePoint is
3. Lack of information and knowledge management skills
4. Vision, the business case, and measuring success
5. Executive support
6. User adoption
7. Individual choices derail SharePoint initiatives
8. Information Management
9. Defining requirements
10. Technical skills

The Art of SharePoint Success framework of Governance, Strategy, Architecture, and Transition addresses all of these issues. The following sections discuss each of these challenges.

Politics

Politics is the biggest barrier to SharePoint success.

If you're thinking, "*Not in my case*", then you're the most at risk!

There are a number of reasons why SharePoint can become a political football. Firstly, SharePoint has many potential uses and that can often lead to it being perceived as a threat. For example at a major international insurance business I saw an IT led SharePoint collaboration project lose its £350,000 budget because the Marketing and Communications department responsible for the existing Intranet felt threatened by the introduction of SharePoint which they believed could become a replacement intranet.   They spoke to the right people and the collaboration initiative didn't win project approval.

Secondly SharePoint can be a catalyst for extensive change within an organisation including changes to power structures, and processes. This type of change is usually accompanied by political manoeuvring.

Thirdly, SharePoint requires different areas of the business to work together, sometimes to the extent of pooling departmental budgets in enterprise level platforms and solutions.   SharePoint is a shared infrastructure and without some ground rules scuffles usually emerge.

Not knowing what SharePoint is

Can you clearly describe to someone what SharePoint is? In my experience not many people can.   Forrester neatly summarise the problem.

> *"Like the 'Shimmer' product commercial in the old Saturday Night Live skit, SharePoint can be difficult to define.. Without clear definition of SharePoint Enterprises struggle... Lacking appropriate guidance, organisations grapple with SharePoint..."*   (Koplowitz & Le Clair 2008)

Simply put, if you don't know what something is then you're going to struggle to use it successfully; and if you can't write down on a piece of paper what is then you don't know.

Lack of information and knowledge management skills

SharePoint is about three things: people, processes, and information. Of course you need experienced IT professionals to design, build, and maintain the technical solution, but you need an information and knowledge management professional to design the business solution first. Have you got someone who fits this description on your SharePoint project? If you're working with a Microsoft partner then do they have the soft skills and experience as well as the technical skills?

Vision, the business case, and measuring success

Many organisation embark on SharePoint initiatives without clearly understanding what they are trying to achieve. I have enclosed below an extract from a document I received from a client talking about their aims for a collaboration project:

> *"In essence, staff want to work better together, to share knowledge, to work informally, to communicate, to connect across boundaries and to innovate. They want to move from a set of happy families defined by organisational structure to a networked community".*

This type of high-level and abstract narrative can be a useful motivational tool because the lack of detail invites us to form our own ideas as to how this vision might be realised. Although we might all intuitively agree with the vision at first we soon need more detail. If you can't answer the questions, *"What are we trying to achieve?"*, and, *"How will we know when we've done it?"*, then you're not ready to start.

Many organisations struggle to define a clear business case or to measure the success of SharePoint initiatives. For example at a major UK retailer the communications team struggled to gain approval for their Intranet because the £75,0000 per annum value realisation from printing and distributing savings was outweighed by the £450,000 cost of deploying the SharePoint platform and purchasing licences. Although they intuitively knew that there were long term gains to be realised from the investment beyond the reduction in printing costs they found it difficult to quantify and articulate these intangible benefits in the boardroom.

Executive support

Executives are in a unique position to be able to drive change in an organisation. Visibly active and participatory Executive support gives credibility to a programme or initiative. Without such support SharePoint based initiatives can fail either because the proposed projects don't gain approval and funding, or because solutions are delivered but aren't adopted or used by the business.

User adoption

Achieving success with SharePoint requires long lasting changes in behaviour of workers. Weaning information workers off their addiction to email and file shares and away from long established ways of working with line of business applications and Excel is a long term war not a short term battle.

For example an international insurance business invested £1.5m in developing and maintaining a SharePoint based portal for underwriters, which aggregated information from several line of business systems into a single consolidated user interface. Two years after launch the IT function estimated that of the 100 potential users of the system only 8 regularly used it. The others preferred to continue working in the old ways.

Individual choices derail SharePoint initiatives

SharePoint is a shared infrastructure and as such requires agreements on how it should be used and operated. At a technical level a lack of agreed policies, processes and responsibilities can quickly lead to failure of the SharePoint platform. At the business level inconsistencies between the way different departments or teams design the layout, navigation, and structure of their SharePoint sites can make it difficult for users moving between sites.

Information management

SharePoint implementations can very quickly become chaotic without the appropriate levels of control and training. Thousands of SharePoint sites can spring up making it difficult for people to find information. People don't know which is the authoritative version of documents. Time and money are wasted as people work on duplicate, un-coordinated developments and customisations. Vital information can be lost as SharePoint sites are deleted in an uncontrolled manner.

It is a truism that with SharePoint, *'Content is King'*. Content must be up to date, accurate and be easy to find otherwise users will quickly lose confidence in the system. The quality of content relies on the users rather than the IT department

Defining requirements

The real value of SharePoint lies not only in improving what you are already doing, but in changing what you do because you have new capabilities. Simply asking the business what they want, or what their requirements are doesn't seem to work for SharePoint. Henry Ford summed the problem up nicely when he said, *"If I asked people what they wanted they would just say 'faster horses'."*

Technical skills

SharePoint is a vast technology platform comprising of several enterprise class products, and it has the ability to integrate with an almost endless number of external systems and data stores. It requires infrastructure, database administration, data storage, security, software development and end user skills. Properly implemented it provides a high performance, scalable and reliable infrastructure. Technical issues such as poor performance, system failure, or extensive down time will quickly impact upon user confidence and reduce adoption rates. Has your SharePoint Administrator completed the appropriate training?

Governance

Governance has become one of the most widely discussed and overused terms in the SharePoint community. Yet it is still widely misunderstood and poorly implemented.

SharePoint governance: What it is

In a nutshell SharePoint governance aligns the use of SharePoint technologies with enterprise objectives and strategy; it defines accountability and responsibilities for the SharePoint success; and it specifies the measures by which success will be measured.

The best way to understand SharePoint governance is to look at it in the wider context of enterprise and IT governance. Figure 1 illustrates the relationship between the three disciplines.

Figure 1: SharePoint, IT & Enterprise Governance.

Enterprise governance consists of the processes, customs, policies, responsibilities, and organisational structures which affect the way an enterprise is directed, administered or controlled. It includes the relationships between the stakeholders; the goals of the organisation; and most importantly it ensures accountability.

IT Governance is a subset of enterprise governance. It is:

> "...*The leadership and organisational structures and processes that ensure that the organisation's I.T. sustains and extends the organisation's strategies and objectives."* (Wikipedia 2010)

In modern organisations IT is of huge strategic importance either as one of the largest cost centres, or arguably as an enabler of competitive advantage. It is widely recognised that IT governance should be an integral part of enterprise governance, and should be the responsibility of the board and executive management rather than the Chief Information Officer or other IT managers.

The relationship between enterprise and IT governance is illustrated by translating common enterprise governance questions into specific IT governance questions (Oudi 2010).

Table 1: The relationship between Enterprise & IT Governance

Corporate Governance Questions	IT Governance Questions
How do the suppliers of finance get managers to return some profit to them?	How do the board and executive management get their CIO and IT organisation to return some business value to them?
How do the suppliers of finance make sure that managers do not steal the capital they supply or invest it in bad projects?	How do the board and executive management make sure that the CIO and their IT organisations do not steal the capital they supply or invest it in bad projects?
How do the suppliers of finance control managers?	How do the board and the executive management control the CIO and the IT organisation?

Enterprise governance should drive and set IT governance. IT in its turn can influence strategic opportunities as outlined by the enterprise and can provide critical input into strategic plans. In this way IT governance enables the enterprise to take full advantage of its information and can be seen as a driver for corporate governance.

SharePoint governance is a subset of IT governance. One of the most commonly cited definitions is that SharePoint governance:

> *"..Uses People, Policy, Technology and Process to resolve ambiguity, manage short and long range goals and mitigate conflict within an organisation. It covers usage and design; structure and a framework to measure success"* (Roth 2009)

Another way to think of SharePoint governance is in terms of its objectives which in broad terms are:

1. Assure that investments in SharePoint generate business value
2. Mitigate the risks that are associated with SharePoint I.T projects

Much of the confusion over SharePoint governance is concerned with the relationship and differences between the related concepts of management and operations.
In simplistic terms (Liu 2010):

- governance is concerned with vision and the translation of vision into policy
- management is concerned with making the decisions needed to implement policy
- operations are about implementing managerial decisions

Table 2 illustrates an example of SharePoint governance, management and operations.

Table 2: SharePoint Governance, Management and
Operations

Vision & Policy (Governance)	SharePoint will support our objectives for greater innovation; increased sales; and improved operational efficiency SharePoint will be our Enterprise Collaboration platform
Decision (Management)	We will implement a Project Management Portal based on SharePoint
Implementation (Operations)	Implementation and on-going maintenance of a project management portal

Many of the topics commonly associated with SharePoint governance in Microsoft's literature, published material, and blogs and websites actually relate to management, operations, or a combination of both. For example:

- technical '*best practices*'
- information architecture
- user interface design or branding
- technology customisations
- training
- site lifecycle management

All of these topics are vital to the success of SharePoint within an organisation.   A SharePoint governance framework should define who is responsible and accountable for them but the detailed policies and processes do not relate to governance.

SharePoint governance: How to do it

A robust SharePoint governance model should address relationships between three key elements:

1. strategy
2. business change
3. IT operations

Strategy is concerned with the **accountability** for the return on investment in SharePoint technologies. It defines the scope of SharePoint use within the organisation, links the use of the technology to high-level organisational objectives, and defines the success measures and the means by which they are monitored and reported.

Business change is concerned with the **responsibility** for management decisions which implement the high-level strategy. Two key elements of business change are people and processes. The people aspect relates to user adoption - changing behaviours to ensure that the technology is used positively. The process aspect relates to changes in business processes, either re-engineering of the processes enabled by the new technology, or embedding the technology within existing processes to improve effectiveness and efficiencies. It is also vital that the business change level provides feedback from the business into the strategy level to shape the on-going evolution of the strategy.

IT operations are responsible for the **implementation** and on-going maintenance of the SharePoint environment.   This includes data storage, database administration, platform services, support, software development, and security.

Every organisation is different, and will need to develop and evolve a SharePoint governance model that fits with its existing enterprise, and IT governance.   But a robust model must address the three key elements of strategy, change, and operations

Experience shows that there are five broad approaches which organisations typically take to SharePoint governance. Figure 2 illustrates these five models as a progression from the simplest de-centralised model to the most complex and comprehensive, the Information Worker competence centre model. Many organisations naturally develop either a centralised and de-centralised approach as a starting point but these have inherent weaknesses and ideally you should plan to progress to one of the other three models.

Figure 2: Progressive models for SharePoint governance

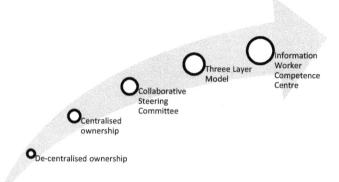

The following sections describe each of these models.

De-centralised ownership
In the de-centralised approach separate teams, departments or business units implement their own SharePoint environments with no co-ordination. This is common in large organisations and often results in site sprawl. Ultimately within the de-centralised model SharePoint has no single owner. There is no strategy or vision to guide, and no way of measuring success or return on investment.

Although on the positive side it could be argued that this approach promotes maximum freedom, it also promotes a sprawling mishmash of servers, sites, and content and an increasing amount of resources are required to create and maintain many separate and disparate implementations. Some short term benefits may be realised at the tactical level by individual teams or departmental level, but it is unlikely that the organisation will benefit at the strategic level. In fact overall the costs are likely to outweigh the benefits as each implementation is subject to individual learning curve costs and the disparate solutions make co-ordination, communication and collaboration between different areas of the organisation more difficult rather than improving them.

Centralised ownership

In the centralised model a single team or business function takes sole ownership of SharePoint. This is common in the early stages of SharePoint development or within smaller organisations. Which department assumes ownership is often determined by the use of SharePoint. IT departments often drive collaboration initiatives; Marketing usually own web site projects; Internal Communications or Human Resources often drive intranets projects.

There are two common scenarios where the IT team assume centralised ownership for SharePoint, and both are ultimately doomed to failure. In the first scenario the IT team take the '*build it and they will come*' approach. This will either result in failure due to low user adoption or a failure in information management chaos and compliance terms where there is high user adoption but no control. In the second scenario the IT team thinks, '*We will implement SharePoint for our own purposes, and when the rest of the business see how good it is they will all want to use it*'. This approach will fail because most people will only adopt a new technology when they first see it being adopted by people they perceive to be like themselves. In simple terms, the IT team playing with technology will not usually convince the business to use that technology themselves.

Human Resources, Communications and Marketing are other functions within an organisation which often assume early centralised ownership of SharePoint, typically through a requirement to develop intranet or web site solutions. They will of course need to work with the IT team to implement the technology but because the business is usually the budget holder in these situations ownership is seen to lie with them. These implementations may produce successful tactical solutions such as a publishing intranet used as a centralised communication tool. As scope of the intranet expands away from communication and into collaboration or document management it becomes impossible for a single business function to have the vision and reach to influence change across the organisation.

It has been claimed that

> *"The biggest ownership mistake involving large mutli-disciplinary intranets is to appoint a single department such as IT or Communications as the sole governing body of the system.. An Intranet has so many facets that it is next to impossible to run properly with a single owner, whether it be a person or a department"* (Ward 2007)

Collaborative steering committee

The next stage of SharePoint governance is a collaborative model which most often manifests as a project board established to oversee a SharePoint implementation. To be successful the committee should consist of around 6 to 8 members that represent different areas of the organisation. Human Resources and Internal Communications or Marketing are important members because they have the ability to begin to influence changes in behaviour necessary for effective user adoption. IT is required to bring knowledge of the technology and its capabilities. A senior Executive stakeholder brings authority, leadership and the strategic perspective. Business unit or team leaders bring the users perspective which research has shown to be a key element of any successful technology related business change initiative. A committee such as this has all the ingredients necessary to begin to address the three elements of the governance model. This can be a model from which to launch your first SharePoint project, and can be a long term approach for smaller organisations or limited SharePoint implementations. If you currently recognise yourself as being in a de-centralised or centralised model, then evolving to a collaborative steering committee model should be your first priority!

Three layer model

The Three Layer model for SharePoint governance uses three (or more) inter-related teams one for each of the three elements of SharePoint governance. Figure 3 illustrates the model.

Figure 3: Three layered model for SharePoint governance

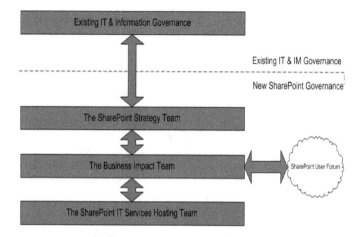

Table 3 briefly describes each of the three SharePoint governance teams.

Table 3: Overview of SharePoint governance teams

Team	Purpose	Membership
SharePoint strategy	'Owns' SharePoint within your business. It defines policy and strategy relating to the SharePoint platform and is accountable for a return on investment in SharePoint. It aligns the use of SharePoint with the corporate strategic objectives and defines the success metrics and how they will be monitored.	It is vitally important that the Strategic Team is a multidisciplinary, cross functional team which represents all areas of the organisation. Ideally the team will have very strong business representation to ensure it remains focused on delivering business value. Potential roles on the team could include: IT Executive, Senior Business Representatives; Senior HR and Training Representative; Executive Financial Stakeholder;

		Senior Information Manager; Senior User Representative; Lead Supplier.
Business Impact	Responsible for ensuring that the SharePoint Services deliver benefits and value at the organisational, team, and individual user level. They ensure that the SharePoint Services are adopted, and used in line with the policies defined by the SharePoint Strategy Team.	Typically mid-level management or users. Roles on the team may include; IT representative, HR & Training representative; Compliance & Auditing representative; Business Unit or Team user representative; Change Management representative.
IT Service Hosting	The SharePoint IT Service Hosting Team are responsible for the technical, administration and development tasks relating to the SharePoint platform.	Typically the SharePoint IT Service Hosting Team is a virtual team made up of representatives from different areas of the IT function. This includes; Data Storage, Database Administration, Infrastructure, Software Development, Support, and SharePoint Administration.

Information Worker Competence Centre
An Information Worker Competence Centre is:

> *"A coordinating function providing strategic oversight and decision levers across its portfolio of programs. As an administrative entity it logically groups "people with interrelated disciplines, domains of knowledge, experiences and skills [...] generally focusing on crucial expertise for the business" (Ruppertz-Rausch 2009)*

Governance is a key element of a competence centre. Figure 4 illustrates the structure of an Information Worker Competence Centre. Microsoft Enterprise Strategy Services have produced a whitepaper, which gives an overview of an Information Worker Competence Centre and describes how to establish one. The paper can be downloaded from:

http://go.microsoft.com/fwlink/?LinkId=157169

This approach is typically associated with the largest organisations and SharePoint implementations with investments that run into millions of pounds. For example an insurance business implemented one of the world's largest SharePoint online implementations consolidating 27 business unit intranets into a single solution serving approximately 77,000 users globally. Co-ordinating the implementation and on-going evolution and maintenance of such a massive solution requires a dedicated business function to handle the user adoption challenges, receive and assess requests from the business for new solutions and customisations and to manage the budget.

Figure 4: Structure of Information Worker Competence Centre

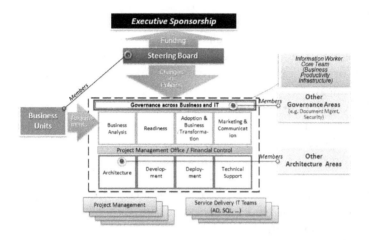

Strategy

A SharePoint strategy is a written statement of how SharePoint technologies will be used in order to achieve specific business objectives.   If you don't have one that you can print off, pick up and wave around then you are going to struggle!

> *"Achieving business value with SharePoint investments requires methodical strategic planning to minimize risk and maximize potential benefits."*
> *(Koplowitz & Le Clair 2008)*

This section discusses the following key considerations in developing your SharePoint strategy:

1. What is SharePoint?
2. The case against the business case
3. Strategic lenses
4. Defining your SharePoint strategy

What is SharePoint?

SharePoint is notoriously difficult to define. For example in the keynote presentation at the Microsoft SharePoint Conference 2009 Microsoft's CEO Steve Ballmer said:

> *"What is SharePoint? This is still a question I get asked when out visiting customers... It's kind of magical in a certain way. It's a really special kind of product... It's kinda like an operating system"* (Ballmer 2009)

Not very helpful. Here's my attempt:

> *"SharePoint is an* **set of integrated technologies** *which provides a* **platform** *upon which an organisation can build a flexible, long term* **information and knowledge management infrastructure."**

A bit of a mouthful! But it includes what I believe are the most important elements.

SharePoint is an integrated set of technologies

SharePoint is an umbrella term (and license) for a set of technologies that could be packaged as individual products. Performance Point Server, Portal Server, and Content Management Server are three former products that are now part of the SharePoint brand, and it's easy to see how technologies such as Excel Services, document management, and MySite could be stand-alone products. Microsoft has an explicit strategy to develop these technologies as an integrated set. The strength of SharePoint is in its breadth more than its depth. A SharePoint licence provides a full range of information management capabilities and the more of those capabilities an organisation uses the greater the return on investment. If you already use SharePoint for your Enterprise Search then why invest in another document management system? Understanding the breadth of SharePoint and the extent to which you anticipate leveraging the range of different capabilities is one key element of developing a SharePoint strategy.

SharePoint is an application development platform

SharePoint is a rich platform for building multi-tiered web applications. It possesses the three defining characteristics of an application development platform (Lele 2007):

- extensibility
- scalability
- reliability

Extensibility refers to the hooks which enable integration with other systems and applications, and the mechanisms for expanding the platform by developing new capabilities. SharePoint's many such hooks and mechanisms include but aren't limited to the following:

- Provider model
- HTML standards
- Business Intelligence Integration with SQL Server technologies
- ADO.NET
- Silverlight
- Federated search
- ASP.NET
- CMIS
- REST
- Workflow integration
- Business Connectivity

Scalability is a characteristic of a system, which enables it to handle growing amounts of work in a graceful manner. SharePoint is a highly scalable platform at both the physical and software layers. At the physical layer SharePoint can be scaled up by adding additional resources to the servers in the farm, or scaled out by adding additional servers to the farm. At the logical or software layer the key to SharePoint's scalability is the containment hierarchy and the service application model.

Finally, reliability refers to the ability of a system to perform consistently, on demand, without degradation or failure. SharePoint exhibits this characteristic by supporting redundancy at the physical layer, with multiple servers at the web front end, application, and database level.

There are two key questions that arise from viewing SharePoint as an application development platform:

1. What is SharePoint's role in your application development strategy?
2. What applications are right for SharePoint?

There are three basic strategies when considering SharePoint's role in your application development strategy:

1. application
2. application and Intranet
3. enterprise portal

The simplest approach is to view SharePoint as an application only. Under this approach SharePoint is deployed as-is, customisations are probably limited to either configuration through the web browser, or no-code customisations using SharePoint Designer.   Typically the your internal IT team will manage the deployment alone.

Next SharePoint can be used as an application and an intranet platform. In this model an intranet application is built on the SharePoint platform. Often this includes significant customisations, and you may work with a partner during the initial deployment.   Once the deployment is complete you may limit in-house customisations to no-code solutions through SharePoint Designer.

Finally you can adopt SharePoint as an enterprise portal, a core component of its application development strategy. Under this model you are likely to have a fully-fledged and experienced internal software development team, and SharePoint is considered for all web based applications.

If you decide that SharePoint will play a role as an application development platform then you'll need to be able to determine when to use SharePoint and when not to use it, so what are the key considerations?

Firstly,   SharePoint   is   best   suited   to   managing unstructured information, i.e. documents as opposed to data. If your solution is entirely data driven then perhaps SharePoint isn't the best way forward?

Secondly, if you're not using any of the SharePoint workloads such as search, content, communities, insights, sites, or composites then why would you use SharePoint?

Thirdly, SharePoint is an excellent tool for situations when you need to create multiple instances of a web site based on a common template. For example a site for every supplier, every customer, or every project. If you only need one site that displays different data then again perhaps SharePoint isn't the right tool for the job?

SharePoint is an Information Workplace platform

In 2005 analysts at Forrester Research Inc. coined the term "*Information Workplace*" to describe the work place of the future for information workers (Driver and Moore 2007). They define the information workplace in terms of seven tenants. Table 4 summarises the seven tenants of the information workplace.

Table 4: Seven tenants of the information workplace

1. Contextual	Workers shouldn't have to keep clicking and opening different applications. Instead, technologies such as RSS will push information to the end-user's portal. Also, users will make use of virtual worlds where co-workers can interact with one another (in the form of avatars). Inside these worlds, they can view technologies such as presentations, word processing documents and spread sheets like they would in the real world
2. Individualised	This is predicated on the idea that users are at the centre of their own universe. To enable these individualized experiences, core Web 2.0 technologies can be employed by IT, including, mash-ups, RSS, tagging, social networking, podcasts and virtual worlds

3. Seamless	Right now, the information worker who deals with multiple applications lives off the "ALT + TAB" command to toggle between them. In the new information workplace, good RIAs will replace traditional desktop applications but hold on to some of the great functionality, including control, instant feedback and efficient task flow—functions its older brother, HTML-based Web applications, tried but often failed to address. Tagging will also allow the individual user to categorize information in a way he wants, preventing the need to thumb through electronic folders
4. Visual	Traditionally, information in business has been delivered to end-users primarily through texts and numbers. The future workplace will deliver it through 3D (again, often through a virtual world) or through RIAs and mash-ups. The ability to show information graphically (instead of textually) will cut down on "information overload" and deliver it in a more user-friendly way
5. Multi-modal	Simply, this tenet means mash-ups. The user can take whatever aspect of various applications she likes and squish them into one
6. Social	This tenet cuts to the core of what the information workplace means to the modern day worker. It incorporates all of the big Web 2.0 technologies—including profiles of workers, tagging, shared bookmarks, blogs, wikis and community members. In a social environment, information doesn't get moved to neat and tidy repositories (like folders). Instead, it lives much more freely and is found through tagging and search. Users gravitate towards social groups that interest them and contribute to them accordingly
7. Quick	The old information workplace operated on on-premise software that took forever to install, and sometimes just as long to update. The new workplace will operate on principles of SOA and hosted services that promote speed-to-user rather than tiresome command-and-control architecture. The beauty is, if a CIO does this right by using enterprise-worthy vendors, they can have a fast delivery model but keep administrator access to ensure compliance and security.

To realise the vision of the information workplace an organisation needs a technical platform which provides the following set of capabilities:

- content management
- collaboration and communication

- portal framework
- pervasive business intelligence
- office productivity
- search
- human centric business process management
- information rights management

This presents us with a basic strategic choice:

1. Select best of breed products for each area and integrate them
2. Select a unified infrastructure that delivers the breadth of capabilities

Option 1 has the benefit of delivering best of breed functionality across all capabilities, but do you really need the best? On the downside the IT function has to maintain several different technologies from different vendors who may all have different strategies and roadmaps for their products; integration can be difficult, costly and time consuming; and for the users learning to use several different technologies can be a barrier to adoption.

Option 2 has the benefit of lower costs as a single licence and technology platform delivers the breadth of capabilities; integration is simpler; and users only have one technology to adopt. On the downside the single platform may not have the same depth of functionality as the best in breed products.

If you follow strategic option number 2 and select a unified infrastructure then your next challenge is to select the technology and vendor.

SharePoint is infrastructure
Infrastructure can be defined as,

> "*Substructure or underlying foundation; esp., the basic installations and facilities on which the continuance and growth of a community, state, etc. depend, as roads, schools, power plants, transportation and communication systems*" (Yourdictionary 2011)

SharePoint is your information management infrastructure and infrastructure has a number of defining aspects.

Infrastructures are open. There is no limit to the number of users, stakeholders or vendors that can be involved. There is always something on the outside of the infrastructure that could be connected. With SharePoint this could refer to opening up or connecting your SharePoint platform with partners, suppliers, customers. The openness of the SharePoint platform could be a problem when defining your SharePoint strategy. Where do you draw the borders? How do you define the scope of your SharePoint implementation and how do you define the scope of its use?

Infrastructures have a supporting or enabling function. SharePoint is an enabler as it provides a set of capabilities which can be used and reused in many ways and for many purposes. For example a transport infrastructure consisting of road, rail, and air links enables commerce, education, health services, and social activity. The benefits are derived from the services that are implemented on the infrastructure rather than from the infrastructure itself and so it is with SharePoint. This is one contributing factor to the difficulties that many organisations face in creating a business case for SharePoint. There are significant costs involved in deploying the base infrastructure of servers and software, yet this base platform does not deliver any direct business benefits. Often the first SharePoint project in an organisation has to bear the costs of implementing the infrastructure, even though the benefits are spread across the multiple solutions it enables.

Infrastructure is shared by a larger community. A single SharePoint platform can appear to the users in many different ways. A shared infrastructure requires commonly understood guidelines, or rules of the road, to co-ordinate the multiple groups of users. This underlines the need for effective governance and management of SharePoint.

Building large infrastructure takes time. As time passes requirements will change and evolve and the infrastructure needs to adapt. Infrastructure is never complete, and your SharePoint implementation will never be finished.

Infrastructure is never developed from scratch. Infrastructure will always be integrated with or replace existing infrastructure. For example SharePoint often replaces or integrates with existing collaboration and file sharing tools and methods such as email and mapped network drives.

The case against the traditional business case

Most organisations seem to struggle with the business case for SharePoint investments, and some experts argue that you shouldn't even try! There are two main arguments against the traditional business case for SharePoint:

1. Traditional business cases are ill suited to the knowledge economy
2. The cause and effect chain is too long

Typical project approval and budget allocation processes involve a business case built on a financial analysis and expressed in financial terms such as, Return On Investment, Internal Rate of Return, Net Present Value, and Total Cost of Ownership. These measures rely on being able to estimate the outcomes from an investment in financial terms.

Some people argue that this industrial age approach is ill suited to today's knowledge based economy. They argue that a traditional business case is well suited to a situation where the inputs and outputs are tangible and can be measured in financial terms, but that knowledge economy is driven by intangible factors that can be difficult to define, difficult to measure or too costly to try to define or measure. How do you define the productivity of an information worker? Is it the number of documents they write? The number of tasks they complete? The number of hours spent in meetings? And how do you measure the benefits of collaboration or social computing?

A second argument often used against the traditional business case for SharePoint is that the cause and effect chain is so long that it makes it impossible to map costs to benefits. For example an investment in social computing that leads to two people meeting, exchanging ideas, solving a problem, delivering a reusable solution or best practice which results in ongoing costs reduction across the organisation can be difficult to predict, estimate or measure.

Strategic lenses

Organisations approach SharePoint from many, many different perspectives. I've identified a number of different lenses through which organisations view SharePoint:

- Value
- Enterprise Content Management
- Knowledge Management
- Collaboration
- Intranet

Value

How is value defined in your organisation? Where is value created in your organisation? Answering these two questions is a great start in developing your SharePoint strategy. For example in 2009 I worked with a UK public sector agency that was investigating how they could use SharePoint. We soon identified cost reduction as a strategic driver. But which costs? Case handling turned out to be the core business process within the organisation, and the teams of highly paid lawyers and economists that handled the cases were a significant cost centre. Investigation into the working practices of the lawyers revealed familiar problems relating to the use of email, and file shares for collaboration and document management. The decision was made to develop a prototype to demonstrate how a SharePoint based solution could improve the core case handling process and improve the productivity of the lawyers.

In many commercial organisations value will be measured in terms of revenue and profit but there are other measures. For example, a police force that used detection rates as their key measure; a not for profit organisation measures how many of its volunteer workers would recommend the organisation to another potential volunteer; and a leading legal firm has a mission statement based on delivering high quality. Understanding how value is measured, the processes that create it, and the role of information in those processes is the platform from which to build your SharePoint strategy.

Enterprise Content Management

Many organisations approach SharePoint from an Enterprise Content Management, or Document Management perspective. A key element of enterprise content management is understanding the content lifecycle. Figure 5 illustrates the key stages in the lifecycle of unstructured content.

Figure 5: The content lifecycle

Potentially each of these stages could be supported by a different SharePoint based solution.   A collaboration solution could provide an environment for people to create sites for live projects or group working. A set of departmental or process based portals could provide long-term storage for the completed or published content. A records centre could provide archiving and disposal services. Finally of course there is search to glue it all together.

To the user these could all be presented as different tools for different jobs but under the bonnet they are all built on SharePoint.

Knowledge Management
If your organisation has a strategic focus on knowledge management then SharePoint provides you with the set of tools that you need to implement your strategy, plus Knowledge Management gives us food for thought in developing a SharePoint strategy.

There are two types of knowledge: explicit knowledge which can be codified, perhaps as documents, process maps, or calculations; and implicit or tacit knowledge which is experienced based and can't easily be codified. Understanding which of these two types of knowledge are associated with the value creation in your organisation can help to shape your SharePoint strategy. SharePoint facilitates the management of explicit knowledge through search and content management. Strategies for the management of tacit knowledge are likely to include SharePoint's social features including MySite, blogs, and people search.

Knowledge Management is a mature discipline with over twenty years of experience and empirical research. There are a number of well-established practices and techniques and SharePoint can be used as the toolset to implement them with. Amongst the knowledge management practices that can be implemented using SharePoint are:

1. best practices
2. communities of practice
3. lessons learnt
4. expertise location

These are KM strategies that can be implemented using SharePoint but implementing SharePoint is not the same as implementing the strategy. You need to buy into the strategy first, the technology is a secondary concern.

Collaboration
Collaboration is not something that happens as a result of installing software.

Nor is it something that you're going to achieve overnight.

Strictly speaking collaboration is a human activity where people work together to achieve jointly valued results. A project team is the classic organisational example. But within the context of SharePoint planning collaboration is often mixed up with related concepts such as communication, cooperation, and co-ordination.

In modern organisations people work together in a number of different ways.

Table 5: How people work together within organisations

Working style	Description
Teams	Cross functional groups that come together to achieve a jointly held goal or objective. Typically a team will only exist until the goal is achieved
Departments	Organisational units defined by functional specialism.
Communities	Groups of people who share a common interest or area of expertise
Networks	A group of people who want to stay in touch for their mutual benefit

These ways of working are very different in terms of their objectives, time frames, leadership, authority, and membership; they have different requirements in terms of how they work together and share information; and they create value in different ways. An individual employee may be a member of many different teams, communities and networks. No one solution will meet all of their requirements and needs, but SharePoint can be used to create an integrated set of solutions.

When defining your SharePoint strategy consider which of these ways of working is most closely associated with value in your organisation, and identify examples. Project teams are often the easiest to tackle because they are very visible and their results are obvious so it comes as no surprise that one of the most common uses of SharePoint is to facilitate team collaboration. Creating SharePoint sites for departments can facilitate corporate communications and information sharing; community sites are often associated with the identification and sharing of best practices; and networks can play an important role in problem solving and innovation.

Intranet

Many organisations select SharePoint as the technical platform for their intranet, and intranet projects are often driven by IT, HR or Internal Communications or Marketing departments.

Intranet business solutions have been around for about 15 years and almost every organisation has one. But how many are successful business tools? In my experience not that many. Why? Because an intranet is an information management tool and typically IT, HR, and Internal Communication teams have limited expertise in information management.

Let's start with the basics. What is an intranet? Usually people use the term to describe an organisations internal web site. But in the purest sense an Intranet is:

> *"...A private computer network that uses internet protocols and network connectivity to securely share any part of an organisation's information or operational systems with its employees"* (Wikipedia 2008)

In other words an Intranet is a private internet, and the internet isn't a single web site with a top level landing page and a tree like structure that users navigate through. It's a vast network made up of many different web sites, applications and services. It has no centre, top or starting point. It is the world's largest information management system and most people find it pretty easy to use and are able to find what they need use search engines. Perhaps we can learn some lessons from this when designing our corporate Intranets?

Razorfish (Avenue A Razorfish 2008) have produced an Intranet maturity model which I find useful in talking to clients that approach SharePoint from an Intranet perspective. It gets them thinking about what they mean by "intranet", and how their intranet will create value for them.

Figure 6: Intranet Maturity Model

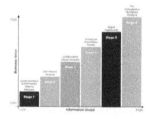

At stage 1 the intranet is a corporate communications mechanism. It is centrally managed, benefits accrue from savings in printing and distribution costs, and adoption is not an issue.

At stage 2 the intranet becomes a vehicle for employee self-service. FAQ's, HR policies and procedures, and template documents are classic examples. Benefits come from standardisation and increased productivity through self-service. Adoption is not an issue as the value proposition is easily understood by all.

In stage 3 the addition of document management and collaboration tools such as team calendars, discussion boards, and task lists address the needs of project teams. Adoption at this stage can be more difficult.

At stage 4 the intranet becomes an enterprise portal. The key characteristics of a portal are the integration with other systems and applications to provide a single point of entry, and personalisation and customisation. Personalisation describes the system's ability to present the right information for the individual user and customisation describes the ability of the user to determine which information they see.

Stage 5 takes the enterprise portal further by integrating real time information from data warehouses or business intelligence systems to create pervasive dash boards and decision support systems.

Finally at Stage 6 the intranet becomes the single interface into all corporate systems and information stores. The research notes that there aren't many intranets which have reached this stage yet.

SharePoint provides a platform which enables organisations to move all the way along this maturity model.

Defining your SharePoint strategy

There are two broad approaches: enabling specific processes or delivering general capabilities (that then enable processes!).

For example, a major bank and a UK not-for-profit organisation use SharePoint to improve their project delivery process. An asset management company has improved their client on-boarding process, and a private bank has improved their credit application process. These are all examples of specific process improvements.

A European central bank and a global manufacturer have implemented SharePoint as a generic collaboration service that allows any employee to create SharePoint sites for any purpose, and a number of organisations have implemented SharePoint for enterprise search. These are examples of general capabilities. With the right leadership, motivation, and support people will adopt these tools and use them in their own way. There's no need for a detailed central view of the business processes. The individual workers determine for themselves how best to use the new tools.

Targeting business processes makes creating a business case much easier, because the business case for IT is only as predictable as the use.

Architecture

Installing a SharePoint farm is one thing. Architecting and building business solutions on it is an entirely different thing.   How do you even decide what it is that you're going to build?

The answer relates to the strategic approach that you have selected.   If you have managed to identify a specific business process that you want to target then traditional solution design methods work well. Start by investigating the current situation, identify the pain points, and design a solution that addresses them. But what do you build if you want to deploy SharePoint as a set of general capabilities?

This section presents an approach to deploying SharePoint as a set of generic business services.   It contains the following:

1.   The services concept
2.   Intranet and collaboration services with SharePoint
3.   The user centric intranet – beyond the services model
4.   Why the services architecture works

The services concept

Imagine that you run the facilities service for a large office block.

On the ground floor are meeting rooms that can be used by people in your company when working with 3rd party visitors such as customers, suppliers and partners. Anyone in your company can book one of these rooms by completing a short request form. It takes one working day to process the requests, set up the room, and add your visitors to the guest list.

On the first floor there are a rooms that have been designed for teams. Anyone in your company can go to the first floor and book out a room for a period of time from an hour up to a month. The rooms are equipped with whiteboards, projectors, screens, flipcharts, and telephones. If your team need to keep the room for longer than a month then you can renew your booking for another month, but if you forget to renew then after a month all your materials will be cleaned out of the room, kept in a cupboard for six months and then destroyed unless you ask for it to be returned.

On the second floor every employee can have their own personal office. The offices are quite small, just enough room to store your files and books, and equipped with a table and chairs in case you want to invite a colleague in for a quick chat.

On the third floor are the departmental offices. To be allocated a departmental office a head of department has to fill in a form, the request has to be approved by the central facilities team. The office has to be paid for from the departmental budget. Each department office has a front of house area where visitors to the department can find the documentation and resources created by that department, and a back house area only accessible by members of that department where departmental meetings are held and departmental resources and content are stored. Since these offices are paid for from departmental budgets they can be decorated and equipped to order.

On the fourth floor is the project management office. Here project managers are allocated a project room for their teams to work in for the duration of their projects.

Finally, on the top floor is a series of large meeting rooms that are used by special interest groups, or communities, for regular meetings and seminars.

As the facilities manager you don't need to know the detail of exactly what people are doing in the rooms, you don't need to understand the projects, or what the meetings are about. You don't need to sit down with the people in your company and ask them what their requirements are, you are able to provide a set of basic, generic services or capabilities and let people use them as they see fit, but within the framework of the service levels that you offer.

Intranet and collaboration services with SharePoint

I hope that the metaphor is obvious? In this scenario we have taken a building (SharePoint) which consists of rooms (collaboration areas, or SharePoint site collections) and divided it up into floors (web applications). Each floor (web application) delivers a different service, is designed to support a particular way in which people work, and has its own value proposition. Figure 7 illustrates the concept of delivering SharePoint as a set of services.

Figure 7: Example Intranet and collaboration services

Figure 7: Intranet & Collaboration Services

Enterprise Search (People, Content, Expertise)

MySite	Teams	Communities	Portals	Extranet
Social and Ad-hoc collaboration; http://personal/myname; Individual workspaces; Self Service creation; one workspace per employee; Small Storage quota; No Directory listings; Minimal training required; **Benefits:** Share personal learning, find expertise and experience, enhanced problem solving, improved communications	Ad-hoc collaboration; http://Teams; Ad-hoc teams; Instant Self Service; Small Storage quota; Minimal training required; 6 Months then archive; e.g. inter-business unit projects; **Benefits:** Improved team performance	Social learning; http://Communities; Inter-divisional groups with shared interests, voluntary membership; Centralised creation; Medium storage quota; Entry into a Directory; e.g. Technology areas; **Benefits:** Improved intellectual insight around specific subjects from social learning; Improved quality through sharing best practices and standardisation	Corporate communications, document management and vertical collaboration; http://globalservices; Based around organisational units and departments; Entry into a Directory; **Benefits:** corporate communications, employee engagement, reduction in time spent searching for information	Enables collaboration with 3rd parties including suppliers, customers, partners

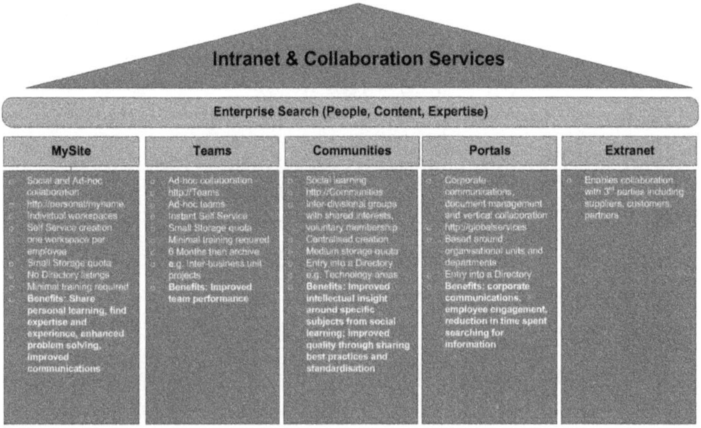

Every organisation I talk to adapts this model, renaming the services and refining their descriptions and purpose, but I've yet to find the organisation for which this model wouldn't work. The following sections briefly describe these baseline services.

MySite Service

MySite provides each user with their own individual home page. The MySite sites are based on the same principles as popular public social computing platforms such as Linked-In and Facebook which will make them intuitive and easy for most users to learn to operate and adopt.

This service offers benefits through accelerated communication through micro-blogging and news feeds; and in sharing tacit knowledge by allowing people to create personal brand identities and to position themselves as experts on certain topics.

Each MySite will provide a public view and a private view. It will contain a profile which could be based on information integrated from the corporate Active Directory, and supplemented with additional fields of information.

The MySite includes a colleagues list which the owners can manage; a list of communities which the owner has chosen to join; and Newsfeed will list activities of colleagues and from communities.

The Teams service

The Teams service allows any users to instantly create collaboration sites. The typical approach is to allow any user to instantly create a site at any time and for any purpose.

To create a collaboration site the user selects a template upon which to base their site. New templates can be developed and added to the Service over time. A directory which lists and describe the collaboration sites, can be a useful way of controlling site proliferation. Another approach is to give each site limited lifetime. Once the site reaches a certain age it can either be automatically archived, deleted, or the site owner can be automatically prompted to either renew the site or delete it.

Collaboration sites are typically based on quick to edit Wiki pages, and can contain a wide variety of collaboration and document management tools and

functionality   including;   document   libraries;
announcement lists; discussion boards; and RSS feeds.

The Communities service

The Communities service is intended to support
communities of practice, or special interest groups. An
employee wishing to create a community must complete
and submit an online request form. Once the request has
been approved the community site is created for them.
Community sites are different from Team sites because
team sites have a limited lifespan, and Community sites
live forever, or at least until the community breaks up and
the community leader deletes the site.

The Portals service

The Portals service enables authorised users to create top
level intranet sites that consist of rich HTML based
content. Typically this service is based on a on a site
request and authorisation model where users wishing to
create a new portal complete an online form which is
routed to a central team for approval.

The most common use of a Portals service is to create
intranet sites for business units and processes. For
example an HR site might be created as HRWeb, or a
credit application portal might support a core business
process at a private bank.

Typically Portal sites are used to store and present
corporate information such as news, policy documents, or
forms. This service allows each business unit or
geography to create and maintain its own internal Web
site.

The Search service

The Search service provides a method to find both tacit and explicit knowledge. It acts as a people directory enabling users to search for individuals either by name or by area of expertise. Search terms are matched against the information held in the profile and content of each users MySite. It also provides the ability to search across documents and content held in any site within the MySite, Teams, Collaboration, and Portal services.

The Extranet Service

The Extranet service is similar to the Teams service except in this instance the SharePoint sites are created so that they are accessible by 3rd parties such as partners, suppliers and customers.

You may prefer to base the extranet sites on publishing portals, making use of the content management features and rich web based content. Or you may prefer to base the extranet sites on collaboration sites, favouring functionality over aesthetics. SharePoint licensing is a particular discussion point with extranets as both CAL and FIS licensing models can be used.

The user centric intranet – beyond the services model

The services based approach to SharePoint deployments works. For example a European central bank deployed a Teams style service and within nine months the service was achieving 160,000 site visits per month from just 2,500 employees, and the project manager told me it was one of the most successful projects she had worked on at the bank in her fifteen years there. It's also the basic premise behind Microsoft's' own intranet.

One characteristic of the services model is that there is no obvious home page, or starting point unless you count your enterprise search page. I think that this is a good thing. Remember the early days of the Internet when internet portals like Yahoo tried to create a taxonomy of web pages? Figure 8 illustrates a 1990's Yahoo portal for those too young to remember.

Figure 8: 1990's Yahoo portal

It wasn't long before the amount of content made this approach of navigating the internet impossible. Along came Google and the rest is history. Organisations are facing the same challenges. A client commented to me recently that a top level landing page and fixed hierarchy for an intranet just doesn't work anymore.

I believe that the services model; having hundreds or thousands of SharePoint sites organised into a few top level services; and using Search to glue it all together mirrors the way that we use the internet and provides a flexible and scalable model for an Intranet.

But the services model doesn't work for everyone. Some of my clients have just been uncomfortable with the idea of no home page, and others have pointed out that with no home page it can be difficult to ensure that corporate communications pushed out through the Intranet are seen by everyone.

The solution is to use a customised MySite as every employees personalised homepage. Figure 9 illustrates the idea. The global navigation bar that gives access to any of the services from anywhere within your SharePoint deployment. The activity feed can be extended to allow the user to subscribe to team sites or portals so that any activity on those sites appears directly onto the home page. The beauty of this approach is that the information the employee sees first is that which is most relevant to them, and it is based on popular consumer sites like Facebook and Linked-in which could be a massive boost for user adoption.

Figure 9: The MySites concept.

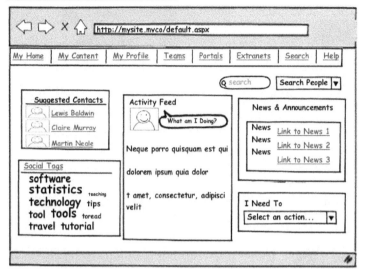

Why the services architecture works

To understand why the services model works so well let's examine the approach using the strategic lenses we discussed in the Strategy element of our framework.

The first lens was Value; understanding how value is defined and measured in your organisation and focusing SharePoint in those areas. The services model allows us to do this at two levels; in the selection of the services we choose to deploy, and then the area in which we pilot and introduce the use of the service. For example in an event management business where value is related to revenues and profits an extranet service which created an extranet site for each event booked at a venue enabled the business to cross sell products and services such as merchandising and security.

From a content management perspective different services can be used to facilitate the different stages of the content lifecycle. A Teams service for the dynamic creation of content, a Portals service to create areas for the storage and management of published content, a Search service for the retrieval of content, a Records service for the archiving and disposal of content.

From a Knowledge Management perspective Team, Community, Mysite and people search services facilitate a KM strategy based on the management of tacit knowledge. Portals, Records, and content search services facilitate a KM strategy based on explicit knowledge.

From a collaboration perspective the services support the different ways that people work together. The Teams service supports project teams; the Portals service supports workgroups or departments; The Mysites service enables networks; The Communities service support communities of practice or special interest groups; and the Extranet service support working with partners, suppliers or customers.

Finally the full services model enables an organisation to progress along the intranet maturity model from a publishing intranet using just portals to a consolidated workplace interface using a user centric intranet.

Transition

There is no such thing as a SharePoint project; there are only organisational change projects.

The final element in the Art of SharePoint success framework is Transition which relates to the management of change at both the organisational and individual levels. Although presented last it is probably the most important element, after all if no one uses the technology then it delivers no value.

This section contains the following:

1. SharePoint, change, and change management
2. The diffusion of innovations
3. Brining it all together – building your adoption plan

SharePoint, change, and change management

SharePoint can bring a number of different types of change to an organisation. It's not unique in that respect, the same can probably be said of nearly all information technologies. But SharePoint's potential as a catalyst for change is bigger than most other technologies. It can:

- facilitate changes in information centric **business processes** by enabling new ways of working
- be instrumental in changing **organisational structures** such as the evolution from hierarchies to networks
- enable a shift of **power** from formal positions of management authority to community based experts
- require changes in individual **behaviour** such as a move away from sending emails and attachment to using SharePoint sites

- enable new **relationships and interactions** with customers, partners, and suppliers through extranets, web sites and social computing

According to Wikipedia, change management is a structured approach to transitioning individuals, teams and organisations from a current state to a desired future state in a controlled manner (Wikipedia 2010).

A structured approach means that we have a plan. Transitioning from the current state means that you understand the current situation and know where you are starting from. A desired future state means you know what you are trying to achieve and how you will know when we have done it. A controlled manner means that you have some means of measuring your progress.

If you don't have all of these elements in place then you're not ready to start. You might not have all the answers at the beginning, but if you're going to leave the house you should at least have some vague notion of where you are going.

There are different types of change and it can be helpful to understand which you are attempting. The following sections briefly discuss the main types of organisational change.

Organisation wide versus sub-system
Your SharePoint strategy should determine the scope of SharePoint usage within your organisation. Are you deploying a set of general capabilities to a wide audience? Or are you focusing on very specific use case? If you deploy SharePoint using the services based model then

you could find yourself working at both levels. For example you may choose to deploy a team service or a portal service which is available organisation wide, but your Business Impact team (remember the governance model?) might work with individual business units or process to find specific sub system level use cases for the services.

Transformational versus incremental change

A Transformational change is a radical or fundamental change to the organisation. In SharePoint terms this might mean trying implement a complete suite of services in one go.

Good luck with that!

In my experience incremental, or gradual change is the secret to success with SharePoint, and this is the basis of the services model. Each service can be introduced as a distinct project. Figure 10 illustrates the concept of incremental change whilst deploying SharePoint as services.

Figure 10: Incremental change with SharePoint services

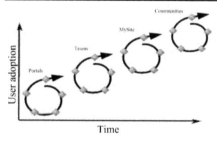

Remedial versus developmental change

Are you trying to remedy a known issue or problem or are you trying improve or develop an already successful situation? If you're attempting the former then your SharePoint strategy will probably be focused on developing a specific application or solution, probably related to a specific business process. Using SharePoint to resolve quality issues in your project delivery process is a typical example. If you're attempting the latter, such as improving the way teams collaborate within your organisation then you're probably going to adopt the services based model.

The diffusion of innovations

The diffusion of innovations (Rogers 1962) is a theory that offers an explanation of how, why and at what rate new ideas or technologies spread through social groups. Although the evidence for the theory came from a study of the seed technology amongst North American famers in the 1940's it provides a great basis for understanding the SharePoint adoption problem! There are four key lessons from the theory that should shape your SharePoint adoption planning:

1. the adoption lifecycle
2. the adoption process
3. factors that affect adoption
4. user adoption requirements

The following sections summarise the key points.

The adoption lifecycle

In any social group there are five different categories of adopters. Table 6 briefly describes the five groups.

Table 6: Categories of adopters

Category	Description
Innovator	The first group to adopt a new technology or innovation. These are the people who love technology for technologies sake, the ones camping outside the shop for the latest release of the new phone
Early adopter	The second fastest category of individuals who adopt technology. These are the visionaries who first see the opportunity for the application of technology. Often these are the opinion leaders in an organisation
Early majority	The third group to adopt a new technology. Will only adopt once they see and understand the value proposition
Late majority	The fourth group to adopt a new technology. Typically this group are sceptical about innovations.
Laggards	The last group to adopt. Often the oldest group and resistant to change.

Figure 11 illustrates the adoption lifecycle. The bell curve shows the percentage of the population represented by each of the categories of adopters. The s-shaped curve shows the cumulative adoption rate of a technology as each group adopts.

Figure 11: The adoption lifecycle

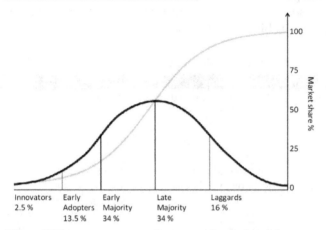

The different stages of your plan should target the successive adoption by the different categories. Innovators are passionate about technology so focusing on the technical aspects of your solution will be important in winning them over. Next, the early adopters are interested in the application of the technology so work with them to understand how a teams service, for example, can be applied to specific business problems. The early adopters will be your pilot groups.   The early and late majority will typically only adopt a new idea when they see it first being adopted by people that they perceive to be like themselves. This is why piloting a SharePoint solution in the IT department first is not a good idea. The business are unlikely to adopt something just because IT think it is a good idea. Pilot it in the business and promote the success stories. Finally, don't even bother with the Laggards, the best strategy for winning them over is to surround them. Once they see everyone else adopting a new technology or innovation they will come round. Eventually.

Innovators and early adopters make up about 16% of the population and these groups are likely to readily adopt your SharePoint based innovation. The trick is to move beyond these groups into the early majority. You haven't reached a critical mass of adoption until you get past the 16% mark.

Understanding the S-curve is key to understanding the value or return on investment from your innovation. Quite simply as adoption increases so does the return on investment.

The adoption process
Individuals go through five stages when deciding whether to adopt or reject a new idea or technology. Table 7 describes each of the stages. A user adoption strategy should use specific techniques or tactics move people through these stages.

Table 7: Five Stage of the adoption process

Stage	Description
Knowledge	In this stage the individual is first exposed to an innovation but lacks information about the innovation. It should be noted that during this stage of the process the individual has not been inspired to find more information about the innovation.
Persuasion	In this stage the individual is interested in the innovation and actively seeks information/detail about the innovation
Decision	In this stage the individual takes the concept of the innovation and weighs the advantages/disadvantages

	of using the innovation and decides whether to adopt or reject the innovation. Due to the individualistic nature of this stage Rogers notes that it is the most difficult stage to acquire empirical evidence
Implementation	In this stage the individual employs the innovation to a varying degree depending on the situation. During this stage the individual determines the usefulness of the innovation and may search for further information about it.
Confirmation	Although the name of this stage may be misleading, in this stage the individual finalizes their decision to continue using the innovation and may use the innovation to its fullest potential.

Factors affecting adoption

There are five key factors that affect the adoption of innovation:

1. the idea is perceived to have more value than existing methods
2. the idea is not overly complex
3. the idea results in visible, measurable, positive outcomes
4. the idea is testable before implementation
5. the idea is compatible with existing values, past experience, and current needs

Let's briefly consider how we can ensure that these factors are present in our SharePoint implementations.

Firstly, it's important that you clearly communicate the value proposition of your SharePoint solution and that means that you know what it is! Why are we doing this? If you don't know then don't start.

Secondly, keep it simple! Over time your SharePoint infrastructure may grow to become large and complex, but successful complex systems usually start out as successful simple systems. Not many start out as successful complex systems.

Thirdly, you need to be clear about your success measures, and how they will be measured and reported. This goes back to knowing how you will have achieved your goals. If your goal is simply 'improving collaboration', then you are almost certainly going to fail!

The idea must be testable before implementation. In SharePoint this might mean beginning each SharePoint solution with prototypes and pilots.

Finally the idea must be compatible with the existing values, experiences and needs. Implementing a SharePoint collaboration solution in an organisation that has just wasted millions on a failed content management system implementation will be very difficult. Equally implementing a collaboration solution in an environment where people typically work alone probably won't get you very far either.

User adoption requirements

There are five key requirements for user adoption:

1. corporate advantage
2. personal advantage
3. useability

4. social culture
5. operational support

Corporate advantage means that people need to understand why the organisation is making the change. What's the problem? And how does the change help? At central European bank that I worked with the SharePoint Strategy team (remember that governance model?) reviewed the organisations 10 strategic objectives listed on their own web site and tried to map the use of SharePoint to them.

Personal advantage answers the question, '*What's in it for me?*', how does the individual employee benefit from the change. The services model helps here because each service is designed to address a particular issue. The teams service is intended to improve team performance and address the issues associated with collaboration via email and file shares for example.

Useability relates to the user interface design and branding, and the navigation and ease with information can be found. The services model helps with the latter because the services become your top level information architecture. Dynamic, in progress information is in the teams service; static, published information is in the portals service; personal information is in MySite, and so on.

Social culture refers to how the new technologies and services are perceived, and the incentives for using them. For example at the European central bank I worked with they awarded business improvement bonuses for good ideas that improved the way the organisation works and in one month 5 of 15 awards were for the innovative use of the Teams service they implemented. If you are implementing a Communities service then studies show that rewarding and encouraging people to participate in the community is vital. For example you could allow consultants to enter community activity onto their time sheets. Finally, visible executive leadership such as the CEO creating their own Mysite, or writing a blog can be powerful tools in changing culture.

Finally operational support includes initiatives such as a help desk, training courses or materials, and including an introduction to your solution or services as part of your staff induction process.

Brining it all together – building your adoption plan

For every service or solution that you deploy on your SharePoint platform you should plan and budget for creating and executing an adoption plan. An adoption plan is quite simply a written statement of how you intend to ensure that your people use the new tools you provide in the way that you intended.

The following list provides a good structure for an adoption plan:

1. Aims and objectives
2. Transition team
3. Overview of the approach

4. Project plan
5. Success criteria
6. Metrics, monitoring and reporting
7. Risks and issues
8. Appendix A: overview of selected approaches

Section 1 should give a simple overview of what the adoption plan is trying to achieve. Section 2 identifies the individual members of the transition team, and defines their high-level responsibilities and ownerships.

The nitty gritty of this is in sections 3 and 4; the approach and the plan. Table 7 presents a very simplified overview of my recommended approach.

Table 7: Simplified adoption plan

Phase	Example adoption measures
Awareness	Pens, posters, intranet bulletins, user workshops
Availability	Easy first steps, sandpit environments, launch day events
Usage	Training, support desk, Stop Doing and Start Doing, Success Stories
Adoption	Service updates, new employee orientation, staff incentives

In the Awareness phase the aim is to first raise awareness that the current situation, tools, or working practices are undesirable and that change is required. Once the need for change has been established then the focus shifts to an emphasis on the solution that is coming, and on the corporate and personal return on investment. Use your existing corporate communication channels to get the message out.

The Availability phase is focused on making sure that peoples first experience of the new solution is a positive one.   There's plenty of research to show that first impression count when it comes to the adoption of new technologies.   Easy First Steps is a great technique. Create a simple one page set of instructions so that someone using your service or solution for the first time can quickly and easily achieve something useful. Creating a team site is a good example. Another useful technique is the Sandpit environment. This involves creating a complete copy of your service or solution in a non-live environment so that people can experiment without fear of doing anything wrong or breaking anything. By careful that the purpose of the Sandpit environment is clear! You don't want people using it for real work by mistake.

The Usage phase is the first few weeks and months of the solution being live in the organisation. The aim is to encourage people to use the solution. The availability of materials such as FAQ's, and How To guides, and a support desk are crucial at this stage. Stop Doing and Start Doing is a fantastic technique for driving changes in specific behaviours.   The idea is to create a set of handouts, or flyer that identify 'bad' behaviours, such as sending emails to multiple people with documents attached, and suggest alternative 'good' behaviours, such as creating a team site and storing the document there. If you're clever you can map these behaviours to your success metrics. The innovators and early adopters will naturally adopt your solution first, work closely with them to document and promote their success stories in order to win over the early majority.

Finally, the Adoption phase aims to cement the changes into the fabric of your organisation. Regular updates to the service or solution in response to user feedback, following through with staff incentives, and ensuring that an introduction to the services is part of your induction process.

Conclusions

It has been said that:

> *"To make knowledge work productive will be the great management challenge of this century; just as to make manual work productive was the great management task of the last century... The productivity of knowledge and knowledge workers will not be the only competitive factor in the world economy. It is however likely to become the decisive factor, at least for most industries in developed countries"* (Drucker 1992)

SharePoint is an enterprise class technology platform that provides the tools with which we can begin to address this challenge, but the tools are the smallest part of the solution.

With SharePoint its very much a case of 10% tools and 90% people.

Good luck!

S☺

References

Avenue A- Razorfish (20080), *"Describing the Intranet maturity framework"*, Avenue A- Razorfish, [online] Available from: http://intranetmaturity.pbwiki.com/The%20Framework [accessed 04/12/2008]

Ballmer, Steve (2009), Keynote speech at the Microsoft SharePoint Conference 2009, Las Vegas, USA

Driver, Erica and Moore, Connie (2008), *"Information Workplace platform vendors light up the world of work"*, Forrester Research Inc., USA

Drucker, Peter (1992), *"The Age of Discontinuity"*, Harper & Row, USA

Koplowitz, Rob & Le Clair, Craig, (2008), *"SharePoint success will take a village"*, Forrester Research Inc/, USA

Leganza, Gene (2010), *"Topic Overview: information Architecture"*, Forrester Research, [online] Aailable from http://www.forrester.com/rb/Research/topic_overview_information_architecture/q/id/55951/t/2 [accessed 16/06/2010)

Lele, Vishwas (2007), *"Microsoft Office SharePoint Server 2007 As an Application Development Platform"*, Applied Information Sciences Inc. [on-line]

Lui, David (2010), *"Governance vs. Management"*, [online], Available from: http://grault.net/adjunct/index.cgi?GovernanceVsManagement [accessed 20/08/2010]

London Management Centre (2008), "Lewin's 3 stage model", [online] Available from http://www.lmcuk.com/management-tool/lewins-3-stage-model [accessed 17/09/2011]

Rogers, Everett M. (1962), *"Diffusion of Innovations"*, Glencoe, Free Press

Roth, Criag, (2009), *"Governance, Politics, and Diplomacy with SharePoint: Success Factors Beyond Technology"* (presentation), SharePoint Conference 2009, Las Vegas

Ruppertz-Rausch, Simone (2009), "*Information Worker Competence Centre - Achieving Business Success with your Collaboration Infrastructure*", Microsoft, Available from http://technet.microsoft.com/en-gb/library/ee213565(office.12).aspx   [accessed 16/05/2010]

Oudi, Sudesh (2010), *"I.T. Governance vs Corporate Governance vs I.T. Management"*, [online], Available from: http://servicexen.wordpress.com/2008/06/01/it-governance-vs-corporate-governance-vs-it-management/ [accessed 01/08/2010]

YourDictionary (2011), "Infrastructure", [online] Available from http://www.yourdictionary.com/infrastructure [accessed 11/08/2011]

Ward, Toby (2007), *"Intranet Governance"*, Intranetblog.com, [online], Available from: http://intranetblog.blogware.com/blog/Governance [accessed 04/12/2008]

Wikipedia (2008), *"Intranet"*, [online] Available from: http://en.wikipedia.org/wiki/Intranet [accessed 03/12/2008]

Wikipedia (2010), *"Change Management"*, [online] Available from: http://en.wikipedia.org/wiki/Change_management, [accessed 23/05/2010]

Wikipedia (2010), *"Information Technology Governance"* [online] Available from: http://en.wikipedia.org/wiki/Information_technology_governance#cite_note-2 [accessed 07/08/2010]

6.   Exploring Different Options for Implementing SharePoint Solutions

Introduction

An important decision to make while planning the implementation of any SharePoint solution is how exactly it should be created. Two commonly used options are leveraging the out of the box available functionality through customization in the browser and development of solutions using custom code.

SharePoint's out of the box functionality empowers end users to create simple solutions with little effort and in a short time frame, however with a limited customization scope. Development of custom code solutions provides the most flexibility, however at a higher cost in terms of complexity and resource requirements.

Another option is to extend the standard SharePoint functionality with customizations that make use of JavaScript and the Data View Web Part. Using JavaScript has become a very popular way of extending SharePoint without having to rely on custom code. It allows users with some basic development knowledge to create their own more advanced solutions easily.

Considering all these possibilities, when evaluating the correct course to take for a solution implementation, organizations need to take into account the pros and cons of the different approaches, and weigh them against each other. This chapter will compare these approaches with each other and describe the capabilities, as well as the benefits and the drawbacks of each approach, allowing a decision maker to better understand which method is useful in which situation and choose the best option.

Overview of the different approaches

What is a solution? Simply said, a solution helps to manage a business problem with some specific functionality in SharePoint. Possible solutions can range from simple lists that are created for a specific purpose, design changes where a custom branding is applied, simple or complex workflows that help to automate and improve business processes, to backend solutions that run additional processes to capture and act upon events that occur in the SharePoint environment they are running in, and many more.

Some examples of possible customisations are:

1. The HR department requires a library through which they can share existing HR policies. They want to classify these policies according to different audiences that are affected, as well as provide some information on when the individual policy takes effect. The suggested customisation is a Document Library with appropriate metadata.

2. The Sales department requires an overview of on-going and completed sales activities. The data is already stored on SharePoint and should now be displayed on a single page with graphical

indicators. Users should also be able to apply different filters. A recommended solution is a Sales Dashboard.

3. The company's intranet doesn't match the corporate branding. Corporate communications initiates a project to create a new design.

4. The HR department wants to improve their hiring process by automating the internal decision making process. So far, it is tracked manually whether a potential candidate should be invited for a second interview and afterwards whether he should be hired or not. The HR manager wants to keep track of candidates, their corresponding hiring status and able to see at a quick glance the current status for all of them. It is proposed to implement a workflow combined with a custom list and a page that displays all open candidates with their current status.

Solutions can be created in a lot of different ways, depending on the required functionality, the available internal knowledge, the overall scope, and other factors.

Each approach has benefits and drawbacks, which will be explained in more detail in the following sections. Furthermore, the different approaches will be analysed under the following aspects to allow a better comparison:

1. Required Knowledge – how much knowledge is required within the organisation and in which areas.

2. Customisation Scope – what can be achieved with the particular approach.
3. Ease of development – how easy is it to create customisations with the approach.
4. Portability – can solutions be ported over to other SharePoint sites, servers, etc., and to what extent.
5. Maintenance effort – how much work is required to maintain (e.g. make modifications) a solution developed under the given approach.
6. Implementation time – how long can implementations take on average.
7. Software Tools – which tools can be used or are required for the implementation.
8. Other Requirements – if needed, which other requirements are there.

Note: In this chapter, it is assumed that an internal implementation is planned, excluding any possible existing third party solutions and support from external consultants. Additionally, it is possible to purchase third party tools to solve existing problems or to get external support when it comes to development, however the discussion on the benefit and drawbacks of these go beyond the scope of this chapter.

Out of the box Customisation

The easiest way to create a solution in SharePoint is to make use of the out of the box functionality. SharePoint makes it quite easy for users to modify sites and pages by allowing them to create predefined or custom lists and libraries, adding new pages, and editing these pages by adding content. With the use of the available Web Parts, which in their simplest state display specific content, users can create as well as maintain interactive and dynamic pages. Combining all these functionalities, simple solutions can be created quickly and easily with little knowledge, one of the factors that has certainly contributed to the success of SharePoint.

Required Knowledge
The biggest benefit of approaching the development of a solution with using out of the box functionality is that users can get started with it quickly, as only basic SharePoint knowledge is required for simple solutions and no development experience is needed. Any user who has been using SharePoint for a while and who has been given appropriate permissions can maintain a page or a site and leverage lists, libraries, web parts, etc. It is also possible to create a different branding for a SharePoint environment with this approach, as all relevant files can easily be created with the appropriate free software tools and then be applied to a SharePoint site collection.

With a minimum amount of training and practice, it is even possible to create slightly more complex solutions which make use of multiple pieces of functionality, for example an approval workflow that gets started when a leave request form is filled out. It is in fact even possible to customise and maintain a small SharePoint environment with this approach only.

Customisation Scope
Within the scope of this approach are the creation of libraries and lists, setting up Content Types, basic workflows, adding pages and modifying and enhancing

them with Web Parts, and the development of forms. These individual parts can be combined to create a slightly more sophisticated solution, such as a workflow that starts whenever a form is completed, with the data of the form also being shown in a custom Content Type.

However, this also means that customisations are limited in their functionality. Therefore this approach is not the best one to use when implementing more complex solutions, such as the development of custom Web Parts, complex workflows, or event handlers that react upon events.

Ease of development
It is relatively easy to create such customisations. SharePoint provides a varied set of options to create solutions through the browser. Furthermore, with the use of SharePoint Designer, InfoPath, and Visio it is possible to create more advanced solutions.

Portability
Solutions created with this approach are only partially portable. Lists, libraries, and sites can be stored as templates and then be reused in the same site collection, or transferred to other site collections and be used there. However, not all content can be ported over this way, a notable example of this are sites that makes use of SharePoint's Publishing functionality, another example are running workflows and their associated tasks.

Maintenance effort

Maintaining solutions is relatively easy, similar to the way they are created. As changes usually occur directly on the production server, extra care should be taken. Changes usually cannot be retracted, thus a preferred way is to create such solutions first on a test server, and then either port them over to the production server if possible, or recreate them the same way on the production server once the final solution on the test server is deemed suitable enough.

If similar solutions are created in multiple locations, there is a risk that a change needs to be executed in all these locations individually, thus increasing the maintenance effort.

Implementation time
Another benefit of this approach is that the time it takes to implement a solution is reasonably short. Existing functionality such as document libraries, which has been created for a specific purpose only, is leveraged in a straight-forward approach. Furthermore, the solution complexity is usually quite low, resulting in a shorter creation time.

Software Tools
The most commonly used tool for this approach is the browser, usually Internet Explorer. For more advanced modifications SharePoint Designer can be used. InfoPath is used to create and modify forms, which can be opened in the InfoPath client or in the browser (if the license permits).

Lastly, one can also create workflows for SharePoint 2010 with Microsoft Visio, which then need to be imported into SharePoint Designer for further processing. This approach is preferred if the workflow is to be designed by end users or business users first, and then developed by a site owner, or somebody else with the appropriate workflow knowledge.

Extending SharePoint through Development in the Middle Tier

The term Middle Tier has been used by Marc D Anderson in this case to describe an approach that can be seen as in between the first approach, where SharePoint was customised with out of the box functionality only, and the third approach that goes all the way to developing solutions in custom code. Some development can be part of this approach, which is done in JavaScript and not in .NET. The entry level for this, as well as the difficulty and the time to implement solutions is fairly low compared to custom code development. Also, existing knowledge of SharePoint, such as the knowledge that can be used for the first approached, can be leveraged here as well.

As a matter of fact, solutions built with this method usually build upon some of the customisations developed with the first approach, extending them with additional features.

With the use of JavaScript and the Data View Web Part, valuable and complex solutions such as interactive Dashboards can be built.

Required Knowledge

As mentioned, this approach can be seen as an extension of the first approach, thus the same knowledge is required. Additionally, experience in JavaScript development is needed, as well as some knowledge about XML and in particular XSLT.

The Data View Web Part uses XSLT extensively, providing the developer with a huge flexibility in terms of how information can be displayed. Some additional basic CSS knowledge is beneficial for the formatting of the output but not essential.

As for JavaScript, it is possible to get started even with basic knowledge only. Knowing the basic concepts such as variables, loops, and functions is sufficient enough to create simple solutions that enhance SharePoint.

Customisation Scope

Solutions developed this way usually make use of the Data View Web Part and SharePoint's available web services. The web services provide various functionalities such as the possibility to modify list and library items, look up user data, and more. The web services are called through JavaScript, and provide the developer with a wide range of options, such as retrieving specific information from lists, or getting information about a user.

The Data View Web Part displays information from one or multiple libraries or lists. With the use of XSLT, how the information is displayed can be controlled entirely. This Web Part is thus more flexible than the standard List

View Web Part, and allows the developer to define which
information should be displayed, as well as the layout of
the output.

Another customisation option that is used often is the
modification of SharePoint's user interface with the help
of JavaScript. A popular library to use is jQuery which
allows selecting and modifying elements in a HTML page.
For SharePoint, this could mean that all Web Parts with a
specific title are selected and their header style is changed
to a different one. Another example is the modification of
the quick launch menu by transforming it in such a way
that it is shown as an accordion, and individual groups of
items are expanded when the mouse hovers over them.

It should be noted that the result of this approach differs
from the other two in the sense that the code actually gets
executed on the client-side. This basically means that the
JavaScript code does not run on the server directly, but
rather in the user's browser. As a result of this, the scope
of these solutions is still limited, extending the first
approach only partially.

Any solutions that may require code to run on the server
directly cannot be developed with this method. Examples
for this are a timer job that needs to run regularly or a
custom Web Part.

Ease of development
While more knowledge is required for this approach, it is
still not too difficult to create solutions with it. Even with
basic JavaScript knowledge one can get started very fast

and develop some first sample solutions. The results of the development can also be seen immediately, as changes to the code files can be executed directly on the server. While having a test server and implementing the solutions on it is still the preferred approach, it is also possible to implement solutions with this approach on the production server on a test site first, and then move them to the correct locations once complete and tested.

As for development with the Data View Web Part, even with basic XSLT knowledge one can already create some adequate implementations in SharePoint Designer. As editing occurs on a page with the Web Part added to it, the result can be seen and verified immediately.

Portability

Solutions that use JavaScript can be ported easily if they are developed with reusability in mind. Best practice is to create a dedicated JavaScript file in a library on the SharePoint server, add a Content Query Web Part on the page where it should be used, and link the CQWP to the code file. That way, the same code can run on multiple pages, and it is easy to migrate the file to another location as well.

As the Data View Web Part is a regular Web Part that is added directly to a page, it cannot be ported as easily as the JavaScript files. Some of the XSLT can be stored in a dedicated file and then be referenced in the Web Part, however most of the time the Data View Web Part needs to be seen as a single implementation with little reusability.

Maintenance effort

As already said, the files that are part of a solution are stored directly in libraries on the server. Therefore, making changes can be done fairly quickly with little effort, resulting in a small maintenance effort. Furthermore, these changes can be verified immediately.

Implementation time

While the implementation time is longer than for the first approach as some development time is required, the development life cycle is faster than the third approach. Less time needs to be spent on debugging, packaging, and deploying solutions than with the third approach.

Software Tools

As with the first approach, common development tools are Internet Explorer and SharePoint Designer. In addition to that, browser tools such as the Internet Explorer Developer Tools or the Firefox extension Firebug are frequently used when developing with JavaScript. To see the communication between the client and the web services, a popular tool for debugging these requests is Fiddler, a web debugger.

One of the most popular JavaScript libraries is jQuery, which has found a lot of usage in the SharePoint community as well.

Another commonly used JavaScript library is SPServices, which provides some good functions for interacting with SharePoint's web services, as well as some other useful functions.

Creating custom solutions in .NET

The approach that offers the most flexibility and functionality is also the most complex and resource-intensive. It is possible to create custom solutions for SharePoint in .NET, the software framework that SharePoint is built on, and deploy these solutions to SharePoint.

Required Knowledge

To create a solution with this approach, development knowledge is required in either of the programming languages C# or Visual Basic.NET, and as already mentioned knowledge about the .NET framework is needed. As SharePoint development still differs from regular .NET development, experience in this area is required as well.

Customisation Scope

This approach offers the most options when it comes to creating solutions; not only can it encapsulate the solutions from the two other approaches, it is also possible to create solutions that cannot be developed otherwise. Examples for this are very complex workflows that integrate with other systems, custom web parts that extend existing out of the box web parts with additional functionality, administration tools that allow the administrator to manage certain aspects of the environment, and many more.

As development is done directly with the official SharePoint API, any customisation of SharePoint that is

made available by Microsoft can be developed with this
approach.

Additionally, quite complex solutions that include
multiple features, such as a Customer Relationship
Management system built on SharePoint, are best
developed with this approach.

Ease of development
Due to the use of .NET and the SharePoint API and the
corresponding required knowledge, this method is more
difficult than the other two. Development tasks not only
include development, but also debugging the solutions,
intensive testing, as well as packaging and deploying them
to the server.

Portability
The output of each development can be a reusable and
distributable package that can easily be installed and
activated on any other SharePoint environment.
Whichever customisation is developed in this way can be
ported over to any another system, be it internal or
external. Compared with the other two approaches,
solutions developed this way are the easiest ones to reuse
in other systems.

Maintenance effort
As the development is more complex and the
requirements in terms of knowledge and resources are
higher, the maintenance of these solutions is higher as
well. Even small changes require some time to implement

as the solution should go through the whole development life cycle each time.

Implementation time

The time it takes to implement custom solutions in this way is longer than the previous approaches. The reason for this is that one should follow development best practices and include enough time for the development, testing, and deployment of a solution.

Software Tools

The standard tool to develop solutions with this approach is Visual Studio. Visual Studio provides all required functionality to develop all kinds of solutions, and supports the developer by providing useful tools to create specific SharePoint features such as web parts, custom lists, and many more.

Additionally, a wide range of useful third party add-ons for Visual Studio 2010 are available, that enhance the development experience even further.

Other Requirements

It has already been mentioned that this development approach is also the most resource intensive. The development laptop or computer needs to have a local SharePoint installation to be able to leverage all development functionality, thus all this is best done in a virtual machine.

Additionally, a code versioning system such as Microsoft's Team Foundation Server is recommended to keep track of changes, and to be able to revert back to a previous snapshot in the development history. This also makes it easy for multiple developers to work on the same solution.

Overall this means that a higher up-front investment needs to be made, driving up the total cost to develop solutions with this approach.

Decision making process

Given these three implementation approaches, which one should be used in which case?

Before any decision is made on which technical approach to follow, it is of uttermost importance to first define the business problem to get a better understanding of which issue needs to be solved and then to define a desired solution independent from any technology. This also provides an opportunity to verify if a solution is required, or if the problem can be dealt with otherwise, for example by using an already existing system.

As a last step, the required functionality that implements the proposed solution needs to be defined. Here, the requirements for the SharePoint based solution need to be listed in detail. Once these functional requirements are available, it is possible to decide which approach to follow. For this, several questions need to be asked.

The first question should be: do the functional requirements restrict one approach? For example, how big is the scope of the proposed solution, and can each

approach be used for it? If it is known that web services
need to be used, the first approach cannot be followed.

The complexity of the proposed solution can also serve as
an indicator to rule out approaches. For a simple solution
such as a document library with multiple Content Types,
the first approach may be more than enough. At the same
time, if the solution project is planned to last several
weeks with a large amount of requirements, this can be a
good indicator for a project that is best developed with
the third approach.

What kind of knowledge is required to implement the
solution, and is it available internally? If there are no
SharePoint developers with .NET knowledge in the
company, it is obviously not possible to follow the third
approach. At the same time, if there's no one available
with JavaScript experience, developing solutions with the
second approach may not be possible.

How much budget is available to implement the solution,
and is it possible to implement it under a given approach
with the given budget (Note: while usually a company
would not proceed with a solution implementation if the
budget is not available, there is a chance that a different
approach may result in a similar solution with less cost
involved).

These are some of the most common questions to answer
when   evaluating   the   different   implementation
approaches. As the individual situation differs from
organisation to organisation, it is best to evaluate them

for each solution, even if similar solutions were developed before.

Summary

This chapter provided an overview of different approaches for developing solutions in SharePoint. The various benefits and drawbacks of each approach were examined, providing the reader with a better understanding of them. Lastly, a decision making process that helps to determine which approach to follow in which situation was described.

7.   SharePoint Server-based Data Access and Storage

Introduction

This chapter guides readers through the basic storage and data access options available in SharePoint 2010 application development projects. The matching of application business requirements with the appropriate storage and data access technique is vital for achieving a successful project. We begin by contrasting SharePoint lists with SQL Server database storage. Thereafter, we shall consider using blob storage and web services for an agnostic storage provider. It is also necessary to consider the limitations of SharePoint to help better understand why particular storage strategies are preferable. Lastly, we examine various data access options that are available for server-side application development projects. SharePoint's server-side object model is reviewed as well as LINQ, LINQ to SQL, LINQ to SharePoint, Web Services and Business Connectivity Services.

The Logical Layout of SharePoint

There are four object models in SharePoint 2010. These are API's that work with a SharePoint implementation programmatically. The Server Object Model is the most powerful and commonly used object model, and therefore it will be described in more detail in this

chapter. The other three Object Models, collectively referred to as the Client Object Models (Client OM), offer a subset of the Server OM's functionality. The Client OMs are used to write applications off the SharePoint 2010 farm, which manipulate and work with the farm. The three Client Object Models are the:
1. .NET client object model,
2. Silverlight client object model, and
3. *ECMAScript* client object model.

SharePoint consists of a logical hierarchical relationship between objects in the Server OM as is shown in Figure 1.

Figure 1 – Server Object Model hierarchy on a SharePoint Farm

SharePoint Lists are for Data Storage

Applications traditionally store data in database tables. SharePoint's basic building blocks for storage are SharePoint lists, as opposed to database tables. When training C# developers to use SharePoint, it is often useful for developers to think of lists as being a direct one-to-one replacement for database tables.

Once the SharePoint team, including the developers, understand that lists are the storage mechanism then they are able to recognize that the data needs to be added, manipulated and consumed from lists. SharePoint provides standard (out-of-the-box) screens to perform the read and write operations on lists. Web Parts, such as the Content Query Web Part, aggregate data and display it to the end user allowing for further customisation of the user experience. Web Parts provide for a richer *pluggable* UI experience. Tools such as SharePoint Designer and InfoPath allow business users to refine the UI further. However, the exact business requirements are often not achievable using all these options.

Developers have multiple options for accessing SharePoint resources using the Server OM. Application data is usually stored in SharePoint lists if the data is to be stored within SharePoint. The lists can be accessed directly through the Server OM hierarchy, but this is not the way to access data efficiently in SharePoint 2010 projects.

Except for the smallest of projects, lists used in application development should be created using a deployable *wsp* package. This is because the lists need to be created identically throughout the Development, Testing, Acceptance and Production (DTAP) environments.

Lists built using Visual Studio, and deployed via *wsp,* always consist of the following four components:

1. Site Columns – also referred to as 'fields', are the smallest building blocks. An example of site columns could be a telephone number for a comment field.

2. Content Types – are used by SharePoint to describe the structure of data. A content type is a collection of site columns that tell SharePoint how data is structured.

3. List Definition – is information telling SharePoint what a list should look like and how to add pages to edit the data.

4. List Instance – is the actual instance of a list definition. This is the equivalent of a table in the SQL Server world.

Lists can be setup to have relationships and the list instances can have referential integrity enforced (i.e. setup cascading delete on lists). After having stored application data in SharePoint lists, it is necessary to query and manipulate the list.

SPQuery and CAML

CAML is the SharePoint specific language that when used with the SPQuery object by developers to query SharePoint lists. In Microsoft Office SharePoint Server 2007 (MOSS), this was the de facto mechanism for retrieving list data. CAML is analogous to T-SQL as it is a structured language for querying SharePoint list data.

CAML is XML-based and particularly difficult to construct and debug. U2U is a tool that helps build up CAML queries. However it is not a complete tool and has relied on developers stringing different bits of working CAML to create complete CAML queries in MOSS.

In MOSS and SharePoint 2010, lists can be queried using CAML queries, which are weakly-typed since there is no compile time checking. A developer will therefore not know whether the query is valid. In MOSS the code deployment used to take up to several minutes. This coupled with the poor feedback resulted in time-consuming development efforts. In addition, if there was an error, which was often the case due to the complexity of the CAML query, little error information was provided. The whole process was slow and ineffective. LINQ to SharePoint is a greatly improved technique to query data as compared to the traditional CAML-based approach. Thus, it is no longer necessary to write CAML by hand unless the developer wishes too.

SharePoint Lists or SQL Server tables to store Application data?

SharePoint lists are ultimately stored within a SQL Server database (i.e. a content database). One cannot directly query the list using T-SQL. Instead, a developer has to perform retrieval and modification of list data via the Server OM when developing applications on the SharePoint farm. One technique is to use the SharePoint OM API hierarchy and perform a *SPQuery* or to use

LINQ to SharePoint. However, certain types of data do not lend themselves to storing data within SharePoint lists. The table in Figure 2 below compares the use of SharePoint lists with SQL Server database tables. Another technique that is perhaps generally more useful is opting for a LINQ to SQL code solution, which manipulates and queries the SQL data. This idea will be expanded upon later in the chapter.

SharePoint Lists	Database tables
SharePoint security and permissions	Transactional
Workflow	Performance
Versioning	Distinct queries and aggregations
Office integration	Greater flexibility
Native / Easy setup	Easy for .NET developers
SharePoint generates User Interface	

Figure 2 – Comparison of SharePoint 2010 lists vs. database tables

Generally, it is best to opt for database tables if the system is either transactional, has a performance requirement or performs complex queries. However, many applications do not completely fall into this situation. Using native SharePoint lists makes for a stable configurable application and so picking the appropriate storage mechanisms is vital.

Data can be stored in SQL Server and can be surfaced using External Content Types (ECT) via Business Connectivity Services (BCS), which makes the data appear like native SharePoint lists.   BCS is the improved replacement for BDC (Business Data Catalogue) on MOSS.   BCS can connect to SOA (Service Orientation Architecture) or to Web Services so that almost any architecture can be built using any storage mechanism.   A personal suggestion would be to use BCS to offer up the data from SQL Server (or Web Services) and to use LINQ to SQL to have programmatic access for the application's custom web parts.

Content databases have restrictions in that they should be less than 200GB each and site collections should be under 100GB each.   However, there are exceptions and depending on the SQL IOPS (speed of transactions), bigger content databases and site collections are performance wise viable.   If one is storing pictures or any other form of blob storage such as videos or sound, such data thresholds are exceeded quickly.   SharePoint allows for Remote Blob Storage (RBS), which takes the blob stored in the content database and inserts a pointer to cheaper disk storage.   The net effects include storage is cheaper, performance of the SQL Server is improved and the content database is drastically reduced in size (up to a 95% size reduction depending on the storage type). However, RBS brings disaster recovery complications. Therefore, RBS is only valid for large farms with suitable storage requirements.

In summary, one should select the option that is most suitable to the business situation. Generally, a good first option would be to store data within SharePoint, since this drastically reduces development time.

Data Access Options

There are a plurality of data access options that depend on the storage mechanism used. It is therefore useful to review some of the most common options that are available on a project for both SharePoint list and database table storage.

LINQ

Language Integration Query is a mechanism for performing Create, Read, Update and Delete (CRUD) operations against any data source. LINQ is useful in that you only need to learn one mechanism for querying any data source that supports LINQ. The logic used in LINQ happens to be similar to T-SQL, which fortunately is what most developers are already familiar. Therefore, if LINQ to SQL is used, the same query logic is performed and LINQ works out the T-SQL needed to perform the queries. Similarly, using LINQ to XML allows the same LINQ syntax to perform CRUD operations on an XML data source, which means the developer does not need to learn an XML-specific query language such as *xPath*. There are many LINQ flavours such as LINQ to Objects and obviously LINQ to SharePoint.

SharePoint Lists Data Access Options

There are generally three options for working with SharePoint list data using the Server OM:

1. Using the Server OM hierarchy to find and update data. This technique can be slow for retrieving data and should be avoided.

2. CAML queries using SPQuery. This is the fastest way to access SharePoint list data. However, it uses CAML with its aforementioned drawbacks, i.e. complexity and lack of compile-time checking.

3. LINQ to SharePoint. This is the recommended way to access list data. A proxy of the list data is generated, which enables the developer to write LINQ to SharePoint statements. *Intellesense* is available so that the developer knows the code being written will work at compile time (even if the logic is wrong the query will run). Thus, the combination of *intellesense* and compile-time checking result in a more efficient development life cycle. However, some limitations exist with doing a LINQ to SharePoint.

Note. It is possible to use combinations of the three options above to build applications. Such flexibility combined with web parts and the out-of-the-box capability for generating UI's, results in a powerful way to build application platforms.

LINQ to SharePoint

LINQ to SharePoint was a Codeplex addition for MOSS and had multiple limitations. In SharePoint 2010 LINQ to SharePoint is available out of the box (OOTB).

There are various steps needed to code LINQ to SharePoint queries programmatically. Firstly, a list is needed in the current site collection. In the example shown below a list is created for Customers, which contains three fields.

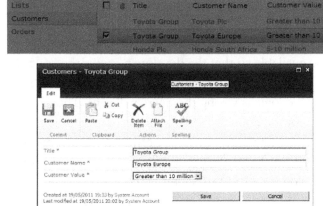

Figure 3- Two lists with site columns

Secondly, the LINQ to SharePoint proxy needs to be generated for these lists. There are two options for doing this. The first option uses the OOTB command prompt to generate the proxy using the SPMetal.exe tool from PowerShell (or the command prompt) on the SharePoint development server. The second, and perhaps more preferable option, is using Visual Studio (VS) 2010 to generate the proxy code. This allows the developer to remain in their Visual Studio (VS) IDE. There is a very useful project called *CKSDev*, which has a lot of useful functionality that developers should explore. A particularly interesting piece of *CKSDev* functionality is using the SPI to generate a new LINQ to SharePoint proxy. In order to make use of this functionality, it is necessary to check that *CKSDev* (http://cksdev.codeplex.com/) has been installed as a VS extension (you can get this through the Visual Studio gallery. Open VS2010, click "Tools", and click "Extension Manager" (as shown below).

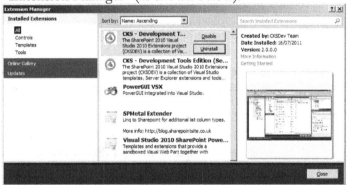

Figure 4 – Adding the CKSDev VSIX extension

Right click on a SharePoint project, click "Add", select "New Item", click "SPMetal Definition" (CKSDev), then edit the "Name" and click the "Add" button (as shown below).

Figure 5 – Generating the LINQ to SharePoint proxy using the CKSDev SPI

The final part of this walk through demo shows how to use LINQ to SharePoint in order to select and delete a customer from a drop down list using a web part as shown below.

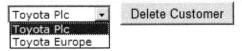

Working Demo

Figure 6 – Working web Part that requires coding logic implemented with LINQ to SharePoint to perform data access against the SharePoint 2010 list.

In the code shown in the screenshot of Figure 7 below, the web part has been implemented, a dropdown list has been added and the list has been populated using LINQ to SharePoint:

```
protected void Page_Load(object sender, EventArgs e)
{
    if (!Page.IsPostBack)
    {
        PopulateCustomersDropDown();
    }
}

private void PopulateCustomersDropDown()
{
    ddlCustomers.Items.Clear();
    SPMetalContext dc = new SPMetalContext(webUrl);
    var customerItems = (from c in dc.Customers
                         where c.CustomerValue == CustomerValue.GreaterThan10Million
                         select c);
    foreach (CustomerCT item in customerItems)
    {
        ddlCustomers.Items.Add(new ListItem(item.CustomerName, item.Id.ToString()));
    }
    ddlCustomers.DataBind();
}
```

Figure 7 – LINQ to SharePoint code to populate the drop down list control on the custom web part

Note: The *SPMetalContext* object is the proxy code generated by the *CKSDev* LINQ to SharePoint proxy class.

The code in the screenshot of Figure 8 below shows an example of a simple LINQ to SharePoint that was added to the delete button to remove a specific customer record from the Customers list.

```
protected void btnDelete_Click(object sender, EventArgs e)
{

    int custId = Convert.ToInt32(ddlCustomers.SelectedValue);
    SPMetalContext dc = new SPMetalContext(webUrl);
    var customerItem = (from customers in dc.Customers
                        where customers.Id == custId
                        select customers).Single();
    dc.Customers.DeleteOnSubmit(customerItem);
    dc.SubmitChanges();
    PopulateCustomersDropDown();

}
```

Figure 8 - LINQ to SharePoint code snippet to delete a specific customer.   Note that the delete behaviour is set by the referential integrity that is setup against list instances.

As you can see from the code snippets above, performing CRUD operations programmatically is relatively straightforward. For more information, please see my blog posts on *SPMetal* at http://blog.sharepointsite.co.uk

Summary

SharePoint is a good tool to build enterprise applications and solution architects are not restricted to using SharePoint lists for data storage. SharePoint lists are improved and should be the preferred option when selecting data storage for SharePoint. SharePoint has multiple advantages for building applications such as: speed to production, shared stable existing infrastructure and multiple re-usable modules. LINQ to SharePoint has evolved into a highly usable mechanism, which when coupled with the improvements of SharePoint 2010 lists, makes SharePoint an excellent choice for data storage.

8.   SharePoint 2010 Automated Code Deployment

Introduction

This chapter guides readers through a variety of SharePoint Code Deployment methodologies for 7x24 production intranet and internet facing farms. SharePoint farms requiring high availability often constrain and challenge the method of deployment and site administration due to customizations, full development and deployment documentation, and 100% reproducibility. In most deployments (old and new), the focus of planning and governance applies to the users and application management of power-users to ensure a deployment is successful immediately after an upgrade or new solution release. However, the same standards and planning guidelines should also apply to the SharePoint development lifecycle.

By defining the development lifecycle, IT organizations may utilize SharePoint's rapid-development platform while minimizing the risks and surprises. The following guidelines help with the implementation of successful deployments to SharePoint farms:

1. Create a development process life-cycle so that contextualized requirements are prioritized and approved by all stakeholders.

2. Train and require developers to use good programming models for .Net and SharePoint Object Models. Having developers learn as they go can often cost twice as much money and time to find, troubleshoot and re-write poorly written code that slows down the site.

3. Inventory your current customized code and re-use functionality as much as possible. Create customized common libraries for core business functionality for replication.

4. Take the time to fully understand the application being developed. This includes details on how the application interacts with other SharePoint services and/or databases and will ensure a shorter downtime during unplanned outages and installations.

SharePoint Internet facing sites often have additional requirements, network bottlenecks, and limited downtime constraints which make deploying code from the development arena through QA/staging, and finally into production SharePoint farms more restrictive. One of the major reasons deployments fail is the lack of standardized deployment processes and environments.

The defacto-standard SharePoint development environment consists of a local (or shared) development virtual machine (VM), a UAT/QA set of VM's which are similar in functionality to the production farm, a set of

Staging VM's which imitate production in functionality, and the production farm itself.

For example, a mid-sized SharePoint farm may have the following configurations.

Environment	Server Setup
Development	One virtual machine that includes basic SharePoint functionality and databases as needed for development. Usually this will be located on a developer desktop or development VM server and limited to a small number of simultaneous projects.
QA/UAT	Should include at least one web front-end (wfe), an application server, and a database VM. This environment tests the interaction of multiple development projects with each other and existing production content/applications. Deployment consists of a combination of developers and system administrators who easily transfer knowledge.
Staging	Should mirror the number of production servers/VM's: 2 wfe's, 1 application VM, and database VM. Script deployment process when possible and treat the process as if deploying into a production farm. Address deployment issues in QA and re-test in Staging.
Production	2 wfe's, 1 application server/VM, 1 database server/VM. Continually script installation and deployment for speed to ensure minimal downtime into production applications and systems.

Note. To determine which SharePoint farm architecture is right for your environment please go to http://technet.microsoft.com/en-us/library/cc261834.aspx.

The above environments initiate the framework for a standards based development lifecycle and save companies, no matter the size, time, resources and money. Having a definitive framework reduces the number of bugs, performance related issues, and cross-application conflicts that reach the production environment because they are caught and addressed in QA and staging processes.

- Scripted deployments reduced downtime; installation surprises – ie: human errors – are minimized); and system administrators spend less time in deployment.
- Development lifecycles provide protocols to address, replicate, and fix bugs quickly.

This chapter describes methods to build and deploy custom code into an Intranet or Internet facing production farm by implementing a development lifecycle using standardized tools and utilities.

Development and deployment is easier with the new capabilities provided in Visual Studio 2010, Team Foundation Server 2010, and SharePoint 2010 make the development and deployment process. Further, PowerShell can automate part of the build and deployment process. This automation aides in providing code which is successful, reliable, and reproducible.

SharePoint Deployment Tools

Just as a building contractor requires certain building equipment, the SharePoint developer and administrator also need tools to ensure the successful deployment of projects into production level environments. Searching the web for 'SharePoint Development' and/or 'SharePoint Deployment' will return results from the very basic to the high-level obscure. The mirage of information makes locating relevant information difficult.

A list of relevant tools for the developer and administrator follows:

1. Visual Studio 2010 – provides integrated SharePoint development. An MSDN license will give the developer access to all updated Microsoft applications and development tools.
2. Team Foundation Server 2010 – this version control system includes SharePoint package (wsp) support and updated build mechanics for deploying to production farms even if they are in different physical or logical networks.
3. JetBrains ReSharper – assists in standards based application development. URL: http://www.jetbrains.com/

Free development Tools

4. Microsoft PowerShell – A c# like script development used for administration/deployment

and included in Microsoft Windows server 2008 and higher.

5. PowerGUI - PowerShell editor http://powergui.org/index.jspa

6. Fiddler – browser based debugging tool(s) http://www.fiddler2.com/Fiddler2/version.asp

7. SharePoint manager – SharePoint Object Model Explorer http://spm.codeplex.com/

8. CAML Viewer – assists in writing CAML queries to search lists http://spcamlviewer.codeplex.com

9. UlsViewer – view SharePoint ULS logs easily http://ulsviewer.codeplex.com

Visual Studio Extensions

Note. Some of the following extensions may have similar features and functions, be sure to try out each extension and determine the best fit for your environment.

1. SharePoint Software Factory – easily create, manage and deploy SharePoint solutions http://visualstudiogallery.msdn.microsoft.com/4 c5664f6-fefc-446b-b91c-36bec0c87e35

2. CKS Development Tools – provides advanced templates and tools for developers http://cksdev.codeplex.com/

3. Caml.net.intellisense – IntelliSense for CAML syntax

http://www.sharepointarchitects.us/caml.net/?page_id=148

4. Productivity Power Tools – Visual Studio extensions assisting in code development http://visualstudiogallery.msdn.microsoft.com/d0d33361-18e2-46c0-8ff2-4adea1e34fef/

5. Solution Explorer Tools – Visual Studio Extensions such as expand/collapse projects/solution http://visualstudiogallery.msdn.microsoft.com/ef4ac3e9-d056-4383-8ca2-11721bd879b4/

6. Visual Studio 2010 SharePoint Power Tools – SharePoint extensions and templates for developing sandbox webparts http://visualstudiogallery.msdn.microsoft.com/8e602a8c-6714-4549-9e95-f3700344b0d9

7. C# outline – add braces and outlines to classes, members, and constructions http://visualstudiogallery.msdn.microsoft.com/4d7e74d7-3d71-4ee5-9ac8-04b76e411ea8

The tools above will assist the developer in creating code and assists with adhering to corporate developmental governance policies. However, they by themselves do not ensure development governance is achieved.

SharePoint Deployment Governance

SharePoint development and deployment governance can be defined as the policies, roles, responsibilities, and processes that guide, direct, and control how an organization's business divisions and IT teams cooperate to achieve business goals. In many organizations this is defined as the developers write code then send it to administrators who must figure out how adjust their business plan to deploy and keep the application running. The poorly written code dictates the business plan of the company rather than the business determining the code needed.   By taking the time to define how different departments within an IT or IS communicate during the development and deployment process will greatly reduce (and possibly eliminate) the 'finger pointing' and provide code which complements the business plan.

Note. MSDN has a good governance policy which can be used and/or modify as needed for other uses. http://technet.microsoft.com/en-us/library/cc262900.aspx.

Implementing basic governance concepts can dramatically reduce bugs in the final application, reduce the number of bugs which are created, and provide a positive working relationship with both team members and the application customer. One such methodology for implementing this concept is called Scrum – an iterative, incremental framework often seen in agile software development. An obvious question might be: "What does project management have to do with development lifecycle and successful deployments?" and the answer would be: "Everything".

   Note. This chapter will not go into details of scrum and agile software development; to get more information on Scrum, please see: http://www.scrumalliance.org/pages/what_is_scrum or http://www.scrum.org . For more information on agile software development, see: http://en.wikipedia.org/wiki/Agile_software_develo pment.

By encouraging collaboration and smaller, iterative code development cycles, development teams have the ability to focus and create code faster and the client/customer can see changes and feature requests quicker than by using traditional methods.

When implementing any type of development process methodology it is important to define business process first and implement second. Too many times organizations try to implement development processes without defining the rules of engagement. For example, a manager goes to a software development seminar which hails that Scrum is the answer to his/her problems and wants to immediately change all current projects to scrum techniques complete with burn down charts, backlogs, etc. This approach is doomed for failure because it is likely his staff have no idea what these terms mean and what they are supposed to do with them. A better approach in transitioning to Scrum is to start simple and improve/add Scrum techniques incrementally as business needs require. Scrum can be implemented in its most basic form with an Microsoft Excel Spreadsheet and as complex using Microsoft Visual Studio Team Foundation Server 2010 (TFS) which will create burn down charts, backlogs, and current sprint details. For more information on TFS and how it manages development processes refer to: http://msdn.microsoft.com/en-us/vstudio/ff637362.aspx.

Software and technology is a great start to ensure governance; however, it is important to have a development team surrounding any projects which include customized code. This should include, but may not be limited to, the following participants:

- Technical Architect to ensure technologies and development follow standards and provides guidance on technical schedules
- Business Analyst and/or Project Manager to bridge the gap between the project client and development teams and ensures project schedules remain on time. Often these can be two separate functions, but it should be required that each project have at least one of these roles defined.
- Content owners who oversee the requirements and final sign-off for functionality of the project deliverables.
- IT Team Lead to oversee the deployment mechanics and provide requirements and standards for deployment into production environments.
- Application Users, Developers, and IT administrators may be used in an as needed basis as determine by project needs.

Each of these participants should be involved in determining a development and deployment governance lifecycle to ensure successful deployments across various projects and development teams. Once these governance processes are defined development processes are implemented to ensure successful deployment, monitoring, and maintenance into 7x24 production environments.

The following sections will provide some guidance and suggestions on techniques which have been used on small and large scale SharePoint development and are shown in Figure 1 below.

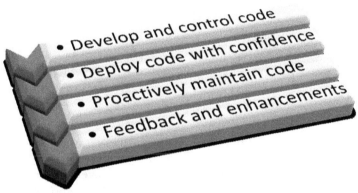

Figure 1 – Development Governance Concepts

Develop and control code

Most companies have unique business processes which require some amount of customization of the SharePoint interface and/or functionality. It is important when beginning a new development project to keep the architecture as simple as possible. Over complicated architectures and designs tend to increase the code development cycle and provide greater risk for bugs and an overall unsuccessful project. Many SharePoint developers have come to love, and hate, some of the adventures when developing SharePoint webparts and custom components. Often times one would expect a feature to take a few hours to code; when in reality it may take several days. Take for example a simple event receiver which will update a list item on update. Unless the event receiver is something one works with on a daily basis, the developer many not know all the variations in which SharePoint will call their event receiver – in short the update event receiver could be called in multiple scenarios and may cause issues with both performance and development workflow i.e. it may get called more times than the developer expected. In short, on any Phase I project – keep it simple and as straightforward as possible. Focus on functionality and architecture as the user interface can be adjusted and changed more easily. The simpler and less code that is developed, the easier it is to deploy and maintain.

It may seem obvious, but ensuring the development team has been trained on the SharePoint object model is as important as writing clean code. Developers should know and be able to understand not only the difference between the following, but also when it is appropriate to use each inside code.

```
properties.ListItem["Title"]
properties.ListItem.Fields.GetFieldByInternalName("Title")
```

Developing and controlling code is the responsibility of each developer and their team leaders. Together, they must learn and understand the current technology, and also work diligently to keep up to date on development concepts, techniques, and software environments. This way they are able to provide guidance and forward-looking code thereby assisting in the prevention of code re-write and/or re-architecture in the future. "Good" code often solicits clients to want additional features and more customized code with even more functionality. This is a true sign of the success of deployed code.

Deploy code with confidence

Deploying code into production environments is, in general, not the same as deploying code in a development environment and it is important to set standards within the organization which are reproducible in order to deploy code with confidence. The more standardized the deployments, the easier code is to maintain over time. Some key objectives with deployment strategies are listed below:

- Be realistic – SharePoint deployment is not a single-step installation.
- Use WSP Packages – When possible, package changes, configurations, and code into WSP packages to prevent multi-step manual processes.
- Require documentation – Often times multiple steps are involved in deployments and it is important to have all developers document all deployment steps such that other team members and SharePoint administrators can easily understand.
- Tools – use Visual Studio 2010, Team Foundation Server 2010, and PowerShell to leverage the latest deployment capabilities for building and deploying package solutions.
- Use a code promotion process – Standardize the process of moving code from development

through one or more stages of testing into production.

As development teams become more comfortable with SharePoint deployment, it is important to review these strategies to determine if there are any areas which can be improved or streamlined. This will ensure deployments are completed in as few steps as possible thus reducing the deployment maintenance windows even further.

Code Promotion

A code promotion model should include both a standard release and patch update (or hotfix) process. The standard process is the methodology for deploying code through the standard release cycle while patch updates are generally defined as a mechanic for emergency code updates due to a production issue found after the project life cycle has ended and cannot be scheduled using the standard process.

Code promotion typically consists of several steps to standardize development processes and provide consistent code deployment into production. These steps are:

- Have developers update code locally on a VM setup and use a version control system such as Team Foundation Server.
- Request a team server build and manually start the build which will build, tab/label, and deploy the SharePoint solutions to QA and/or Staging servers.

- Once the UAT (User Acceptance Testing) has passed by project owners, deploy the tagged build into the production environment.

Figure 2 below depicts an example code promotion process.

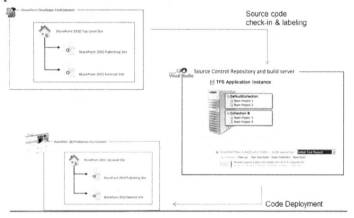

Figure 2 – Code Promotion Process

Microsoft's latest suite of development tools answer the call to address code promotion easily. Using Visual Studio 2010 and Team Foundation Server 2010, a code promotion scenario can be shown as in figure 3 below:

Figure 3 – Code Promotion Scenario

The above diagram depicts different versions of code in various SharePoint Farm environments.   The latest version 4.0 is actively being developed by an engineer. If the development team consists of more than a few team members, an integration development environment may be setup to allow developers the ability to test their deployment documentation and as a unit ensure compatibility with existing features as well as other team members updates and/or enhancements. The QA and Staging environments are v2.7 and v2.5 respectively while production deployment version is 1.0.

NOTE: Using multiple environments are important as they ensure reliability and stability of your production farm(s).

It is important to note that undocumented or unaddressed issues generally do not disappear when new code is deployed. Issues should be resolved (if possible) in the development environment.   The following are some guidelines to ensure new issues do not appear during the promotion process.

- Verify your existing SharePoint environment is up to date with patches
- Check for broken links in existing sites
- Review and identify all customizations – make sure the code and/or installer is available for each!
- Optimize large lists
- Optimize content databases
- Understand any/all UI changes and authentication methods
- Use as much production content as possible

Deployment strategies
The SharePoint 2010 framework allows developers the flexibility to create applications and tools which assist in providing answers to corporations' needs and requirements. This flexibility has its benefits and disadvantages. It is important before beginning any custom development project to determine what, if any, can be utilized out of the box. This will ensure continued compatibility as new releases of the product are available. If it is necessary to customize SharePoint the following is a description of development components which may be required.

Creating and Deploying Solution Packages
A *solution package* is the ability to bundle custom components as a single file and provides a unified infrastructure for deploying custom solutions, unified deployment and localization. Solution files can contain

site definitions, assemblies, application pages, user controls, and other customizations as necessary. The following are some major components which could be found in a solution.

- Solution Project SPI – be sure to use the proper project type to ensure optional performance. Some common project types are: common function dll's and web parts and visual web parts.
- Features and Feature Activating/Deactivating Event Handlers. It is important to increment feature numbers and feature deactivating event handling is setup.
- Configuration XML files such as Elements.XML, be sure to use Type="GhostableInLibrary" as needed -- it not inserted by default.
- Webpart files -- be sure to change webpart name, description, location as needed
- Package files – In the Manifest.XML it is often necessary to prevent application server resets. To prevent application pool resets set the ResetWebServer="FALSE" parameter.
- Information for build/deploy scripts which will be described later in this chapter.

In SharePoint 2010 solutions can be deployed as either a farm or sandboxed solution. This gives administrators more control over the deployment and resource utilization of customized code and/or applications. For more information on how to create a solution package, see: http://technet.microsoft.com/en-us/library/cc262995.aspx

Creating Custom Features

A *Feature* is designed to reduce the complexity involved in making simple site customizations as well as ensure necessary pre-requisites are completed prior to feature activation or deactivation. Features are composed as a set of XML files which are deployed to front-end Web and application servers. Feature deployment is part of a solution package and can be scoped to the SharePoint Farm, Site Collection, or Web Site. For more information on features visit http://technet.microsoft.com/en-us/library/ff607680.aspx.

Creating Custom Web Parts:

SharePoint Web parts are reusable components that display content or perform other functions and displayed on Web Part pages. Web Parts can represent any type of web-based content and can have customized settings, display SharePoint or other external data, and provide access to other features and services within the SharePoint farm. For more information visit http://msdn.microsoft.com/en-us/sharepoint/ee513148.

Using the three above basic concepts, the following deployment steps may be required during installation of a solution package:

Administrative functions:

Administrative functions such as creating and/or extending web applications, configuration settings etc. are most often deployed using PowerShell on the administration host. PowerShell scripts are easily able to be checked into a TFS source repository and deployed using a custom TFS build definition.

With the release of SharePoint 2010, administrators of large scale or highly available SharePoint farms should require all modifications to configuration be completed via PowerShell and not SharePoint Designer or the Central Administration GUI.

Site Customizations:
Site customizations such as themes, master pages, page layouts, site templates / definitions, list definitions, security groups, and navigation can be deployed via a WSP. With SharePoint 2010 and Visual Studio third parties have been able to create default templates which makes this process much easier than ever to ensure these components are deployed and configured via the SharePoint solution model.

Farm services:
Often times it is necessary to deploy custom timer jobs, event receivers, and other service components. These deploy via a solution package and it is important to create feature receivers to verify and configurations as needed. For example, timer jobs should have an activating event handler to ensure the timer job is activated and scheduled as required. Further, a deactivating handler should be created which will remove timer job from the schedule and is deactivated.

Site and Page Customizations:
There are many ways to deploy customizations to site and site pages through web parts, workflows, custom application pages, InfoPath forms, and controls. A simplistic method to deploy these customizations is using SharePoint Designer or the InfoPath client connected directly to the production databases. However, when

changes are applied using these methods, unknown and/or unwanted changes can occur without going through proper governance processes. Further, when performance is a concern, editing files through SharePoint Designer (SPD) can un-ghost files and cause the SharePoint engine to perform additional work as it loads the original file template and applies the customizations. If at all possible, development in production should be avoided. The following depicts some of the problems which could be encountered if customizations are made using a development in production model.

- A republish of the site using SPD over-writes list data.
- Modifications have to be manually completed on all environments.
- SPD workflows cannot be easily modified in development environments and promoted through the various testing / production farms. Although SPD 2010 has the ability to export workflows as wsp that greatly improves the deployment process.
- Editing pages in SPD breaks the SharePoint ghosting feature.
- Mistakes in production environments can cause unwanted downtime.

An ideal code promotion process should provide solutions where the SharePoint administrator runs a script to configure pre-requisites (create list, SQL database, etc.), deploys features, creates sites if needed, and configures security. However, often times the development team is not mature enough and this complexity does little to improve code promotion for the farm and its configuration. However, as developers and administrators gain more experience deploying with solution packages, the process becomes easier and full automation becomes more of a reality.

It is also important to understand the content approval policies and governances in place for an organization. For example, if a wsp is created which includes site logos and/or custom css styles and are deployed into the farm into the site collection style library. It is possible a marketing person may be responsible for those images/styles and will update them on a periodic basis. If the wsp package were re-deployed all changes to the styles and images would be lost and as a result, have a very upset marketing department. WSPs have great value in simplifying deployments, but be sure they support the organizations governance policies. Further, the following should be kept in mind during the development lifecycle.

- Detect and discuss issues early and report critical issues early.
- Do NOT implement a solution which will lose data, try to keep as much of your content and settings as possible.
- Minimize downtime.
- Continue when possible.
- Be reentrant.
- Keep the administrator / architect informed of any architecture changes required by the application and its associated wsp's.

Deployment strategies

When deploying wsp's, there are some strategies which can be put in place which will assist in smoother deployments and more reliable results. Firstly, it is important to organize your wsp's into groups based generally on functions – do not put all content in one feature. In general it is best to keep site definitions in one wsp, web parts and controls in another (often larger deployments will separate these), workflows, and common utilities. Also, it also a good idea to separate out larger projects – especially ones which will likely have updates to ensure those components can be deployed separately from other site customizations. These projects can be further sub-divided into site configuration, controls/web parts, and workflows as it may not be necessary (or wanted) to re-create custom list definitions, etc.

WSP installation can vary depending upon a number of factors:

- Feature scope to either web, farm or site
- Pre-requisites (site collections, external databases, service configuration such as Business Data Catalog)
- Site customization requirements
- Number of features
- Security

Deployments can be generalized from simple to advanced. A simple deployment which has little or no custom code can be described as taking a site template (or backup of a site) and restoring it into the destination farm. This solution is viable only if there is no content in the destination data or the content can be completely overwritten during each promotion process. In general this solution is used when the site is based upon a template already in production, such as a Publishing Site, and the site has been developed in SharePoint Designer. More often than not, this deployment process will not work in production environments. Developers need to provide some mechanism for sending the administration the deployment scripts information required to install successfully. There are a few choices to ensure deployment scripts are successful. One method is to have each developer create a customized install script for their individual components. This method works as long as development teams are small; however, an alternative is to have each developer create an XML file which defines required information for the deployment scripts. An example XML file could be as follows:

```
<solution>
  <features update="true">
    <featurename force="true">
      WSP.Solution_Feature</featurename>
  </features>
  <runonfrontends>true</runonfrontends>
  <runscriptonlyonfrontends>true
  </runscriptonlyonfrontends>

  <overrideLocalInstall>true</overrideLocalInstall>
  <runscript>true</runscript>
  <scriptname allservers="true">
    PostInstallScript.ps1</scriptname>
  <scriptdir>C:\Program Files\Common Files\Microsoft
Shared\Web Server Extensions\14\TEMPLATE\LAYOUTS\
WSP.Solution_Feature\powershell
  </scriptdir>
</solution>
```

The above script provides required information to the administration deploy script. The PowerShell commands which install the solution uses these scripts to determine the deployment steps needed. Since a solution will likely have more than one feature, the name of the feature is identified. To date, there isn't a way to extract the feature name from the wsp without breaking it apart and parsing through the contained files. There is an option for the feature name which will force the feature to activate even if it has already been activated. When a solution component has been upgraded to version two and a feature reactivation process is required, this will tell the script to apply the force parameter on the Enable-SPFeature PowerShell command.

The next component of the XML file is the <runonfrontends> tag. This will identify if the wsp should be installed on the front-end web servers or just the application server. There are occasions, such as timer jobs, which should only be installed on the application server.

The <overrideLocalInstall> tag will force the global installation of the wsp and will ensure the all application pools in the farm are reset. It is important to note that by default all application pools in the SharePoint farm will be reset after each wsp installation and for highly available production farms, this may not be a desired effect especially if more than one wsp is being installed. One way to prevent the production farm from resetting is by installing the wsps one server at a time. This is configured by the –local:true parameter of the Install-SPSolution PowerShell command.

There are occasions where additional configuration is required (such as updating the web.config) and the developer has created a custom PowerShell for this process. If the script needs to be run, the script XML parameters identifying when the script should be run are provided. To see a full copy of an example script which utilizes this code, see http://suzincode.wordpress.com.

NOTE: The WSP deployment process is not perfect and there are some issues when deploying using this method. Be sure to fully test any new wsp implementations before releasing into a production environment.

- Even if the –local:$true setting has been applied, the IIS application pool will likely reset!! Keep this in mind when scheduling maintenance windows.
- WSPs do NOT deploy like Visual Studio, be sure to test the installation using the script process in QA or Staging environments.
- Items in SharePoint lists do NOT always get updated! They may have to be updated manually delete/upload or deactivate/re-activate feature.
- GAC deploys often 'hang up' you may need to delete from GAC, reboot, and re-install.
- Feature Activations do not always 'activate' cleanly, use –force:$true to force activation.

More information on deployment scripts can be found at: http://msdn.microsoft.com/en-us/library/aa544500.aspx. For the purposes of this chapter, the following PowerShell could be used to deploy a solution called WSP.Solution.wsp.

```
#Add the solution
Write-Host "Adding solution $name..."
$solution = Add-SPSolution $path
#Deploy the solution
if (!$solution.ContainsWebApplicationResource) {
  Write-Host "---Deploying solution $name to the Farm... using localinstall:$localInstall"
  $solution    |    Install-SPSolution    -GACDeployment:$gac    -CASPolicies:$cas
    -Confirm:$false -Local:$localInstall
  } else {
  if ($webApps -eq $null -or $webApps.Length -eq 0) {
  Write-Warning "The solution $name contains web application resources but no web
applications were specified to deploy to."
    return
  }
  $webApps | ForEach-Object {
    Write-Host "---Deploying solution $name to $_... using localinstall:$localInstall"
    $solution    |    Install-SPSolution    -GACDeployment:$gac    -CASPolicies:$cas    -
WebApplication $_ -Confirm:$false -Local:$localInstall
  }
}
#enable the feature
Write-Host "---Enabling feature: " $featureid " on host " $SiteCollectionURL
Enable-SPFeature $featureid -Url $SiteCollectionURL -Force:$force
```

This PowerShell is for example purposes only; it will require additional code to function completely. For more information on PowerShell visit: http://technet.microsoft.com/en-us/sharepoint/ee518673.

The techniques described in this section should provide strategies for deployment of code into a production environment along which in turn will improve reliability and increase confidence in promotion of code throughout the development lifecycle.

Proactively maintain code

Once solutions have been deployed into production environments, it is important to maintain these applications during the application lifecycle. Have a process in place which will support the locating of bugs quickly, clearly defined workflows for the standard promotion of code process as well as the out-of-cycle emergency patch process.

The processes defined in this chapter are fairly rigid and a well defined taxonomy needs to be in place beforehand. As with SharePoint these code promotion and deployment techniques will help automate an existing process and make it more efficient; however, it can also create chaos and frustration when implemented on the fly without proper planning. Additionally, these considerations should be kept in mind:

- Be sure to have a roll-back strategy in case an application needs to be un-deployed.
- Administrators deploying should be familiar with SharePoint and its architecture. It is advisable the administrators also be familiar with the applications being deployed in case there are issues which were not encountered in the previous environments.
- What is the development teams threshold for creating packages versus manually deploying objects in SharePoint.
- Who are the individuals responsible for the various components of development and deployment?

Microsoft Team Foundation Server is able to assist in deployment and code promotion process by providing administrators the ability to tag code as it moves through the code promotion process using the build process. Build templates define the mechanics for building code and wsp's out of the box. These templates can be edited with Visual Studio 2010 using the standard workflow mechanics. There are some caveats using TFS, namely, it is important that the build server be installed with the SharePoint binaries this will allow the build server to compile the source code. It would be necessary to either copy the required binaries into the project hierarchy or copy the entire SharePoint 14 hive to the build server.

When creating the build definition for a SharePoint 2010 solution it is important to select the appropriate solutions from the TFS server, Identify workspaces (or destinations for the build/checkout processes), select the build server, choose a trigger, use the MSBuild arguments /p:IsPackaging=True, and finally, select a retention policy. For detailed instructions visit http://msdn.microsoft.com/en-us/library/ff622991.aspx.

Additional changes can be implemented by customizing the build template to execute PowerShell on the remote system. Use something similar to the following PowerShell commands:

```
Connect-WSMan $remotemachine
$s = New-PSSession $remotemachine
try
{
```

```
Write-Output "---scriptdir $dirToProcess"
 Invoke-Command -Session $s -ArgumentList $powershelldir -ScriptBlock {param($a)
cd $a}
 Invoke-Command -Session $s -ArgumentList $dirToProcess -ScriptBlock {param($a)
cd $a}
 Invoke-Command -Session $s -ScriptBlock {Write-Host "here"}
 Invoke-Command -Session $s -ScriptBlock {Get-Location}
 Invoke-Command -Session $s -ScriptBlock {attrib -R $powershellbasedir /s}
}
catch
{
}
finally
{
 Remove-PSSession $s
 Disconnect-WSMan $remotemachine
}
```

Note: The above PowerShell commands are listed for
example purposes and may need additional modification
in order to work in your environment.

All teams involved with developing/deploying
applications for the SharePoint platform should follow
the processes described in this chapter and summarized
below:

- The Change Management process which controls
  changes and provides traceability.
- The Build process which automates the creation
  of installation packages.
- The Deployment process which controls the
  deployment of the SharePoint applications.

- The Promotion process which moves SharePoint applications through the various environments and ultimately into production.
- The Continuous Integration process and tools which pull together the previous processes in a manner that can be triggered by specific development events and automated from build to deployment and verification testing.

Microsoft Team Foundation Server 2010 has improved its ability to build and deploy SharePoint solutions. Additionally, by using PowerShell code deployment can be automated much more than with previous versions of SharePoint and Visual Studio.

Summary

This chapter provides engineering teams with basic concepts needed to allow code to be deployed into SharePoint farms both large and small in a predictable fashion. It is not intended to cover all the possible scenarios and is designed to help organizations get started and determine what it means to deploy code using SharePoint 2010.

This chapter reviewed concepts for code promotion, development governance, and tools used to ensure consistent and reliable releases into production environments. The following items will assist development teams with the above concepts:

- Learn SharePoint and its out of the box functionality as well as how best to customize its features.
- Build a business justification for projects and ensure the appropriate business interests are represented.
- Develop a roadmap to ensure consistent governance.
- Plan / Test / Implement.
- Validate new development at each stage in the code promotion process.
- Review and evolve process to find improvements which can be implemented.

Finally, a successful deployment into a highly available internet or intranet farm can only be developed with the commitment of management and staff.

- Access – provide access to business and technical teams that have the knowledge to provide the necessary input.
- Flexibility – grant flexibility to team members schedules to attend meetings and collaborate on concepts.
- Responsive Decision Making - empower teams to make responsive decisions on behalf of the organization.
- Governance Board – oversight of a governance board to review and provide direction.
- Collaboration – engage in the roadmap process with a highly interactive approach.

SharePoint farms that require high availability have unique constraints and development challenges to ensure site administration, customization, and development. These concerns can be addressed using Microsoft Visual Studio 2010, Microsoft Team Foundation Server 2010, and customized PowerShell scripts.

9.   SharePoint Security and Authentication Notes

Introduction

SharePoint 2010 provides various options for user authentication as well as passing authentication information to external line-of-business systems. During the design and implementation of a SharePoint 2010 solution, the chosen authentication method could affect or restrict the availability of some SharePoint functionality and the options for interacting with external systems.

This chapter will discuss the different options and architectural considerations for user authentication and for further authentication to external systems.

Classic mode authentication vs. claims based authentication

When planning or creating a web application one of the first decisions you have to make is whether the web application must use Classic Mode or Claims Based Authentication. On the surface, it is a simple question. Classic mode authentication provides only Windows authentication. Claims based authentication can provide Windows authentication, forms-based authentication or authentication using a trusted identity provider such as

Windows Live ID, Google OpenID or Active Directory Federation Services (ADFS).

It seems obvious that if you will only ever use Windows authentication it might be the simplest to choose classic mode authentication or, if you have any chance of using other authentication methods, to choose claims based authentication. Some recommendation state that you should always choose claims based authentication as it provides more options. Unfortunately, the decisions are sometimes more complicated. Subtle differences between classic mode and claims based Windows authentication might cause unexpected behaviour or limitations. There are also other options to providing users with a forms based login screen even when using Windows authentication as discussed later in the chapter.

Authentication is the process of determining or ensuring a user's identity. Classic mode authentication always relies on Internet Information Services (ISS) to generate a Windows identity for the current user, normally using NT LAN Manager (NTLM) or Kerberos to verify a user name and password against Active Directory. SharePoint then uses the Windows identity to determine the associated SharePoint user. The user identifier is stored in the format DOMAIN\username.

Claims based authentication is more complicated. It uses Windows Identity Foundation (WIF). WIF provides the basic functionality for identity management. In the case of claims based Windows authentication IIS is still responsible for creating a Windows identity. Instead of using this Windows identity directly, SharePoint converts it to a claims identity using a Security Token Service (STS). The STS is a web service that creates a security token for the user. By default, SharePoint uses Security Assertion Mark-up Language (SAML) tokens. SAML is an open XML standard for exchanging authentication and claims information. SharePoint will then perform any additional claims augmentation that might be required. It then uses this claims identity as the user's identity. The user identifier for a claims based Windows user is stored in a format similar to i:0#.w|domain\username, with the w before the pipe denoting that it is a windows user.

Some SharePoint functionality, such as multi-tenant support for service applications, depends on claims augmentation and so is not available when classic mode authentication is used.

The difference in the way the user identifier is stored provides another good example of the implications of the chosen authentication model. Any custom code, developed with classic mode authentication in mind and that tries to use the user identifier will not understand the claims identifier format and could produce unexpected results when executed against claims based web applications.

An important example of this is that SQL Server Reporting Services is not claims aware. It will be unable to pass the user credentials to a backend data source even when Kerberos delegation is configured correctly. This means that when using claims based authentication the connection to the back-end data source must always use a service account, as it cannot authenticate using the current user. This restricts some functionality such as per user permissions in the backend data store.

At the other end of the scale, some service applications are fully claims aware. Excel Calculation Services is an example. It uses the Claims to Windows Token Service (C2WTS) to convert claims to Windows tokens when connecting to external data sources. Through this mechanism it can authenticate the current user to back-end data sources even if Kerberos constrained delegation is not used.

Web Applications originally created to use classic mode authentication can be converted to use claims based authentication through PowerShell scripting. During this process, all Windows user identities are converted to claims identities. This process is not reversible, and claims based web applications cannot be converted back to classic mode web applications.

The authentication mode also applies to the entire web application. Although you can create different zones using different authentication methods, all the zones in a web application must use the same authentication mode. Claims based authentication allows multiple authentication methods to be available in a single zone. In this scenario users must choose an authentication method (e.g. Windows or Forms) when they connect to the site.

Windows Authentication: NTLM vs. Kerberos

Through the SharePoint user interface, you can configure two types of Windows authentication: NTLM and

Kerberos. For very specific purposes, you could configure clear text and digest authentication but this must be done directly in IIS on each web front-end server.

NTLM is simplest Windows authentication option to configure but does not support any complex authentication scenarios. It does not require any additional configuration steps to work. Microsoft also recommends using NTLM when crawling SharePoint sites for search, so it is always a good idea to have at least one zone of your web application that uses NTLM and to configure that as the URL for search crawling.

NTLM uses an encrypted challenge/response protocol to verify a user's credentials without passing the password over the network. The client passes the username in clear text to the server. The server then presents the client with a challenge (a random number). The client then encrypts the random number using a hash of the user's password and sends the result as a response. The server then verifies that the result is identical to the same calculation made on the server using a hash of the password, thus proving that the client knows the user's password. Because of backward compatibility with older versions of Windows, NTLM does not provide the same advanced security features as Kerberos.

Kerberos is a more secure protocol and supports advanced security features. The Kerberos protocol also allows passing the current user's credentials from one service to another (forwarding or delegation), such as authenticating the current user to an external line of business system. The downside is that Kerberos requires additional configuration to work and clients must have access to a Kerberos Key Distribution Centre (KDC – in a Windows scenario this is an AD DS domain controller). Client machines normally have access to a KDC in a corporate network environment but opening up Kerberos ports to the Internet is risky. Later in this chapter we will discuss some options for securely exposing SharePoint sites across the internet.

Kerberos uses tickets to authenticate a user against a resource or service. The KDC logically consists of two components: an Authentication Service (AS) and a Ticket Generating Service (TGS). When a client wants to connect to a specific resource using Kerberos it must first obtain a ticket for the resource from the KDC. The client authenticates the user using the AS. Once the user is authenticated, the client then requests a ticket from the TGS for the specific resource. To avoid the client having to authenticate the user on every request to a resource, the very first ticket it receives is a Ticket Granting Ticket (TGT). The TGT is a time-sensitive ticket that verifies the client's identity and allows direct requests for tickets to specific resources. The use of the TGT reduces network traffic to the AD servers, and this could cause a noticeable improvement in network traffic to the AD servers in a heavily used environment.

The TGS encrypts the ticket for access to a specific resource or service using a secret specific to the targeted service. This allows the service to verify the identity of the client without anyone else being able to read the ticket. In order to do this, the TGS must be able to identify the target service. Active Directory uses Service Principle

Names (SPNs) to find the target secret. An SPN can either be associated with a user or a computer. For the purposes of this discussion, we will focus on SPNs associated with users (service accounts).

When a user tries to connect to a SharePoint site in a web application that uses Kerberos authentication, the user's browser will construct an SPN based on the URL. For http and https, the SPN will be similar to HTTP/server.domain. To generate the ticket so that it can be decrypted by the web application, the TGS must know which user account will be used to decrypt the ticket. The TGS does not know anything about SharePoint or IIS, so it is not able to find out which user account is the service account for running the application pool for the web application. The only way in which it can find this out is by searching through AD for a user associated with the SPN.

The obvious implication is that the correct SPN must be associated with the appropriate service account in AD. If not, it will encrypt the ticket in a way that only the local service account on the target server can decrypt it. This means authentication will fail, even with the correct username and password. Duplicate SPNs will also be problematic, as the TGS will not know which account to choose when multiple service accounts match the specified SPN.

When troubleshooting Kerberos authentication issues, the two most common culprits are:

- Mistyping of the SPN (some parts of SPNs could be case sensitive)
- Duplicate SPNs

Since Windows Server 2003, AD uses Kerberos constrained delegation for added security. This means that a service will only be able to forward the user's authentication information to another service if it is explicitly configured to allow delegation.

As an example, consider the following scenario: You have developed a custom SharePoint web part that displays information from a separate SQL server database. The data from the server is filtered based on the current user's permissions in the SQL Server database. Assume the database server is named devdb, the domain is dev.local and the URL to the site where the web part is hosted is http://devsp/sites/test

The following SPNs must be configured for the service account used for the identity of the web application:
- HTTP/devsp
- HTTP/devsp:80
- HTTP/devsp.dev.local
- HTTP/devsp.dev.local:80

If using SSL, the following two SPNs must also be configured:
- HTTP/devsp:443
- HTTP/devsp.dev.local:443

Different SPNs are required because users can type different URLs to get to the same site.

The following SPNs must be configured for the service account used as the SQL Server service identity:

- MSSQLSvc/devdb.dev.local:1433

Delegation must be enabled from the SharePoint web application service account to the SQL Server service account.

Forms based authentication

SharePoint 2010 web applications that use claims based authentication can support forms based authentication. Like SharePoint 2007, the support comes in the form of ASP.Net membership and role providers. The big difference is that the SharePoint claims provider provides a layer of abstraction from the ASP.Net membership and role providers. This means that SharePoint does not really care which types of authentication you are using on a claims based web application, as it only ever has to deal with claims. This makes it possible to have more than one authentication type (such as both Windows and forms) running on a single zone of a web application.

Because the claims provider acts as an abstraction layer between the forms based authentication and SharePoint, SharePoint web applications does not directly understand ASP.Net forms based authentication and will not accept standard ASP.Net authentication tickets. The result is that interoperability and single sign-on between SharePoint and other ASP.Net applications no longer works unless the ASP.Net application is modified to also use claims based authentication and WIF. This also means that custom login pages developed for SharePoint 2007 will not work on SharePoint 2010, as they will issue tickets that SharePoint does not understand, and must therefore be redeveloped.

The most common implementations of forms based authentication uses either the ASP.Net SQL Server membership and role providers, or the ASP.Net LDAP membership and role providers. In SharePoint 2007, a membership provider was required for forms based authentication, but the role provider was optional. In SharePoint 2010, the membership provider is also required. For non-standard membership and role stores, custom membership and role providers can be developed quite easily.

Configuring forms based authentication in SharePoint 2010 requires a few different steps.

- Enable forms based authentication on one of the zones in the web application and specify the role and membership providers.
- Register the role and membership providers in the web.config file of the Security Token Service to allow the STS to retrieve information to issue claims tokens.
- Register the role and membership provider in the web.config file of the applicable zone of the web application.
- Register the people picker wildcards for the providers in the web.config file of the applicable zone of the web application.
- Register the role and membership provider in the web.config file of the central administration web

application to allow selecting forms users in central administration.

- Register the people picker wildcards for the providers in the web.config file of the central administration web application.

IIS 7 provides a user interface for making most of the configuration changes (apart from the people picker wildcard settings). They can also be made directly to the web.config file using a text editor. In a farm with multiple servers, the configuration changes must be made on all servers where the applicable web applications are hosted.

Web applications that use forms based authentication have a number of limitations:

- Search based alerts are not supported when using forms authentication.
- The experience when using people picker controls on the site, especially when searching for a user or role, could be limited or provide unexpected results depending on the implementation of the providers.
- SharePoint does not provide any built in support for management of users and roles, such as resetting of password, password reminders, creation of new users etc. This must be custom developed or done using tools such the CodePlex Forms Based Authentication (FBA) Toolkit.

Trusted identity providers

SharePoint 2010 claims based authentication provides the ability to use an external trusted identity provider to provide authentication to a web application (identity federation). Typical scenarios where this would be useful would be when allowing access to the web application to users from a partner organisation using Active Directory Federation Services (ADFS) or using Windows Live ID or Google Open ID as identity providers for members of a public web site.

In an identity federation scenario, there are two types of Security Token Services. The first is an Identity Provider STS (IP-STS) and the second is a Relying Party STS (RP-STS). As the names imply, the IP-STS provides the identity tokens and the RP-STS accepts the tokens and trusts that they are valid, even though the RP-STS is not in control of the identities.

The trust is implemented through public key encryption. The IP-STS issues a SAML claim, encrypts and digitally signs it using the private key associated with an X.509 certificate. The RP-STS can then decrypt it and verify the origin of the token if it trusts the public key for the certificate.

The exact steps in configuring a trusted identity provider depends on the provider that is used, but the main concepts are the same:

- Configure the domain name of the web application on the IP-STS.
- Export the certificate of the IP-STS.
- Import the certificate into the SharePoint farm using the Microsoft Management Console.
- Register the certificate on the SharePoint farm as a trusted root authority using PowerShell.

- Configure the claim type mapping using PowerShell
- Register the IP-STS as a trusted identity provider for SharePoint using PowerShell
- Configure the web application to use the trusted identity provider.

The following figure represents the authentication process in an identity federation scenario:

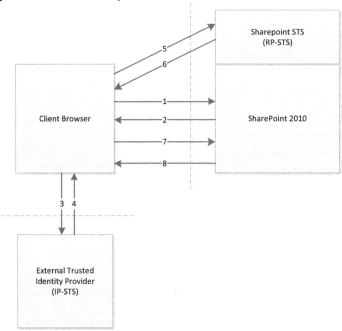

1. The browser requests a resource, such as a page, from SharePoint.
2. The browser is redirected to an authentication page (external page in this scenario).

3. The user authenticates against the external identity provider.
4. The IP-STS issues a token to the browser.
5. The browser passes the IP-STS token to the SharePoint STS (used as an RP-STS) via SharePoint
6. The RP-STS trusts the claims in the token and issues a local token.
7. The browser passes the local RP-STS token to SharePoint on all subsequent requests.
8. SharePoint provides access to resources based on the local RP-STS token.

The Secure Store

Another security related service that SharePoint provides is the Secure Store. It provides secure encrypted storage of user credentials that could be used for single sign-on or authentication to external systems.

The secure store stores credentials per target application. For each target application, it can store credentials per individual or per group of users. The per-individual model is suitable when each user should use unique credentials. Where multiple users must authenticate to the external system using the same service account, the group model will usually work best.

When planning a secure store service deployment, there are some best practice guidelines to ensure the safety and security of the credentials:

- A backup of the secure store database should be taken before and after generating a new encryption key
- The backup of the encryption key should not be stored with the backup of the secure store service application database
- The secure store service application should use a service account that is not used by any other service applications or web applications
- If the size of the farm and the architecture allows, the secure store service application should be hosted on a dedicated application server that does not host any other services
- If the environment and architecture permits, the database for the secure store service application should be hosted on a separate SQL server instance that is not used by other services or web applications in the farm

SharePoint over the Internet

Many companies are using SharePoint for more than just an internal collaboration platform. As the uses of SharePoint evolve and grow, the requirements for access to the SharePoint instances also change. It is quite common now for companies to make SharePoint systems accessible over the Internet. The benefits of being able to access systems from anywhere are clear, but the security risks should be considered thoroughly.

There are many different options for making SharePoint available over the Internet and the optimal solution will depend on the exact purpose of the systems and the audience.

When exposing SharePoint for the sole purpose of enabling employees of the company access to internal SharePoint systems, the best option is usually to stick with the company's current remote access policy. This normally uses a VPN client, remote desktop or SSL VPN technology to provide secure connections to internal systems.

When exposing a single SharePoint based application to users from one or more partner organisations in an extranet scenario, in most cases the best option is to expose a single web application from an internal server through the reverse proxy capabilities of the company firewall. Most enterprise-level firewall products also allow for intercepting the NTLM or Kerberos challenge from SharePoint and presenting the user with a login form. In this way, it is possible to provide end-users with an authentication form without having to implement forms-based authentication.

If the number of extranet users is relatively small, the simplest solution might be to maintain individual accounts for the extranet users in the internal corporate Active Directory store. This quickly becomes unmanageable when more users require extranet access, and might have licensing implications as well. If many users from a specific partner organisation require access, setting up Active Directory Federation Services ADFS to trust users from the partner organisation might be the best option. Another option would be to use a custom trusted identity provider or forms based authentication. I personally would not recommend forms based authentication unless none of the other solutions provide the required functionality.

In a reverse proxy scenario, it is very important to ensure that the correct Alternate Access Mappings are in place. Although most reverse proxy capable firewall products are very good at translating the internal URLs in the pages to external URLs, there are some cases where the URLs used in scripts on some pages are encoded in such a way that they are not recognised as URLs and therefore not translated. This will potentially break some SharePoint functionality, as the external users will not be able to resolve the internal URLs.

When any sensitive information is exchanged (including passwords in a forms based authentication scenario), Secure Sockets Layer (SSL) encryption is essential. Most firewall products that provide reverse proxy functionality also support SSL termination. This means that secure connections using HTTPS is available for use over the internet between the client and the firewall. The internal communications between the firewall and the SharePoint farm is unencrypted as the internal network is normally secure. The SSL certificates configuration happens on the firewall rather than on the SharePoint farm. This can reduce the administrative burden for maintaining multiple certificates by using wildcard certificates on the firewall device. If SSL is configured directly on the SharePoint farm, it must be configured on each web front-end server.

SharePoint can also provide publicly accessible web sites. When allowing anonymous access to the public, the best option is normally to have an isolated farm in the DMZ dedicated to servicing the content. This farm should ideally not have any connectivity back to any internal systems. A typical approach is to have an internal content editing farm where content managers can edit the content and then use content deployment jobs to publish the content to the public facing farm. In this way, the public facing farm can be locked down completely.

In cases where the public facing site allows any user to register, three main options are:
- Using a public trusted identity provider such as Windows Live ID or Google Open ID
- Building a custom trusted identity provider specifically to manage the membership process
- Implementing forms based authentication

In my experience, forms-based authentication has some unexpected quirks and is difficult to troubleshoot and maintain. I would only recommend forms-based authentication when all other options are ruled out.

Summary

SharePoint provides a rich set of options for user authentication. In most common scenarios the choice of authentication mode and method is obvious, but the implications of each choice should be considered carefully.

When the implementation requires the use of service applications or components that are not claims aware, classic mode authentication should usually be the first choice. In cases requiring functionality that depends on claims augmentation, there is no choice but to use claims authentication.

When using windows authentication, NTLM is not as advanced or secure as Kerberos, but is the simplest option to configure. It is normally acceptable in a simple implementation on a secure local network. Kerberos provides advanced features such as identity delegation but requires additional configuration in Active Directory.

The best option for exposing SharePoint via the Internet depends on the target audience. For internal employees VPN, SSL VPN or Remote Desktop options are usually best. For extranet scenarios, reverse proxy implementations usually work best. When exposing SharePoint to anonymous users, the use of a dedicated, isolated and locked down farm is preferable. Sites that allow users to register should consider using a public trusted identity provider such as Windows Live ID or Google OpenID. Forms authentication is usually only an acceptable solution when none of the other options will work.

10.   InfoPath 2010 – What is new?

Introduction

This chapter is about highlighting the massive improvements incorporated in InfoPath 2010. The aim of this chapter is to provide enough information to the reader to be able to understand the products strengths and limitations. I will also review key information such as licensing that companies and decision makers must be aware of before selecting InfoPath as a form design solution.

InfoPath 2010 is fast becoming a mainstream product due to its integration with SharePoint 2010 however; it is unfortunate that there still exist some long trailing misconceptions about the product such as:

- InfoPath web enabled forms need the InfoPath client installed on user desktop to be able to view forms.
- InfoPath forms can only be designed in InfoPath Designer, etc.

These misconceptions will be reviewed and explained for the readers. This chapter covers points I see as being vital to implementing InfoPath SharePoint based solutions.

Overview

InfoPath is a form creation tool that enables technical and business users to create forms using InfoPath designer for gathering business data.

Novice users with basic training can use InfoPath, however; we do not expect advance business users to create complex forms, as we would not expect them to know about data connections, XPath and other technical topics. Leave marketing a side, practically business users design and develop only low to medium complexity forms with trivial lookup columns using InfoPath designer.

Using InfoPath 2010, we can create highly customized, sophisticated forms without writing any code. InfoPath provides pre-built form layouts, form validations, rules and drag and drop form field controls to assist with form design and development.

What InfoPath can do?

To highlight the new features of InfoPath 2010, let us first look at InfoPath 2007 then we will discuss the changes in InfoPath 2010 in subsequent sections.

InfoPath 2007

InfoPath 2007 offers you the capability to:

- Create InfoPath client forms (users fill the form using InfoPath Designer 2007).
- Create web enabled InfoPath forms hosted in MOSS 2007 (Enterprise edition).
- Create Initiation and Association forms for custom workflows.

InfoPath 2010

Microsoft has split InfoPath 2010 into two applications:

- InfoPath Designer 2010
- InfoPath Filler 2010

The main reason for this split is to logically separate design and usage of the forms, however, both applications called the same executable but in different modes.

In addition to the core features InfoPath 2007 offers, InfoPath 2010 comes up with an interesting feature that allows us to edit SharePoint list forms using InfoPath Designer 2010.

Editing forms for SharePoint list

Every SharePoint list contains a set of list forms that you use to view, edit, or add items to a list. Using Microsoft SharePoint Designer 2010, you can customize these forms on the fly, but it lacks the rich experience that InfoPath 2010 offers. InfoPath is a superior form design tool in many aspects with design layouts, data connections to various external data sources, validation and rules management.

Using InfoPath 2010, any customisation applied to any of the forms takes effect to all three forms, and whereas using SharePoint Designer 2010 you have to apply it individually.

If you are planning to modify the HMTL of the list form or looking to add JavaScript then SharePoint Designer 2010 is suitable for these types of tasks.

Launch InfoPath Designer to edit List Forms

There are three possible ways to launch InfoPath Designer 2010 to edit list forms.

1. Using the browser:
Open the list in the browser, click on the *Customise Form* option under <u>List Tools, List</u> tab in the ribbon.

Figure 1 – Customize form option from browser

2. Using SharePoint Designer 2010:
Open the site in SharePoint Designer, select the list or content type, then go to the tab *List Setting* in the ribbon and click *Design Forms in InfoPath*.

Figure 2 – Design Forms in InfoPath option from SPD

3. Using InfoPath Designer:
Launch InfoPath Designer, select <u>SharePoint List</u> then click *Design Form*.

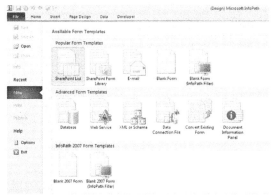

Figure 3 – InfoPath forms templates

Provide the site URL, click *"Next"* and then select the option to create a new SharePoint list or select existing list for customisation.

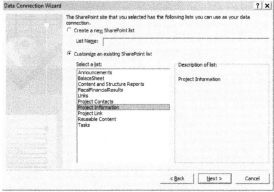

Figure 4 – Select list for customization

Note: You need SharePoint 2010 Enterprise Edition to be able to edit list forms using InfoPath. Additionally, Microsoft no longer provides a standalone forms server for hosting InfoPath forms.

A common misconception is that if you have SharePoint 2010 Standard edition you can modify list forms from InfoPath Designer 2010, you will need the full <u>Enterprise</u> edition to edit SharePoint list forms.

If you try to connect your SharePoint site running with Standard license, you will get the error **"This feature requires SharePoint 2010 or greater with InfoPath Forms Service enabled."**

Figure 5 – Error: InfoPath form service not enabled

We can enable InfoPath form service by activating the feature <u>SharePoint Server Enterprise Site Collection features.</u> You find this feature under Site Collection Administration feature available in Enterprise Edition only.

Could we use SharePoint Designer 2010 to launch InfoPath Designer 2010 that allows us to edit list forms?

Again, the answer is *"no, you cannot"*. When you edit list forms using InfoPath 2010, SharePoint generate three files (*displayifs.aspx*, *editifs.aspx*, *newifs.aspx*), these will appear as an ASPX page as you can see in SharePoint Designer 2010, but the page contains an InfoPath Form WebPart, therefore, when you try to customise list forms on SharePoint foundation or SharePoint Standard you will get "*WebPart missing*" error. This make perfect sense because InfoPath WebPart is only included in the Enterprise Edition.

Key Improvements and New Features

How to edit list forms using InfoPath 2010

Let us take an example of customizing an out of the box link list by adding a dropdown column (Category) and make minor design layout changes and then publish it. Follow the steps below to see how easy it is in InfoPath 2010 to modify your list forms.

- Use any method of your choice, mentioned in the previous paragraph, to launch InfoPath Designer 2010 for list customisation (**Links** list in my case).

Figure 6 – Link list form in design mode

- Add a column (Category) to the list of type ***dropdown list,*** and then enter choices.

Figure 7 – Add dropdown choices

- Change the form design by selecting the *Page Design* tab from the ribbon and choose the design of your choice.

Figure 8 – Link list after customization

- Select the *File* tab and click on the *Quick Publish* option.

Figure 9 – Publish InfoPath form using quick Publish

- Now browse to your list and click *Add new item.*

Figure 10 – Link list add form in browser

Backstage View

InfoPath Designer moves away from typical File menu approach and use the more compact, logically structured and pleasing user interface that provides a single location for all the form and data management options.

Figure 11 – Backstage view

In summary:

- Shows you everything InfoPath Designer 2010 knows about your form.

- Shows you everything you can *do* with your form.

- Programmable like the ribbon.

- Accomplish your task faster.

Quick Publish

Arguably, in spite of Microsoft's best efforts, the form publishing in InfoPath 2007 to MOSS 2007 is not as smooth as you would expect from a non-programmers tool, for every change made to the form you have to go through all the lengthy screens to publish it.

InfoPath 2010 comes up with the immensely useful option: Quick Publish. Most often we develop forms using iterative design approach; this means many iterations; hence, this single click publishes to MOSS 2007 or SharePoint 2010 feature will save valuable time.

InfoPath Form WebPart

The InfoPath form designer or developer can either directly publish the form to the library or attach the **forms** content type to the list. When a user clicks on the Add or Edit option of the list, FormServer.aspx residing under layouts, renders the form for us.

However, users who wanted to embed InfoPath forms in a custom Web Part Page had to call XmlFormView web part in ASP.NET page code using Visual Studio to achieve this. These kinds of restrictions left negative impression about InfoPath adaptability among business users.

 Microsoft addressed this issue in SharePoint 2010. Using the new InfoPath Form Web Part, available in the Enterprise Edition, you can host forms in a Web Part Page without even writing a single line of code, all you need to do is just add the InfoPath Form Web Part to a Web Part page and point it to published InfoPath form. This allows us to connect to other web parts on the page for sending and receiving data.

Portable InfoPath Forms

One of the challenges with SharePoint 2007 was, to republish InfoPath 2007 forms for each host environment separately, this problem surfaced because InfoPath 2007 stores the absolute URL in published (.xsn) file, which made our forms less portable.

Microsoft addressed this issue in InfoPath 2010 by keeping the relative URL in published form; therefore, we do not need to republish it for each host environment.

Quick Rules

One of the big changes in the 2010 version is prebuilt quick (validation) rules for controls. Now we can add new rules, copy and paste rules between controls that require similar validation. All the rules applied on a specific control can be manage and accessed using the **Manage Rule** option in the ribbon.

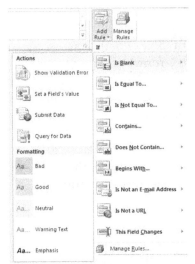

Figure 12 – OOB rules

Ribbon

The concept of the ribbon was originally introduced in Office 2007. Because of the success and attention this feature received, Microsoft incorporated the ribbon in the InfoPath 2010 release.

The ribbon provides only context related options available to the user on top of the screen, which makes the life of InfoPath developer and designer much easier. You do not need to search the options in traditional menus and toolbars anymore that might require several steps to complete a task. The ribbon displays the commands in a tab structure, grouped by type to ensure quick and easy accessibility.

You can customise the availability of commands in the ribbon by navigation to File -> Options -> Customize Ribbon.

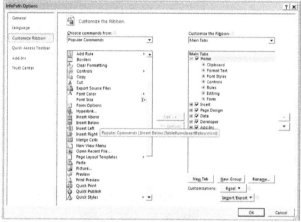

Figure 13 – Customize Ribbon Commands

Hide Ribbon from Web Forms

If you do not want the ribbon to take up valuable screen space when your InfoPath form is displayed in a modal dialog, then:

- Open your form in InfoPath Designer 2010.
- Click on <u>File</u> and then click on the <u>Advanced form</u> options. Form Options dialog comes up, select <u>Web Browser</u> category under <u>User Interface Options</u>.
- If you leave the checkbox *Show InfoPath commands in Ribbon or toolbar* unchecked, the ribbon will not show at all.

Figure 14 – InfoPath form in a browser without the ribbon

Filtering

Control filtering is one of the out-of-the-box features not supported in InfoPath 2007 web enabled forms. Control filtering was a feature missed by form designers and developers. There were a number of workarounds available to tackle this issue but these are not required in InfoPath 2010.

Useful additional features

- Pre-built layouts and themes.

- New Actions:

  ○ Send data to Web Part

  ○ Change REST URL

- TFS / SVN as source control.

- New Controls:

  ○ External Item Picker (BDC)

  ○ Picture Button

  ○ Person and Group Picker

- Improved deployment support (using .wsp).

- Compliant with Web Content Accessibility Guidelines 2.0 (WCAG 2.0) AA.

- Fully XHTML 1.0 compliant.

Licensing

Form Type	License Required
InfoPath forms in SharePoint 2010	SharePoint 2010 Enterprise Edition
SharePoint list forms (customise using InfoPath 2010)	SharePoint 2010 Enterprise Edition
SharePoint Workflow forms (customise using InfoPath 2010)	SharePoint 2010 Enterprise Edition
InfoPath client forms	Microsoft Office 2010 suite for InfoPath filler 2010

Unfortunately, InfoPath and SharePoint licensing is not the easiest thing to understand, it gets complicated with various versions of SharePoint 2010 available and different type of forms you can create using InfoPath 2010.

Note: If you are planning to use InfoPath 2010 forms in your SharePoint (enterprise edition) Intranet sites, then editors and developers of the InfoPath 2010 forms should hold both Standard and Enterprise CAL while users filling web enabled InfoPath forms just need Standard CAL.

Potential Issues

- InfoPath filler comes with the InfoPath licence which means that every user in your organisation needs the InfoPath license to be able to fill InfoPath 2010 client forms. This already put off a lot of companies from using InfoPath who don't have SharePoint 2010 Enterprise.

- Out of the box, there is no way you can specify the target in Hyperlink field.

- You may be in trouble if you don't have a top level site collection in Web Application.

- Tab containers are not available.

- The template part is a good option for static control like header and footer. It is possibly the least used feature of InfoPath. To add any more value to it, developers should have the option to attach code.

Summary

Designing your form and making it look more attractive is now easier with InfoPath 2010, although it is not as simple as perceived for business users to create complex form by themselves. Nonetheless, with some training of the business users: InfoPath offers great capabilities for publishing forms, streamlining business processes, connect with discrete line of business data sources and design sophisticated electronic forms quickly.

InfoPath is emerging as a major tool in the Microsoft stack. SharePoint integration and slick user interface coupled with extensive improvements are ingrained in the InfoPath 2010 version.

11.   Governance in SharePoint

Introduction

Governance is one of the most popular words related to SharePoint today.   For many, governance means management.   Most people use "govern" and "manage" interchangeably.   However, governance and management actually mean two different things, though they do go hand in hand.

Governance is a framework that defines strategic and goals and objectives.   Governance defines who gets to make decisions, how decisions are made and how to communicate those decisions.   Governance defines accountability and procedures for reconciling differences. Define governance in a documented Governance Plan.

Management refers to the action, the processes, the editing process, and the enforcement of the Governance Plan.

Governance is worthless without management, and managing a SharePoint site without a governance strategy is trying to steer a rudderless ship.   You have the tools, you have the personnel, and you will end up somewhere... But is it where you want to go?

SharePoint is destined for failure without governance. If you wish to guarantee the failure of your solution, skip your Governance Plan.

Governance Planning is one of the most commonly overlooked SharePoint implementation steps. It is critically important to establish a solid Governance Plan. Failure to do so is one of the causes of many failed, stalled, or poorly adopted SharePoint solutions.

Your plan determines who does what, how they do it, and where it is done. What are the rules? Who gets to make the rules? Who enforces the rules?

The Governance Plan is a guideline covering administration, maintenance, and support of *your* SharePoint environments. It identifies lines of ownership for both business and technical teams and defines who is responsible for what areas of the system. Furthermore, it establishes rules for appropriate usage of the SharePoint environments.

Your Governance Plan ensures your solution is used and managed in a controlled and consistent manner. Your plan is in place to prevent SharePoint from becoming unmanageable. A successful plan includes both a strategic, business-minded body to construct rules and procedures and a technically competent team to manage the routine operational tasks that keep the solution online.

Developing a Governance Plan does not need to be a massive undertaking. However, adequate time needs to allocated for this task. You can expect this to take between a couple of days and a couple of weeks to develop a fully comprehensive plan. Of course, it depends on the size and complexity of your solution and environment. If you overcomplicate your plan, no one will read it. If no one reads it, your plan will be ignored.

Your Governance Plan will never actually be complete. You need to revisit, update, and revise your plan as your organization grows, changes, and evolves.

Why would you commit so much time to governance? Without a documented plan, your SharePoint solution is at risk. With no rules or guidance to follow, the only logical conclusion is chaos. Chaos is impossible to manage.

Who will have permissions to create new Workspaces and Sites? How long are backups retained? How quickly should backups be available in case of catastrophic failure? How do you handle detractors such as negative comments or organization bashing? These are just some of the questions your Governance Plan should answer.

Your plan will vary slightly depending on the solution implemented and many other factors related to your specific organization. You do not have to write a complex Governance Plan from scratch. There are many fine examples available. You can do a few online searches and follow the examples put forward by leaders such as Sue Hanley or Joel Oleson. There are examples available just about everywhere.

Governance is a hot topic and is not specific to SharePoint environments. There are thousands of great resources online about Governance Plans. One plan specific to SharePoint and can be found on TechNet under "Governance Resource Center."

At a minimum, your SharePoint Governance Plan should include Business Objectives, Technical Requirements, Team Roles, Topology, Policies, and Training.

Business Objectives

The name says it all! Identify and **document** the specific objectives and requirements the SharePoint solution is expected to satisfy. It may be easier to start with a high level business need and keep adding details until the entire scene has been painted.

The Business Objectives section might start with something like "Our company has identified a need to improve collaboration. We feel that the best way to accomplish this is to provide employees with document management tools and improve the overall findability of our content and assets with a highly usable search application."

Expand the objective to include the entire business need and associated solution vision.

"Our organization has identified a need to improve collaboration between departments. SharePoint will be used to provide employees with web-based document storage, document management and versioning tools, and team/department-based workspaces.

Employees will receive SharePoint training to make better use of the available tools to foster communication and improve document-based collaboration.

SharePoint Search will be utilized to improve the overall findability of our content and assets stored within SharePoint and on our existing file shares."

Remember to capture, clarify, and confirm your business objectives. This section is not technical in nature and should be reviewed and approved by the stakeholders.

Technical Requirements

Unlike the Business Objectives, this section **is** technical in nature. Technical Requirements are all about the nuts and bolts of the solution, but only from a "must-have" perspective.

For example, here are some *examples* of technical "must-haves" that should be considered within your Technical Requirements:

- **Planned Downtime**. A two-hour maintenance window for planned maintenance every Saturday beginning at 5:00AM EST.

- **Capacity Planning**. Hardware needs to scale and support your growth. It needs to support

200GB of document storage at launch and scale to 600GB at 12 months. It must support 15,000 users for the first year, and it is expected to grow to 75,000 users at 24 months.

- **Disaster Recovery**. This environment must have a tested disaster recovery environment setup. SQL Server replication to our disaster recovery rack will suffice.

- **Availability**. Must be fault tolerant with load balanced web front ends, dedicated application server, and two-node clustered SQL Server. Availability target must be 99.9% or better.

- **Support calls**. Help desk calls should be received and attended within a maximum of 15-minute hold without a prior "high call volume" notification to the caller.

- **Audits**. Auditing to capture Site delete events should be in place from launch.

Deployment Team Roles

- Who is doing what?
- Do you need a RACI chart defining which individuals or roles are Responsible, Accountable, Consulted, and Informed?

This is an important part of your playbook. It is important to document which roles are responsible for which activities. Without it, you run a high risk of experiencing diffusion of responsibility.

Please keep in mind that simply saying one person is "in charge of SharePoint" is more than just laziness – it's a recipe for disaster!

You may very well have your SharePoint "Go-To" person. This person should certainly play a vital role in your SharePoint planning and deployment. If you place the entire burden on one person's shoulders, you will have created a single point of failure and placed your solution in jeopardy.

You will have a better solution if you enrol multiple people, identify their individual strengths, and request active and focused participation. SharePoint is a *team solution*. Use your team to construct your solution.

Roles will vary widely based on the size of your organization and on your specific SharePoint deployment. At a minimum, you need to account for the following Roles:

➢ **SharePoint Solution Architect**. Person or people responsible for initial planning of the entire solution, as well as for overseeing the proper execution during implementation and deployment. Needs a solid understanding of the business objectives, and must have the knowledge to satisfy these requirements using native SharePoint components, third-party add-ons, and custom development as necessary. Should be capable of interfacing with both business users and IT. Responsible for writing the technical specifications of the solution, and ensuring they are followed accordingly. This role can be outsourced.

➢ **SharePoint Developer.** The person or people responsible for writing custom code as prescribed by the SharePoint Architect. This should only happen after the Solution Architect has exhausted all other avenues of satisfying must-have functionality using native SharePoint components and existing third-party add-ons. This role **can** be outsourced.

➢ **SharePoint Administrator.** Person or people with Site Collection Administrator permissions; and responsible for administrative tasks such as ongoing maintenance, Search, Site procurement, Security, Templates, recovering deleted items from the Recycle Bin and managing the metadata and taxonomy configuration. *Not* responsible for architecting new solutions or writing code. Should interface very well with business users as well as IT, and understand when to call in the Solution Architect. If you have a

Go-To SharePoint person, this would be the role he or she should belong in. This role **can** be outsourced.

➤ **SharePoint Support or SharePoint Governor.** Person or people responsible for helping business users overcome problems they might encounter. Must have a good understanding of the native capabilities of SharePoint from an end-user perspective. Needs to interface well with business users. Requires a level of patience and understanding usually possessed only by mothers. This role **can** be outsourced.

➤ **SharePoint Business Champion or Evangelist.** Person or people responsible for understanding their specific business unit's day-to-day activities, objectives, and inner-workings. The ability to recognize how SharePoint can be used to improve processes and efficiencies is a trait of this role. Lastly, having a positive outlook in general is a plus because they are the people advocating for the solution.

Responsibilities include ensuring that their department understands the benefits of using SharePoint and serving as a liaison between the department and solution stakeholders in order to properly evolve the solution. This role **can NOT** be outsourced.

SharePoint Topology

SharePoint farms come in all shapes and sizes. The Governance Plan will detail your specific farm layout (topology). Topologies range from single server to federated topologies with multiple farms being joined together. When deciding on a topology, be sure to document the layout, including any notes detailing what led to your decision.

Selecting the appropriate topology is a function of the SharePoint Architect role, but here are some sample scenarios.

Figure 1 - Standalone: SharePoint and SQL on a single server

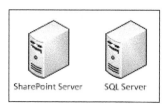

Figure 2 - Small Farm: SQL Server with one, two, or three SharePoint 2010 Servers

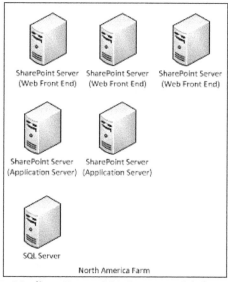

Figure 3 - Medium Farm: SQL Servers with four or more SharePoint 2010 Servers

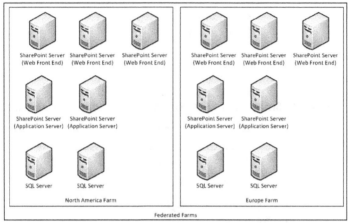

Figure 4 - Multiple Farms working together

Policies

This is the section of your Governance Plan where the rubber really meets the road. For obvious reasons, careful planning and consideration should go into your policies. You may need more policies than identified here.

Customization Policy

The first bullet in this section should describe what your organization considers a customization. It should describe the entire process from start to finish, particularly of how customizations shall be requested, approved, implemented, and all associated roles.

Typically, customizations are considered to be any third-party SharePoint add-ons or custom code (solutions, features, controls, etc.) which are not native to SharePoint. In-browser configuration, SharePoint

Designer configuration, and everything else is considered configuration changes or native SharePoint functionality.

It is unlikely that your users will know exactly what to consider a "customization." Your policy needs to account for requests which may end up being "configuration changes" and not customizations. Your Customization Policy should include the following questions as part of your change management:

- How do users request customizations?

    o Do they use an online form with workflow?
    o Do they send an email?
    o Do you offer and respond to both?

- What role (who) is responsible for reviewing customization requests?

- What is an acceptable time lapse until the user receives a response? Do all requests get a response?

- If it is determined that a request is actually a configuration change, what role approves this change?

- What role is responsible for funding customization efforts?

- What role is responsible for funding configuration efforts?

- How are customization requests tracked and communicated?

- Is the customization localized to a single Site, or is the customization useful across the organization?

- What role is responsible to capture, clarify, and confirm the actual business objectives?

- How are customizations tested prior to being deployed on the Production servers?

Detractor Policy

Due to the social nature of the SharePoint My Sites, many organizations are paralyzed with fear when thinking of it. This is unfortunate because the concepts born out of social networking actually enhance and facilitate collaboration. Adding a Detractors Policy to the Governance Plan instantly relaxes often-unjustified concerns about social features.

Your Detractors Policy can be a simple table with the following column headings:

- What type of Detractor?

  Example: Legitimate complainer.

- Why they make trouble.

  Example: Needs help with or wants to warn others.

- How to recognize Detractor?

  Example: Raises legitimate issue and may use strong language but seems open to reason.

- What is the corrective action?

  Example: Solve problem, provide education, or explain policies. Explain publicly or add to FAQ if possible.

You will be surprised how quickly fears go away when they are written down and accounted for!

Site Provisioning Policy

- How is a new Site requested?
- Who can request a new Site?
- What Workflow is required?
- What role approves the request?
- Where is the new Site created?
- What about unused Sites?
- When and how are Sites archived/deleted?

Site Management and Security Model Policy

- What roles are responsible for which Sites?
- What permissions are associated with which roles?
- What are the Farm Service Accounts being used and the associated passwords?
- Who are the Site Collection Administrators?
- Who are the Site Administrators?
- Who provides backups to Administrators?

Retention Policy

- How long do we keep content?
- What do we do with content we consider old?
- Archive it?
- Remove it?
- Permanently delete it?
- Request the Author to update it?

Name:

Chapter Document Retention Policy

Administrative Description:

This is the content retention policy on
Chapter documents - old documents are
archived after 18 months.

Policy Statement:

This document is subject to the "Chapter
Document Retention Policy" which will
auto-archive this document after 18

☑ Enable Retention

Specify how to manage retention:

Event	Action	Recurrence
Last Modified + 18 months	Send to the Record Center (ECM) location	No
Add a retention stage...		

Figure 5 - SharePoint provides inherent capabilities to create and manage Retention Policies

Figure 6 - SharePoint Retention Policies support various Event-triggered Actions

Training

Do not overlook training. Your Governance Plan should detail initial training, ongoing training, and training levels that are audience specific. Training for administrators is different from training for business users. Training for chapter leaders is different from training for volunteers.

Determine each of the different groups to receive training and the level of training required. Determine the type of training required for each group as well. IT Pros and technical administrators are usually fine with written training. Volunteers and members usually find webinar or video-based training more effective.

Don't stop with training at launch. Ensure your organization supports ongoing training options for new hires, community leaders, business users, executives, and members of all kinds.

Your training can be onsite, offsite, video, online, live webinar, recorded webinar, three days, or three-minute snippets that describe specific actions and activities.

Regardless of the type of training that works for your organization, you need to have a plan for it. Your Training Plan is a part of your Governance Plan.

Summary

Do not neglect your SharePoint Governance Plan. It will not end well. This process does not need to take a long time to complete, but it is vitally important.

Your SharePoint Governance Plan should include the following sections:

- **Business Objectives** define the high level objectives which the solution is expected to satisfy.

- **Technical Requirements** define the technical components of the solution, including integration points with external Line of Business (LOB) systems like your AMS, CRM, and all other non-SharePoint data sources.

- **Deployment Team Roles** define who is responsible for what.

- **SharePoint Topology** defines your SharePoint network and server farm architecture, including number of servers, server roles, specifications, and other relevant information.

Your **Governance Plan Policies** define your business rules that describe how you handle events such as procuring new Sites.

- **Customization Policy** specifies the rules on how third-party products and custom components are identified, tested, and ultimately deployed to the production environment.

- **Detractors Policy** provides guidance in undesirable situations such as members saying less than flattering things about your organization or the solution(s) undertaken.

- **Site Management and Security Policy** specifies ongoing Site and Subsite management and the responsible roles.

- **Retention Policy** defines how long content remains until considered unnecessary, and what to do with it.

- Finally, a **Training Plan** that outlines your official launch, as well as the conduct of ongoing and refresher training with respect to the diverse audiences and their existing workloads.

Creating dashboards using Business Connectivity
Services, SharePoint Designer and other related
technologies   333

12.   Creating dashboards using Business Connectivity Services, SharePoint Designer and other related technologies

Introduction

This chapter guides readers into creating dashboards using some of the key technologies in SharePoint 2010.

Throughout my experience as a consultant, piecing together the various tutorials available on the web to achieve the dashboards Microsoft so heavily advertise alongside the SharePoint product can be daunting. This chapter aims to take you through from start to finish creating dashboards using the following areas:

- Secure Store Service
- External Content Types in SharePoint Designer
- Business Connectivity Services (BCS), Business Data Catalog (BDC) permissions and actions
- Dashboards including:
  - o Business Data, Filter & Excel Web Access web parts

Other technologies are available for creating dashboards within SharePoint including:
- Reporting Services

Creating dashboards using Business Connectivity Services, SharePoint Designer and other related technologies

- PerformancePoint
- PowerPivot
- Visio Services
- Chart Web Part
- List Web Parts

These however will not be the focus of this chapter. An overview of reporting technologies is available on my blog at the following URL:
http://ghamson.wordpress.com/?s=Reporting+Technol
ogies

Creating dashboards using Business Connectivity
Services, SharePoint Designer and other related
technologies   335

Legend		Reporting Technology										
Full Compatibility		Business Data Web Parts	Chart Web Part	Content Query Web Part	Data View Web Part	Excel Services	List Views	PerformancePoint 2010	PowerPivot	Reporting Services 2008 R2	SharePoint KPI Lists	Visio Services
Partial Compatibility - See Notes												
No Compatibility												
Not Applicable												
Data Source	Analysis Services	✕	✓	✓	✓	✓	✓	✓	✓	✓	✓	✕
	Business Connectivity Services	✓	✓	✕	✓	✕	◐	✕	✕	✕	✓	✕
	Excel Services	✕	✓	✓	✕	●	✕	✓	●	✕	✓	✕
	External List	✓	✓	✕	✓	◐	◐	◐	✕	✓	✓	✕
	List / Library	✕	✓	✓	✓	◐	✓	✓	✓	✓	✓	✕
	PowerPivot	✕	✓	✓	✓	✓	✓	✓	●	✓	✓	✕
	Reporting Services	✕	✓	✓	✓	✓	✓	◐	✕	●	✓	✕
	SQL Table / Query	✓	◐	✕	✓	✓	◐	✓	✓	✓	✓	✕
	Visio	✕	✓	✓	✓	✓	✓	✓	✓	✓	✓	✓
	Web Service	✓	◐	✕	✓	✓	◐	✓	✓	✓	✓	✕

Created by Giles Hamson

Blog: http://ghamson.wordpress.com
Twitter: @ghamson

Before starting the tutorial, you will need to ensure the following is available:

- SharePoint 2010 Enterprise
    - Trial:
      http://www.microsoft.com/sharepoint

- SharePoint Designer 2010

- o   Full Version (available free):
     http://www.microsoft.com/download/en/details.aspx?id=16573

- SQL Server 2008 R2
  - o   Trial:
       http://www.microsoft.com/sqlserver

- Adventure Works Sample Database
  - o   http://sqlserversamples.codeplex.com/

- Code examples and SQL scripts for this chapter are available here:
  - o   http://ghamson.sharepoint.com/blog/Downloads/SharePointNotesVol1_GilesHamsonDownload.zip

NB: It is assumed that SharePoint 2010 has been setup either using the Configuration Wizard provided as part of the install or the appropriate Managed Service Applications are available and working.

Tutorial Scenario

The aim of this guide to provide a customer dashboard drilling down to high level sales order. This will consist of a list of customers taken directly from a third party database (BCS) with links to the Sales Orders from the customer (BCS & Excel Services).

Creating dashboards using Business Connectivity
Services, SharePoint Designer and other related
technologies   337

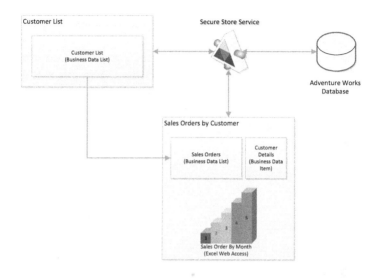

Although in this scenario, we shall be using the
Adventure Works sample database, this could easily be a
customer relationship management (CRM) or
accountancy system within your company.

In each section, the technology is described and the
tutorial follows.

Secure Store Service

What is the secure store service?

The Secure Store Service (previously the Single Sign On
in MOSS 2007) provides an authentication gateway

between end users on SharePoint and third party line of business applications such as databases, web services etc.

It allows end users access to back end data but through a controlled user such as a service account. Administrators only need to manage one user on the third party system, leaving user administration within SharePoint.

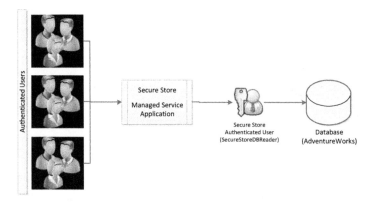

In the tutorial that follows, the Secure Store Service will be setup using the SQL Server user account: SecureStoreDBReader connecting to the AdventureWorks database.

Various technologies in SharePoint use the Secure Store Service including:

- Business Connectivity Services
- Excel Services
- PerformancePoint

Creating dashboards using Business Connectivity
Services, SharePoint Designer and other related
technologies   339

Setting up a Secure Store Application

To start off we need to ensure that we have a service account user that can connect to the Adventure Works database. In this tutorial we shall be using a SQL Server User Account.

Create a user with the following credentials and permissions:

- Username: SecureStoreDBReader
- Password: <of your choosing>
- Permission Role: db_reader
- Database: AdventureWorks

Now that we have a service account setup, we can start the SharePoint configuration of the Secure Store Application.

- In Central Administration click Managed Service Applications:

340   Creating dashboards using Business Connectivity Services, SharePoint Designer and other related technologies

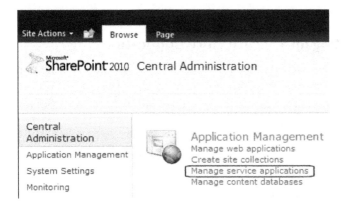

- Locate the Secure Store Service and click on the link provided:

- You are presented with the following screen where you can create and manage your Secure Store Applications:

- Click New in the ribbon:

Creating dashboards using Business Connectivity
Services, SharePoint Designer and other related
technologies   341

Target Application ID

AdventureWorks

Display Name

Adventure Works

Contact E-mail

<administrator email address here>

Target Application Type

Group

Target Application Page URL

○ Use default page

○ Use custom page

⊙ None

- You are required to fill out the following options:

Field Name	Field Value
Target Application ID	AdventureWorks
Display Name	Adventure Works
Contact E-Mail	<your email address>
Target Application Type	Group
Target Application Page URL	None

- Click Next:

342 Creating dashboards using Business Connectivity Services, SharePoint Designer and other related technologies

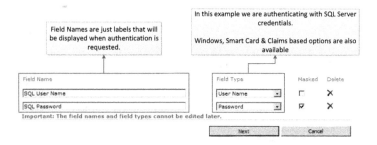

* Click Next:

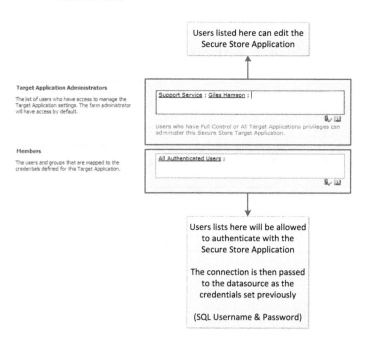

* Click OK

Creating dashboards using Business Connectivity
Services, SharePoint Designer and other related
technologies   343

The Secure Store Application has now been created, but credentials need to be set and the encryption key needs to be applied to encrypt the credential details in the Secure Store database.

Highlight the Secure Store Application and on the context drop down, select Set Credentials:

- Enter your SQL user and password credentials and click OK:

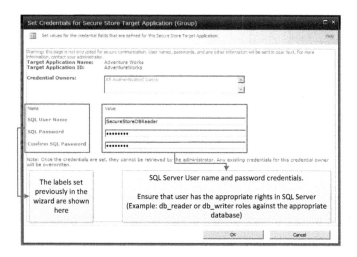

- Now that credentials have been set, we need to encrypt the credentials in the Secure Store database. Select the Secure Store Application and click Refresh Key in the ribbon:

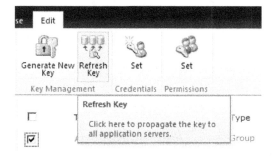

- Enter your pass phrase and click ok to encrypt the credentials.

Creating dashboards using Business Connectivity
Services, SharePoint Designer and other related
technologies   345

- The Secure Store Service is now setup and ready
  for use with Business Connectivity and other
  managed services.

External Content Types in SharePoint Designer

What are External Content Types (ECT)?

External Content Types in SharePoint 2010 are how you
can connect end users to external line of business
applications.

For example if you need to bring data into SharePoint
from a CRM system, you can use External Content Types
to connect to the back end database.

With the introduction of SharePoint 2010, ECT's can
now write back to the database. This is known as CRUD
operations:

- C = Create
- R = Read
- U = Update
- D = Delete

This allows you to use SharePoint 2010 as a front end to
any database system.

NB: Please be aware that if you are writing back to a
database from another vendor, you should either use the

web service / API calls provided or contact their support for advice.

Data is surfaced within SharePoint 2010 in a number of ways:

External Lists (available in SharePoint Foundation)

Just like standard lists within SharePoint, by creating an external list from the ECT. Views, filter connections and the ability to attach InfoPath list forms are available.

Actions can also be created against the whole list in SharePoint Designer

External Data Columns (available in SharePoint Foundation)

Allows external data to be attached to standard lists so that you can merge data stored in SharePoint with data stored externally.

Business Data Web Parts (available in SharePoint Server 2010 Enterprise)

Allows you to surface data from external sources on to dashboard pages, apply actions against individual items.

Custom styles can also be implemented via XSLT. (Covered later in this chapter)

The main focus of this tutorial is the Business Data web parts.

Creating dashboards using Business Connectivity
Services, SharePoint Designer and other related
technologies   347

NB: The full feature comparison of SharePoint 2010 can
be found here: http://sharepoint.microsoft.com/en-
us/buy/Pages/Editions-Comparison.aspx

We are now ready to start the next section of the tutorial.

Setting up the customer External Content Type

In this section we will be using SharePoint Designer 2010
to create the connection to the Adventure Works
database. However beforehand we need to create a view
of customers for us to work with:

SQL

Create a view in the Adventure Works database based on
the following SQL:

- View Name: SP_VW_AdventureWorksCustomers

```
SELECT
            Sales.Customer.CustomerID, Person.Contact.Title, Person.Contact.FirstName
            , Person.Contact.LastName, Person.Contact.Suffix, Person.Contact.Phone
            , Person.Contact.EmailAddress, Person.Address.AddressLine1 as 'Address Line 1'
            , Person.Address.AddressLine2 as 'Address Line 2', Person.Address.City as 'City'
            , Person.StateProvince.StateProvinceCode as 'State / Province'
            , Person.Address.PostalCode as 'Postal Code' , Person.CountryRegion.Name as 'Country'
            , Person.StateProvince.CountryRegionCode as 'Country Code'
            , Person.AddressType.Name as 'Address Type'
            , Person.Address.AddressID, Sales.Customer.CustomerType, Sales.Customer.TerritoryID
            , Person.StateProvince.StateProvinceID
FROM
            Sales.Customer, Sales.CustomerAddress, Person.Address, Person.AddressType
            , Person.StateProvince, Person.CountryRegion, Person.Contact
WHERE
            Sales.Customer.CustomerID = Sales.CustomerAddress.CustomerID
            AND Sales.CustomerAddress.AddressID = Person.Address.AddressID
            AND Sales.CustomerAddress.AddressTypeID = Person.AddressType.AddressTypeID
            AND Person.Address.StateProvinceID = Person.StateProvince.StateProvinceID
```

```
                  AND Person.StateProvince.CountryRegionCode = Person.CountryRegion.CountryRegionCode
                  AND Sales.Customer.CustomerID = Person.Contact.ContactID
                  AND Person.AddressType.Name = 'Main Office'
        ORDER BY Person.Contact.ContactID asc, Person.AddressType.Name asc;
```

NB: This SQL code is available in the download pack from http://ghamson.sharepoint.com.

SharePoint Designer 2010

- Open SharePoint Designer 2010
- Open your site
- Click External Content Types on the left menu navigation
- In the ribbon, under the New group, click External Content Type

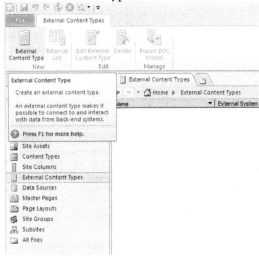

- o   Name: AdventureWorksCustomers

- o Display Name: Adventure Works Customers
- o Leave the namespace and version at the default setting
- o Office Item Type: Generic List
- o Offline Sync for external list: Disabled

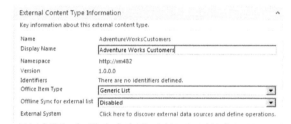

- **External System: Click to create the database connection**

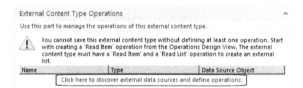

- **Click Add Connection**
- **Data Source Type: SQL Server**

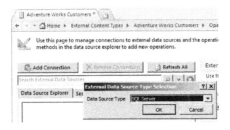

- Enter the SQL Server details
  - o Database Server: <server>
  - o Database Name: AdventureWorks
  - o Name (optional): Adventure Works
  - o Connect with Impersonated Custom Identity – Secure Store Application ID:
    - ▪ AdventureWorks
  - o Click OK
  - o Enter the SQL User and Password credentials and click OK

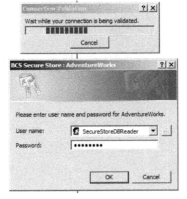

Creating dashboards using Business Connectivity
Services, SharePoint Designer and other related
technologies   351

SharePoint Designer 2010 is now connected to the
database server. Although the Secure Store Service is
being used, to avoid double hop security issues, you are
asked to authenticate when connecting to the database
server from the local client.

Later on in this exercise, the secure store service
credentials entered will be used to access the data.

- On the view created in the database, right click
  and select New Read List Operation

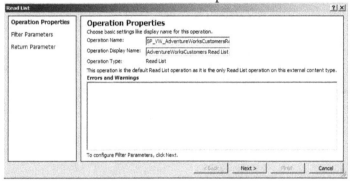

- Click Next

- To stop errors and avoid hitting BDC limitations,
  we need to set a LIMIT filter with a default value
  of 2000.

NB: To avoid the SharePoint server being flooded with
data, limits are put in place that restrict the amount of

records returned from a query via the BDC to 2000 records. This limit can be updated via PowerShell.

- Click Add Filter Parameter
  - Data Source Element: Customer ID
  - Filter: Click Link
    - New Filter: Limit
    - Filter Type: Limit
    - Filter Field: CustomerID
  - Click OK

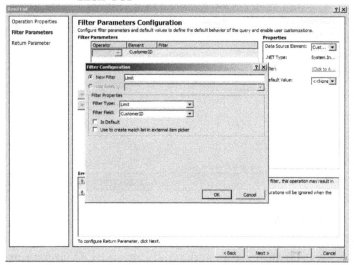

- Default Value: 2000
  - This should clear all errors and warnings

Creating dashboards using Business Connectivity
Services, SharePoint Designer and other related
technologies   353

- Click Next

Read List - Return Parameter

- Highlight the CustomerID field
  - o Select Map to identifier
  - o Required: Unchecked
  - o Show In Picker

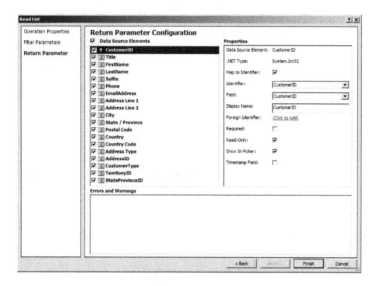

- On the following fields, highlight, change the display name to be more appropriate to the end user and check show in picker.
  - FirstName
  - LastName
  - EmailAddress

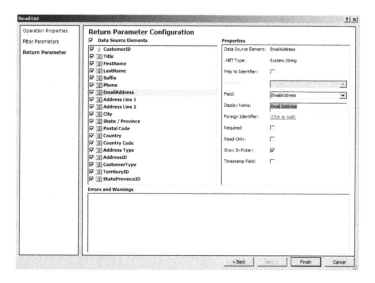

NB: Notice how the labels on the address fields take the SQL display name into account.

- Click Finish

- On the view created in the database, right click and select New Read Item Operation

- Click Next

Read Item - Input Parameter

- Field Settings:

- CustomerID

- Map to Identifier: checked

- Click Next

Read Item – Return Parameter

- Field Settings:

- CustomerID
  - o Map to Identifier: checked
  - o Required: Unchecked

Creating dashboards using Business Connectivity
Services, SharePoint Designer and other related
technologies   357

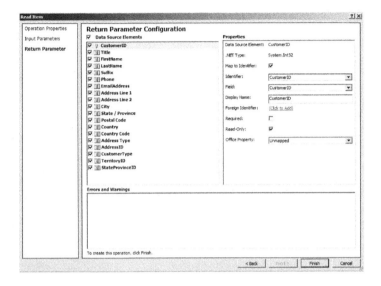

- Update the FirstName, LastName and EmailAddress fields with an appropriate display name for the end user.

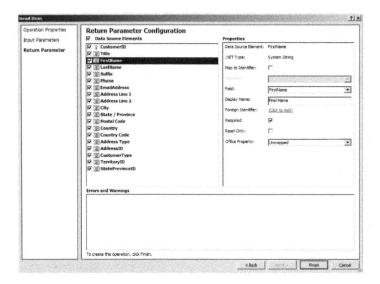

- Click Finish

- In the top corner of SharePoint Designer 2010, click the save icon

The External Content Type and BDC Application Model is now being saved to the Business Data Connectivity (BDC) Managed Service in Central Administration.

Creating dashboards using Business Connectivity
Services, SharePoint Designer and other related
technologies   359

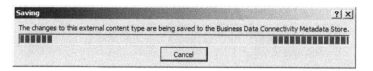

It is here where we shall set the permissions for the BDC
Application Model access and also later in this chapter,
BDC actions.

Please close the External Content Type screens in
SharePoint Designer 2010. Use the small black 'x' in the
top right to do this.

NB: Please note that after adding BDC permissions, if we
re-save the External Content Type without closing and
re-opening first. BDC permissions will be lost and will
need to be re-applied.

Setting the BDC permissions

Now that the External Content Type is in the BDC, we
need to give permission access to the BDC application
model.

NB: Please note that permissions cannot be set in
SharePoint Designer 2010.

- Open Central Administration
- Click Managed Service Application

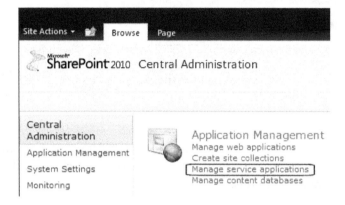

- Click Business Data Connectivity Service Application

- You will notice the External Content Type we have been creating in SharePoint Designer 2010 is now available in the BDC as an Application Model

Service Application Information

Name: Business Data Connectivity Service

Search [   ] 🔎

	Name↑	Display Name	Namespace	Version	External System	Default Action
☐	AdventureWorksCustomers	Adventure Works Customers	http://vm482	1.0.0.0	Adventure Works	

Creating dashboards using Business Connectivity
Services, SharePoint Designer and other related
technologies   361

- Click the check box next to AdventureWorksCustomers and click Set Object Permissions in the ribbon

Set Object
Permissions

For permissions we need to ensure that at least one administrator exists and a more generic all authenticated users with *execute* and *selectable in client* permissions.

This will allow the admin account to have full access:

All other users will be able to execute the BDC Application Model.

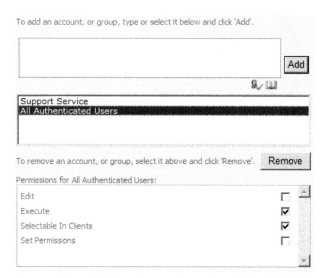

- Click OK

If you re-open the External Content Type in SharePoint Designer 2010, you will now see that the permissions have been applied to the External Content Type.

Creating dashboards using Business Connectivity
Services, SharePoint Designer and other related
technologies   363

Setting up the sales order External Content Type

Now that the ECT has been created for the Customer
details we can now setup the Sales Order ECT.   The
process is the same as before and the details are provided
below and in the download pack.

SQL

Create a view in the Adventure Works database based on the following SQL:

- View Name: SP_VW_AdventureWorksSalesOrders

```
SELECT
          Sales.SalesOrderHeader.SalesOrderID, Sales.SalesOrderHeader.OrderDate as 'Order Date'
          , Sales.SalesOrderHeader.ShipDate as 'Ship Date'
          , Sales.SalesOrderHeader.RevisionNumber as 'Revision No.'
          , Sales.SalesOrderHeader.Status, Sales.SalesOrderHeader.OnlineOrderFlag as 'Online Order'
          , Sales.SalesOrderHeader.SalesOrderNumber as 'SO No.'
          , Sales.SalesOrderHeader.PurchaseOrderNumber as 'PO No.'
          , Sales.SalesOrderHeader.AccountNumber as 'A/C No., Sales.SalesOrderHeader.CustomerID
          , Sales.SalesOrderHeader.SubTotal as 'Sub Total', Sales.SalesOrderHeader.TaxAmt as 'Tax'
          , Sales.SalesOrderHeader.Freight, Sales.SalesOrderHeader.TotalDue as 'Total Due'
          , Sales.SalesOrderHeader.SalesPersonID, Sales.SalesOrderHeader.CustomerID

FROM
          Sales.SalesOrderHeader

ORDER BY
          Sales.SalesOrderHeader.SalesOrderID asc;
```

SharePoint Designer 2010

We now need to create an External Content Type for the sales order information which relate to the customers we are listing in our dashboards. Create an External Content Type with the following settings:

- Name: AdventureWorksSalesOrders
- Display Name: Adventure Works Sales Orders
- Leave the namespace and version at the default setting
- Office Item Type: Generic List
- Offline Sync for external list: Disabled

The database connection will already be setup, follow the steps from the previous section and create the Read Item and Read List connections for the Sales Order details.

Save the External Content Type and permission the BDC application model as shown previously.

Creating the Customer List dashboard page

Now that we have setup the basis for connecting with the data in our line of business application, we can start to build up our dashboards.

Initially we are going to create a searchable list of customers using the BDC List Web Part.

Before we start using the BDC web parts we need to ensure that a number of features are turned on in SharePoint.

- Under Site Settings > Site Collection Administration, click Site Collection Features

Site Collection Administration
Search settings
Search scopes
Search keywords
FAST Search keywords
FAST Search site promotion and demotion
FAST Search user context
Recycle bin
Site collection features
Site hierarchy

- Activate the following features:
    - SharePoint Server Enterprise Site Collection features
        - BDC Web Parts are available with this feature
    - SharePoint Server Publishing Infrastructure
        - Good practice in case we want to implement custom branding later
    - SharePoint Server Standard Site Collection features
        - Not required for this task, but recommended to have activated

SharePoint Server Enterprise Site Collection features

Features such as InfoPath Forms Services, Visio Services, Access Services, and Excel Services Application, included in the SharePoint Server Enterprise License.

Deactivate   Active

SharePoint Server Publishing Infrastructure

Provides centralized libraries, content types, master pages and page layouts and enables page scheduling and other publishing functionality for a site collection.

Deactivate   Active

SharePoint Server Standard Site Collection features

Features such as user profiles and search, included in the SharePoint Server Standard License.

Deactivate   Active

- Now that the features are active in the site collection, we need to activate them in the site we are working on.

- Site Actions > Site Settings > Under the Site Actions section, click Manage Site Features.

Creating dashboards using Business Connectivity
Services, SharePoint Designer and other related
technologies   367

Site Actions
Manage site features
Reset to site definition
Delete this site
Site Web Analytics reports
Site Collection Web
Analytics reports

Activate the following features:

- SharePoint Server Enterprise Site features
  o BDC Web Parts are available with this feature
- SharePoint Server Publishing
  o Good practice in case we want to implement custom branding later
- SharePoint Server Standard Site features
  o Not required for this task, but recommended to have activated

Now that the features are activated, we can create the Customer List Dashboard Page.

- Click Site Actions > New Page:

- In the pop-up, enter the page name: Customer Dashboard

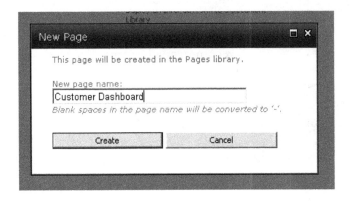

- Under the Page Ribbon, change the page layout to Blank Web Part Page:

Creating dashboards using Business Connectivity
Services, SharePoint Designer and other related
technologies   369

The page layout will change and web part zones will be
available.

- Under the Header Zone click Add a web part.

The page will reload and you will be presented with a
number of web part categories.

- Click on the Business Data category and add
  Business Data List:

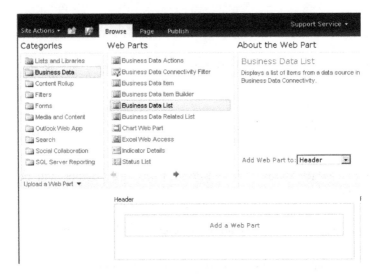

The web part will now be on the page, click open the tool pane and the page will reload. A properties pane will appear on the right.

It is here where we select our Business Data Application Model / External Content Type.

- Click the Select External Content Type button:

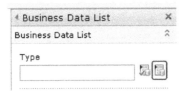

Creating dashboards using Business Connectivity
Services, SharePoint Designer and other related
technologies 371

The External Content Types we created previously are
available for selection.

- Select Adventure Works Customers and click
  OK.

The page will refresh and the properties panel will now
have the External Content Type showing.

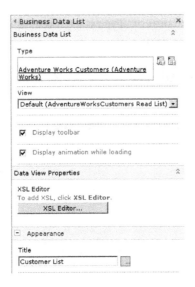

- Name the web part Customer List, Click Apply and Click OK

The web part will now be showing all the fields we have available in our Customer SQL query.

Creating dashboards using Business Connectivity
Services, SharePoint Designer and other related
technologies   373

- We can edit the view shown by clicking on the Edit View button in the top right of the Business Data List web part

You are presented with a view similar to the view options available in lists and document libraries within SharePoint.

- Select appropriate columns. You will also notice a series of radio buttons with the column name "Title". This is the column that will have the context menu for Actions attached.

○ Do not limit the number of items displayed

○ Limit the number of items displayed to:

```
100
```

Display Title	Column Name	Position from Left
☐ ○	CustomerID	1
☑ ○	Title	2
☑ ○	First Name	3
☑ ●	Last Name	4
☐ ○	Suffix	5
☑ ○	Phone	6
☐ ○	Email Address	7
☐ ○	Address Line 1	8
☐ ○	Address Line 2	9
☑ ○	City	10
☑ ○	State / Province	11
☐ ○	Postal Code	12
☑ ○	Country	13

- Select the "Last Name" as the "Title" column
- Click OK
- Publish the page.

After creating the Sales Order dashboard page, we shall use BDC actions to drill down from the Customer Dashboard page, linking the two together.

Creating the Sales Order dashboard page

We shall now create the drill down dashboard page showing Sales Orders for the selected customer.

- Create a page as shown in the previous section with the name: Sales Order Dashboard
- Change the page layout: Blank Web Part Page.
- Add the following web parts to the page:

Web Part	Category	Web Part Zone
Business Data Item	Business Data	Right
Business Data List	Business Data	Header
Query String (URL) Filter	Filters	Footer

Business Data List	Business Data Item
Open the tool pane and choose the type of data to display.	Open the tool pane and choose the type of data to display.

Query String (URL) Filter
(Hidden when the page is published)

Customer Details

Using the Business Data Item, we shall display the Customer details we drill down from:
- Open the tool page
- Select the Adventure Works Customer External Content Type
- Select appropriate columns

- Change the Title of the web part to Customer

- Click Apply and Click OK

The web part will not currently be showing any data.

This is because it is waiting for us to feed a Customer ID parameter. After we have configured the Query String (URL) Filter web part, we shall connect the web parts together to pass the Customer ID parameter.

Sales Order Details

Using the Business Data List, we shall display the Customer Sales Orders.

- Open the tool pane

Creating dashboards using Business Connectivity
Services, SharePoint Designer and other related
technologies   377

- Select the Adventure Works Sales Orders
  External Content Type
- Change the Title of the web part to Customer
  Sales Orders

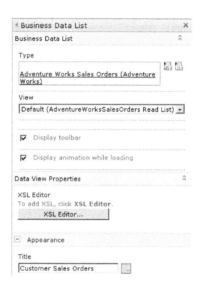

- Click Edit View on the right of the Customer
  Sales Order web part and show appropriate
  columns.

Query String (URL) Filter Web Part

Place the page back into Edit Mode (Site Actions > Edit
Page) if it is not already.

On the Query String (URL) Filter Web Part:

- Click Open the tool pane
- In the properties panel
  - Query String Parameter Name: CustomerID
- Click Apply

The Query String (URL) Filter web part will now look like this:

This web part passes the CustomerID from the query string in the address bar to the other web parts on the page:

- Customer Sales Orders (Business Data List)
- Customer (Business Data Item)

Creating dashboards using Business Connectivity
Services, SharePoint Designer and other related
technologies   379

The web parts will consume the parameter and filter the
data as appropriate.

To connect the web parts together, click the arrow in the
top right of the web part. On the context menu:
- Select Connections
- Send Filter Values To
- Customer

A pop up window will appear with the
AdventureWorksCustomers entity showing

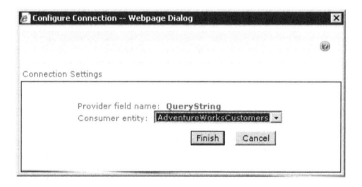

- Click Finish

It will automatically map to the Customer ID because this is the identifier as configured in SharePoint Designer when creating the External Content Type.

The Customer (Business Data Item) web part will now appear like this:

No data will return because no Customer ID value is available in the query string. This is to be added later in the chapter.

Now connect the Customer Sales Order (Business Data List) web part using the same method. When asked what column to filter by, select CustomerID.

NB: you can use the Query String (URL) Filter web part to connect to multiple web parts on a single page.

The Customer Sales Order (Business Data List) web part will now show that it is now connected to the Query String (URL) Filter web part.

Publish the page and we can now test the connections.

At the end of the URL in the address bar of your browser add the following query string parameter and value:

- ?CustomerID=3
- Full URL example = http://<server>/pages/Sales-Order-Dashboard.aspx?CustomerID=3

Press Go to reload the page and you should see the Sales Order and Customer details filter to Customer ID 3

Creating BDC Actions – Customer Dashboard

Now that we have created the top level dashboard (Customers) and the drill down (Sales Orders) dashboard and we have tested it by manually adding parameters to the URL. We now need a mechanism for end users to drill-down.

Earlier in this chapter, whilst editing the Business Data List view on the Customer dashboard, we set the Title field to the last name of the customer record.

We shall now create an Action attached to the Customer External Content Type which will make the Last Name field a clickable hyperlink to drill down into the Sales Order Dashboard for that Customer.

In Central Administration go to the Business Data Connectivity properties page:

- Managed Services > Business Data Connectivity

On the Adventure Works Customer model, click Add Action on the context menu.

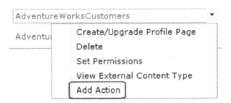

You are presented with various options:

Action Name:
- Displayed to the end user
- Set this to: View Sales Orders

Navigate to this URL:
- The url a user will be taken to when they click on the Action Name. Parameters can be added to this URL. In this scenario, we will be adding the Customer ID as the parameter.
- Set the URL to be:
  http://<server>/pages/Sales-Order-Dashboard.aspx?CustomerID={0}
- NB: Please note that a relative URL will not work. Absolute URL's only.

Parameter Property:
- Click Add Parameter and select CustomerID from the drop down.

Icon:
- An icon can also be displayed next to the Action Name. In this scenario I am using an icon from the SharePoint hive.

Default Action:
- Checked.

- The default action will allow the Last Name column on the Business Data List web part to be clickable.

```
Action Name
┌────────────────────────────────────┐
│ View Sales Orders                   │
└────────────────────────────────────┘

Navigate To This URL
┌────────────────────────────────────┐
│ http://vm482/Pages/Sales-Order-Dashb│
└────────────────────────────────────┘
Example: http://example.com/edit.aspx?id={0}

Launch the action in a new Web browser window (applies to
External Data Web Parts only):
   ○ Yes  ● No


Parameter Property
0        ┌──────────────┬──┐   ┌──────────┐
         │ CustomerID   │▼ │   │ Remove   │
         └──────────────┴──┘   └──────────┘
┌──────────────────┐
│ Add Parameter    │
└──────────────────┘


   ○ No icon
   ○ Standard icon ┌────────┐ ✗
                   │ Delete▼│
                   └────────┘
   ● The image at this URL
┌────────────────────────────────────┐
│ /_layouts/images/checknames.png     │
└────────────────────────────────────┘


   ☑ Default action
```

- Click OK

You will now see that the Action is attached to the External Content Type:

Creating dashboards using Business Connectivity
Services, SharePoint Designer and other related
technologies   385

Now that this is in place, the action link will be set up on the Customer Dashboard.

The Last Name will be clickable and will drill down to the Sales Order dashboard with the Customer ID as the query string parameter.

A context menu will also appear. You can have multiple actions attached to the External Content Type.

NB: if this does not appear straight away, this is because a timer job runs to add the definition to the External Content Type. Either perform an IISReset on the web front-end to force the timer job or wait up to 10 minutes.

Styling BDC List Item Web Parts – Sales Order Dashboard

As an added bonus, the Business Data List Item web part can also be styled with custom XSLT.

As part of this section, we shall be applying a custom style. Due to the size of the XSLT involved, the example code is not provided on these pages but is available to download here:

http://ghamson.sharepoint.com/blog/Downloads/Share PointNotesVol1_GilesHamsonDownload.zip

Please note that you can carry on with the rest of this chapter without downloading the example files.

To apply the custom XSLT style please download the zip file and extract it into a folder on your PC. You will find a file called:

SharePointNotesVol1_CustomerBDCItemStyle.xsl

Please upload this to the style library in the site you are on and ensure to publish the file.

Now that we have the file in place, let's get started.

On the Sales Order Dashboard:
- Site Actions > Edit Page.
- Customer Web Part > Edit Web Part

Creating dashboards using Business Connectivity
Services, SharePoint Designer and other related
technologies   387

You will see the Business Data Item property panel

- Display animation while loading: Uncheck
  - Performance is improved by this
- Actions: Click Choose
  - Uncheck View Sales Orders
    - This appears by default when you create an action and is not required on this page.
- Data View Properties
  - XSL Editor
  - This is where you can get a template for the XSLT to change.
  - NB: do not edit the XSL directly here or you will find after changing other properties in the web part, it will update

the XSL accordingly and you will lose your changes.

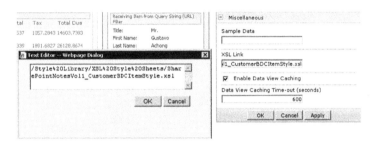

Under the Miscellaneous section, find XSL Link.

- Apply the URL to the XSL file you downloaded here.
- Click Apply, Click OK.
- Publish the page.
- You should now see the style applied accordingly.

Creating dashboards using Business Connectivity
Services, SharePoint Designer and other related
technologies   389

Excel Services – Sales Order Dashboard

To help visualise the Sales Orders on screen we shall use
Excel Services and authenticate with the Secure Store
Service application we have set up.

We shall also be passing the Customer ID parameter so
that we can create a single report that services the
dashboard in the same way as the Business Data List and
Item web parts already on the Sales Order Dashboard.

SQL

Create a view in the AdventureWorks database.
View Name: SP_VW_AdventureWorksSalesOrderCount

```
SELECT
    COUNT(SalesOrderID) AS [Sales OrderCount],
    CustomerID,
    YEAR([Order Date]) AS [Order Date Year],
    MONTH([Order Date]) AS [Order Date Month],
    CAST(YEAR([Order Date]) AS varchar(4)) + '-' + CAST(MONTH([Order Date]) AS varchar(2)) AS [Order Date]
FROM
    dbo.SP_VW_AdventureWorksSalesOrders
GROUP BY
    CustomerID,
    YEAR([Order Date]),
    MONTH([Order Date]),
    CAST(YEAR([Order Date]) AS varchar(4)) + '-' + CAST(MONTH([Order Date]) AS varchar(2))
ORDER BY
    [Order Date Year] asc,
    [Order Date Month] asc;
```

Database Connections / Secure Store Services

As part of the Excel Services solution we are putting
together, we shall be connecting to the Adventure Works
database so that we can refresh the data with parameters
as required.

Best Practice methods suggest that we should separate out the database connection from the report, in case we need to reuse the connection for another purpose.

For this we need a data connection library to hold the .odc (Office Data Connection) file that will be created from Excel.

Under the site actions, more options selection, create a data connection library and name the library Data Connections

Creating the Graph

To create an Excel Services report in SharePoint 2010, the Excel application is used.

Excel 2007 or 2010 can be used for this purpose, but in this instance, we shall be using Microsoft Excel 2010.

- Open Excel 2010 and create a new spreadsheet
- On the data ribbon, click other sources and select SQL Server

Creating dashboards using Business Connectivity
Services, SharePoint Designer and other related
technologies   391

- Enter your server name and use the Secure Store
  Service credentials for the AdventureWorks
  application we created earlier.

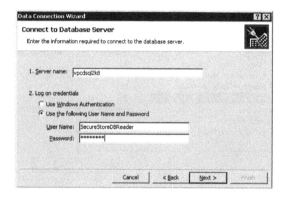

- Click Next
- Select the AdventureWorks database and the view
  you have just created

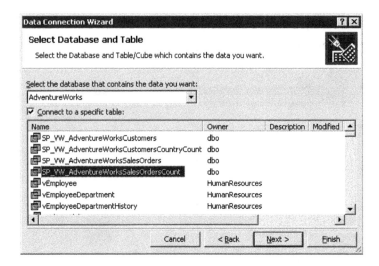

- Click Next
- Check Save password in file
- Check Always attempt to use this file to refresh data
- Click Excel Services: Authentication Settings
- Check SSS – SSS ID:
- Enter the ID of the Secure Store Service Application ID: Adventure Works

Creating dashboards using Business Connectivity
Services, SharePoint Designer and other related
technologies   393

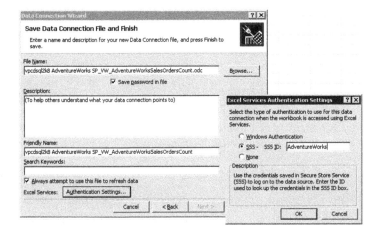

- Click OK
- Click Finish

- You will then see the Import Data dialogue appear
- Click PivotChart and PivotTable Report

NB: Please note that Tables are not supported in Excel Services.

- Click Properties...

- Ensure that Save Password is checked
- Click Export Connection File

NB: This will take the ODC file and place it in SharePoint.

- Navigate to the data connection library
- Click Save

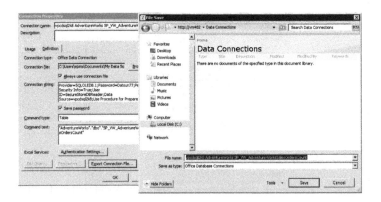

- Fill in the appropriate metadata and click OK
- Click OK on the data connection properties window

Creating dashboards using Business Connectivity
Services, SharePoint Designer and other related
technologies   395

- Click OK on the import data dialogue

Now we set up the PivotChart

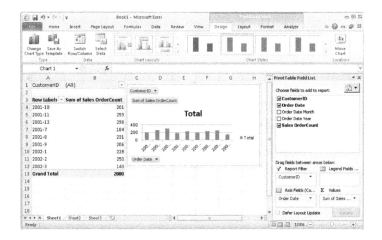

Apply the following criteria:
- Report Filter: CustomerID
- Axis Fields: Order Date
- Values: Sales Order Count

On the Layout ribbon under PivotChart Tools, name the
Chart: Sales Order Count

Now we need to set up a parameter for the chart. This is
a named range in Excel and is used by the Query String
(URL) Filter web part to pass our Customer ID
parameter from the web page.

- Highlight cell B1, the Customer ID Filter for the chart
- Click the Formula Ribbon and press the Define Name button.
  - Definition name: CustomerID
- Click OK

The chart is now complete and we are ready to upload it in to SharePoint.

Publishing the spread sheet

- Click File
- Save & Send
- Select Save to SharePoint

Creating dashboards using Business Connectivity
Services, SharePoint Designer and other related
technologies   397

- Click Publish Options

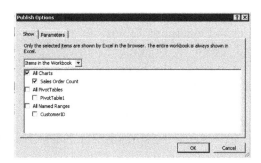

- Select Items in the Workbook under the Show
  Tab and check the Sales Order Count value.

- On the Parameters Tab add the CustomerID
  Named Value we created earlier.

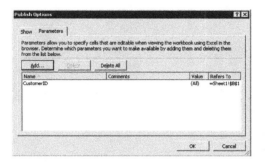

- Click OK
- Browse for a location in SharePoint.

For the purposes of this exercise select the standard Documents – Document Library in the site. Typically you would create a document library specifically for reports, but in reality the Excel file can live anywhere on the site as long as users have at least Reader permissions.

- Click Save As
    o Name the spreadsheet: Sales Order Count
- Click Save

Creating dashboards using Business Connectivity
Services, SharePoint Designer and other related
technologies   399

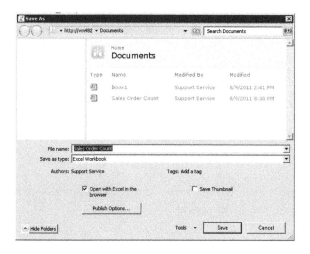

After saving the file, the browser window will open and
you will see your chart in Excel Services working.

Adding to the Sales Order dashboard

For the final practical section of this chapter we just need
to add the report we have created onto our Sales Order
dashboard.

Navigate to the Sales Order dashboard and edit the page.

- Click add a web part in the Footer zone
- Web Part Category: Business Data
- Web Part: Excel Web Access
- Click Add

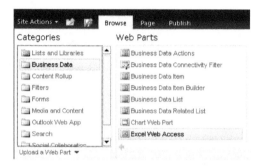

You are presented with the Excel Web Access web part waiting to be configured:

- Open the tool pane

- Click on the workbook selector, navigate to the documents – document library and select the Sales Order Count workbook.

Creating dashboards using Business Connectivity
Services, SharePoint Designer and other related
technologies   401

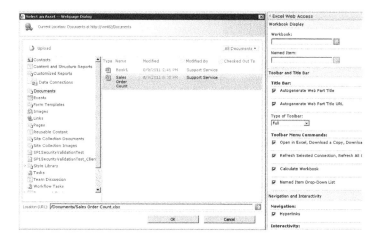

- Click OK
- Click Apply in the properties tool pane

The page will refresh and the chart will appear. We can now connect the Customer ID parameter in the workbook to the Customer ID parameter in the query string.

- In the web part context menu, connect the web parts as we have previously.

402   Creating dashboards using Business Connectivity
Services,   SharePoint   Designer   and   other   related
technologies

> o   Connections > Get Filter Values From >
>   Query String (URL) Filter

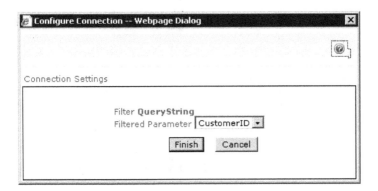

- Click Finish

You can now see that web part is connected to the filter

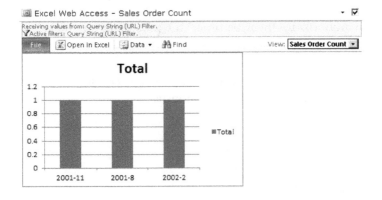

Creating dashboards using Business Connectivity
Services, SharePoint Designer and other related
technologies   403

Publish the page and have a go at drilling down from the
Customer Dashboard. You will see that the chart data
refreshes as the Customer ID updates.

We have now completed the Sales Order Dashboard.

Excel Services – Trouble Shooting

There are a number of factors to making Excel Services
work as described above. This section discusses some of
the common issues that you may come across:

Publish button does not appear in Excel 2010:

To have the publish options available in Excel you must
have at least the Professional Plus edition of the product.

Details: http://office.microsoft.com/en-
us/buy/compare-server-integration-features-between-
office-suites-available-through-volume-licensing-
FX101850719.aspx#c

I am unable to save directly to the SharePoint 2010 document library

If you are working directly on the server, you may not be able to publish directly to SharePoint. This is because the Web Client service needs to be installed so that you can communicate with SharePoint over the WebDAV protocol.

This service is installed and activated on the Desktop Experience pack which is available under features in Windows Server 2008 / 2008 R2.

Please note that this will require a restart of the server.

Excel Web Access error: File / Data Connection is not in a trusted location

Running Excel Services can be quite intensive on the server depending on the size and complexity of the spreadsheet. To combat this, SharePoint allows the administrator to determine which libraries can run Excel Services spreadsheets.

This is controlled in Central Administration under the Excel Services Managed Service.

The same is also true for data connection libraries.

Details can be found here:

Trusted File Locations:
http://technet.microsoft.com/en-us/library/ff191194.aspx

Trusted Data Connection Libraries:
http://technet.microsoft.com/en-us/library/ff191200.aspx

Summary

We have now reached the end of the tutorial; hopefully you have managed to create dashboards using External Content Types, Business Data web parts and Excel Services.

Although this tutorial covers many areas of the Business Intelligence options available in the Microsoft software suite, we have only scratched the surface as to what is possible.

I urge you to start extending the dashboards you have created using other technologies which also support the filter web parts and connections. In particular:

- Reporting Services
- PerformancePoint
- PowerPivot

It is hard to determine which technology is best suited to the business requirement. To aid decision making Microsoft have produced the following page and white paper:

Choosing a Business Intelligence technology in SharePoint 2010: http://technet.microsoft.com/en-us/library/ff394320.aspx

Choose the right Business Intelligence technology to suit your style: http://technet.microsoft.com/en-us/library/gg537617.aspx

Implementing business intelligence for clients is a continual learning process that always depends on end user requirements and environments, having the background knowledge to all the business intelligence technologies available to SharePoint 2010 is imperative to making the right decisions in my projects.

13.   Building Business Intelligence Solutions with SharePoint 2010

Introduction

Business Intelligence is an increasingly desirable commodity in the workplace. IT Managers wish to see how many support tickets are open, executives want to know how the business is doing against their key performance indicators - even I may want to see how much holiday I have remaining to use this year!

However, the answers to simple questions such as those above are rarely self-served, or answered in the timeframe you would expect. These questions often involve multiple people fishing through files or old emails, cutting and pasting figures in Excel or waiting on information to be fed through from an overseas office. Management are often frustrated that they cannot see at a glance how their department is performing without IT spending days developing a custom report, only to be re-engineered the next time the manager wants to know how his department is doing.

The solution to these common problems is a well designed and efficient business intelligence system, and a medium on which to surface dashboards tailored to the needs of the consumer. In the past, such systems have been expensive and generally aimed at the minority of users, however since Microsoft seriously entered the business intelligence market, a BI system can be implemented at an affordable price through SharePoint 2010 and its related technologies for the masses to enjoy.

This chapter explains how SharePoint 2010, and its large suite of business intelligence features, could be used to fulfil the needs of most business intelligence requirements in the workplace. We will explore the pros and cons of the feature set, and look at a couple of example use cases.

The Importance of Data

It is important to stress that the BI features of SharePoint are expecting data to be present. An Excel workbook is not much use without data, and there is not much you can do with PerformancePoint Services if you don't have an OLAP cube at your disposal.

Of all the BI projects I have worked on, I would estimate that at least 75% of the effort goes into ensuring a well-organised, accurate and reliable data source. This is before we even start to think about SharePoint and how its features can visualise and present this data. Many BI projects fall down due to a poor or inaccurate data source. You can have the most amazing dashboard in the world, but users will not use it if the data is inaccurate!

All BI projects should begin with questions such as:

-    What information do I want to display?

- How does this information benefit me, my role or the business?
- What data is required to present this information?
- Where does this data come from?
- How frequently does this data need to be updated?

It is generally good practise to pull your required source data into a data warehouse, modelled specifically for reporting. Multi-dimensional OLAP cubes can then be built from this to allow users to drill down and ask questions of the data with immediate answers.

However, data is not always as well structured as this and this is something we just have to live with. Data can be equally as valuable inside a SharePoint list or a CSV file, but just so long as its there.

The important thing is to recognise where your data exists and in what format, as this will influence your decisions as to which SharePoint BI toolset to use to present it.

Remember that the data layer is the most important factor in a BI solution and the majority of time and effort should be placed on getting it right. The act of building dashboards using SharePoint and its BI features is really the icing on the cake!

SharePoint and BI – A Brief History

Until recently, SharePoint has never really been associated with business intelligence, and neither have Microsoft themselves. Although Excel is probably the most widespread BI tool in the world, Microsoft hasn't traditionally been a serious player in the BI space compared to the likes of IBM Cognos or Business Objects.

BI was introduced in MOSS 2007 with Excel Services. This allowed authors to create workbooks in Excel and publish all or parts of it to SharePoint where users could view without the need for Excel. Filters could be exposed so the users could interact with the data in their own way. This was the beginning of integrated BI in SharePoint.

Meanwhile, two other Microsoft projects were converging. Microsoft had earlier acquired ProClarity, a well-respected BI software company, in order to accelerate their move into the BI space. The code base for ProClarity's Analytics Server product was the lynchpin for a new product to compete in the BI space – Office PerformancePoint Server. This product also brought together the successful Business Scorecard Manager and a long term in house development for planning and forecasting (Biz#). Version 1 of Office PerformancePoint Server launched in 2007, but struggled in the market place and was eventually dropped as a product in its own right in early 2009. MOSS 2007 Enterprise license owners could continue to use PerformancePoint for free, and the analytical and scorecarding components integrated nicely with SharePoint.

Somewhere else in Microsoft the SharePoint team and the SQL Server team were finally coming together to integrate on Reporting Services. An add-in component launched with SQL 2005 SP2 that allowed SharePoint to replace the Report Manager component, and store reports and data sources in SharePoint document libraries. Improved web parts allowed reports to be rendered right there on a SharePoint page!

All of these products and features, albeit disparate, laid the foundations of the BI features of SharePoint, and SharePoint 2010 has taken this a step further with more seamless integration than ever before.

BI Features in SharePoint 2010

This section outlines the core BI feature set included with SharePoint 2010 and discusses the pros and cons of each one and some reasons why you might select one option over another. This is not meant to be a step by step guide to using each component.

Note. With the exception of SQL Reporting Services, which is licensed through SQL Server, all these features are only available through the Enterprise Server edition of SharePoint 2010.

Chart Web Part

Since the deprecation of Office Web Components, prior to MOSS 2007, SharePoint lacked a quick, tactical web part that could chart some data thrown its way.

SharePoint 2010 has attempted to serve this requirement with the Chart Web Part. This web part inherits most of its functionality from the Dundas chart object that Microsoft acquired and provides a rich array of options to customise the chart to the author's needs. There is actually very little information on this web part, and I think the reason for this is its shortcomings highlighted below.

The Chart Web Part can be hooked up to a variety of data sources including a SharePoint List, other web parts on the same page (e.g. another Chart Web Part), an Excel workbook via Excel Services, or any external line of business data exposed via Business Connectivity Services.

There is a huge array of chart types to choose from including pies and bars through to more unusual funnels and bubble charts. The customisation options are equally as extensive and the author can have intricate control over the appearance.

However, there is one **major** drawback. There are no function options to sum or count your raw data. For example, you could chart happily from a SharePoint list laid out as shown below:

📎 Title	Region	Net Sales
Sales North	North	10,000
Sales South	South	11,000
Sales East	East	5,000
Sales West	West	12,000

Figure 3 - Pre-formatted SharePoint List for Charting

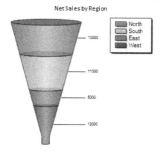

Figure 4 - Funnel Chart of Prepared SharePoint List Data

However, you could not chart the following data as expected and rollup Net Sales by Region:

📎 Customer	Region	Net Sales
Customer A 🌟NEW	North	3,400
Customer B 🌟NEW	North	1,000
Customer C 🌟NEW	South	3,400
Customer D 🌟NEW	West	5,000
Customer E 🌟NEW	East	2,300
Customer F 🌟NEW	South	500

Figure 5 - Typical Raw Data Layout for Charting

In most circumstances, your raw data will not be in an arrangement ready for charting, and will most likely be in raw format requiring some kind of rollup operation prior to charting. This is the Chart Web Part's biggest downfall and, in my opinion, one of the key reasons why it is not more widely used. Another reason for its lack of adoption is the fact that it is not shipped with SharePoint Foundation. Instead, many Foundation or Standard CAL users are reliant on third party solutions that generally do a far better job.

The attraction to the Chart Web Part is the speed of getting something authored and published. I would therefore recommend considering this in the following circumstances:

- You wish to quickly chart data from a SharePoint list that is organised and summarised ready for charting.
- You wish to quickly chart external LOB data, which is organised and summarised ready for charting AND exposed through Business Connectivity Services.

Finally, here is a summary of the pros and cons of using this feature.

Pros	Cons
Quick and easy to set up and configure.	Cannot chart counts or sums of data. Data must be prepared in chartable format.
A large amount of chart types and customisation options.	Charts cannot be reused in other pages of your site.

Static and non-interactive.

Status Lists

Status lists were known as KPI lists in MOSS 2007 but they are effectively the same feature. Essentially they provide a quick way of showing how actual data values are performing against a goal or target. Most organisations are measured against success using a number of key performance measures. Executive management will constantly demand to see these measures reflected as 'green lights' just so they can sleep at night!

At the hard core end of Microsoft business intelligence development, KPIs are constructed deep within SQL Analysis Services and require someone with knowledge of the MDX programming language to develop them. Status lists are at the other end of the spectrum, requiring only some simple configuration.

A Status List is comprised of Status Indicators. Consider these as single line reports. These items can be one of the following types based on their underlying data source:

- SharePoint List (View) based
- Excel Services based
- SQL Analysis Services based (import KPIs already developed in SSAS)
- Fixed Value based

Let's take a common example scenario: the IT manager needs to know the amount of open support tickets, which are currently being worked on and compare this with his goal of 50% being worked on at any one time.

IT support tickets are tracked in a SharePoint list as displayed below:

Summary	Status	Hours Effort
CRM Connectivity Problem ⬜ NEW	Submitted	0
Outlook Not Working ⬜ NEW	In Progress	5
SharePoint Broken ⬜ NEW	In Progress	2
Reporting Services Broken ⬜ NEW	Closed	10
Authentication Problem ⬜ NEW	Closed	3

Figure 6 - IT Support Tickets SharePoint List

The first task is to create a view containing the scope of our data we want to measure. In this case, an 'Open' view filters the list to show only open tickets, as we are not concerned with closed tickets.

We can now quickly create a SharePoint List based Status Indicator to monitor the percentage of open tickets which are currently 'In Progress'.

Figure 7 - Setting Actual Values Based on List Values

On the same screen, we can set values for the target/goal criteria as shown below:

Figure 8 - Configuring the Goal Values

The result is a nice status indicator that serves the IT Manager's requirement and will update itself whenever it is viewed.

Indicator	Goal	Value	Status
Open Tickets in Progress	50%	66.67%	●

Additional indicators could be quickly configured such as the total estimated effort remaining on open tickets, and a dashboard quickly starts becoming a reality.

Pros	Cons
Quick and straightforward to configure.	With the exception of the SSAS status indicator, a user cannot configure the target value to derive from a data source (manually entered only).
Utilise KPIs built in your SSAS cubes and connect to a SSAS filter for interactivity.	Calculation options for actual values are limited.

PerformancePoint Services

It's difficult to describe exactly what PerformancePoint Services (PPS) is as it is a substantial piece of functionality. On one hand, it provides its own suite of charts and scorecards that empower a user to monitor and analyse their data. Whilst on the other hand, it provides an integrated dashboard designer that can integrate native PPS components along with components from other BI tools such as SSRS, Excel Services and Visio Services.

Figure 9 - List of Available Report Types in PerformancePoint

If you are looking to create a dashboard where your targets need to be monitored then PPS is 'the' tool to achieve this. If we compare the KPI features in PPS with those revealed in the Status Lists section, we can see that PPS provides a much more mature offering whilst still providing a code-free development environment.

All PPS content is stored in a special SharePoint list that has content types dedicated to PPS. PPS Dashboard Designer is the client tool used for editing them.

The first building block is the KPI. Again, you can import KPIs from SSAS if developers have incorporated them into your OLAP cube, otherwise they can be configured right in PPS Dashboard Designer.

Figure 10 - Configuring a KPI in PerformancePoint

The scoring pattern, banding method, indicator and thresholds can all be set via the interface. A range of visual indicators come out of the box, and more can be added. You may even wish to plot an actual value against multiple targets, which is all possible.

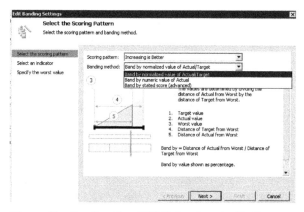

Figure 11 - Configuring KPI Behaviour in PerformancePoint

Once you have the base KPIs created, these can then be displayed on a scorecard. A scorecard allows a KPI to be sliced by cube dimensions to provide greater depth and allow analysis of the KPI. In the example below, a KPI

Details report has also been added to the dashboard and 'wired up' to the scorecard. This is a great way to provide additional meaning to the KPIs on the scorecard.

	Actual	Target			KPI: Financial Profit/Loss Against Plan
Occupancy rates of available student places	78	90	⬤	-13%	Metric: Target
Available student places currently booked	89	90	⬤	-1%	Measure: Resulted
ff Professional development - value	98	90	⬤	9%	Row Path: Financial Profit/Loss Against Plan
nber of Total Active Registered Apprentices	69	90	⬤	-23%	Column Path: Target
TA Market Share (QLD) by Trade Area (ITG)	120	90	⬤	33%	Actual: 29,022,825
nber New Apprentice Sign-ups	98	90	⬤	9%	Variance: 1%
nber of Reported Workplace Incidents	19	90	⬤	-79%	Calculation: Increasing is Better
nber of Non-User Choice Student Enrolments	89	90	⬤	-1%	Banding Method: Band by normalized value of Actual,
Staff Days Lost Through Absence	90	90	⬤	0%	Status Bands: Stoplight E - Small
nmercial Contract Pipeline Revenue	89	90	⬤	-1%	
ancial Profit/Loss Against Plan	29,022,825	28,756,446	⬤	1%	

Figure 12 - Scorecard and KPI Details Report

Another great component of PerformancePoint is the Analytic Chart. If you wish to surface an OLAP cube in a dashboard and allow end users to explore the data – this is the tool to achieve this. Charts supplement a scorecard providing the analytic capability to ask questions of the data and find the reasons for failures to meet targets. The only downside to the charts is the inability to control the rendering or appearance bar a few limited options. This limitation however, is counter-balanced by a huge amount of options for manipulating the data being charted including filters, sorting, multiple chart types, and export features to PowerPoint and Excel (ideal when wishing to print).

Finally, all this can be wrapped up in multi-page dashboards designed right within Dashboard Designer before being deployed to SharePoint as web part pages.

With the inclusion of Filters, scorecards and reports can be connected on the page, providing a complete picture of important business targets and the ability to follow this up with analysis and actions.

Whilst PerformancePoint can be used with a variety of data sources, it is certainly geared around the OLAP cube. It is a fantastic tool for surfacing the power of OLAP without requiring any knowledge of MDX, although intimate knowledge of your OLAP cube structure is highly recommended for report authors. If OLAP is not available to you as a data source, I would personally look to Excel or Reporting Services as an alternative to providing monitoring capabilities.

Pros	Cons
Provides multiple ways of viewing the data.	Limited scope for controlling the appearance of charts.
Export features to Excel & PowerPoint.	Not the preferred tool for non-OLAP data sources.
Preferred tool for creating KPIs from data sources without having to understand MDX.	
Capability to create complete dashboards in a WYSIWYG environment and deploy to SharePoint.	

Excel Services/PowerPivot

Excel Services in SharePoint 2010 is an improved capability to allow real-time interactive reporting and dashboarding of Excel based components through a browser based rendering of Excel.

Most business users are familiar with Excel, and have likely created charts from business data without breaking sweat. The only problem is that these workbooks are stored on users' client PCs and sharing is usually achieved by emailing the workbook around to colleagues or partners.

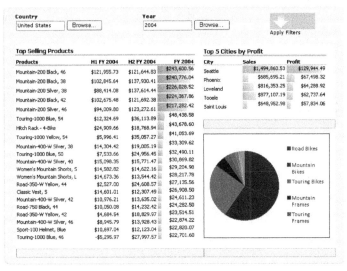

Figure 13 - Excel Services Dashboard

Excel Services allows these same workbooks to be published to a SharePoint document library and displayed through the Excel Web Access web part on a dashboard. This web part can be connected to an entire workbook, single sheet or even a chart or named range. This is great for displaying parts of the workbook in a dashboard for example.

My preferred method would be to use PPS to pull your Excel components into a PPS dashboard where it can be 'wired up' to filters and other web parts – incredibly empowering for dashboard authors.

The advantage Excel has over and above PerformancePoint is the almost bottomless set of visual formatting features which really make your reports come to life. Typically, when executive users are shown a PPS chart they will ask, "Can I have that sales figure shown in pink?" The inability to quickly service such a request in PPS usually has the effect of overshadowing your hard work on the data layer! However, with Excel your executive can have his sales figures lit up like a Christmas tree! The boundaries are limited only to Excel! Conditional formatting, sparklines and slicers will wow your dashboard consumers more than PPS charts in many cases.

In addition to standard Excel features, users can grab the PowerPivot for Excel add-in for free (http://www.microsoft.com/download/en/details.aspx?displaylang=en&id=7609). This enhances Excel to allow it to manipulate huge amounts of data in memory and provide a richer self-serve BI to Excel users. It effectively empowers users to create data models and cubes without the skills of a SQL Analysis Services developer. However to share PowerPivot enhanced workbooks through SharePoint, the server farm must be configured to use a separate product – PowerPivot for SharePoint. This product can incur additional licenses due to its requirement for a special instance of SQL Analysis Services. Just be cautious about using PowerPivot for Excel and its implications when wishing to share these on SharePoint.

Pros	Cons
Users generally familiar with Excel so additional training can be minimised.	PowerPivot for Excel workbooks require additional infrastructure to be published through SharePoint
Author has very fine control over the look and feel of the report/chart.	Graphical fidelity of the Excel client is superb however, there maybe be some differences such as the loss of 3D charts.
Connect to almost any data source with a range of authentication options.	
Use PPS to incorporate Excel components and connect with PPS scorecards and filters.	

SQL Reporting Services

SQL Reporting Services (SSRS) is the one major BI component that does not require an Enterprise SharePoint license. Hence, it is a great tool to make the most of no matter what SharePoint license you have, just so long as you are fully SQL licensed. Heck, SSRS and

Report Builder come bundled with your SQL license – so make the most of this great technology!

When SSRS is configured for SharePoint 2010 integration, some additional content types can be added to a document library to allow SSRS reports and data sources to be stored and managed in SharePoint, and maintained by Report Builder 3.0. Whilst developers can still create reports in the BI Development Studio (BIDS), Report Builder 3.0 really empowers semi-technical business users to author reports and manage them in SharePoint.

The integration features should not be underestimated! Reports are stored in SharePoint like any other document which means all the document management features of SharePoint can be leveraged – check-in/check-out, approval workflow, content publishing and version control. All this allows for a controlled procedure for editing and publishing reports to your audiences.

SSRS 2008 R2 has some great report types - some of which simply are not possible with any other native SharePoint tool. These include gauges, data bars, various chart types and sparklines.

Figure 14 - SSRS Data Visualisation Options

There is also a great map report for plotting geo-spatial data (latitude/longitude co-ordinates) which can be used to plot geographical locations such as customer sites, student addresses or sales regions against an ESRI map shape or a BING Maps background.   Bubble maps take this a step further to show additional information such as the size of sale as opposed to simply a pin in a map.   Such as visualisation is only available through SSRS.

Figure 15 - Example Map Report in SSRS

Where SSRS really comes into its own is the ability to create print quality reports.   Dashboards for monitoring and analytics serve a purpose, but businesses will always have a requirement to serve up print-ready reports that tell a specific story – such as monthly profit & loss.

For all such report requirements, SSRS is the tool to use with its SharePoint integration features described earlier, coupled with the powerful scheduling and snapshot features.   Reports can be delivered to an executive's SharePoint workspace for the end of each month and alerts can be configured as a useful notification mechanism.

Watch out for the next release of SQL Server 'Denali' that will further expand the possibilities, especially the new Silverlight report scratchpad also known as 'Project Crescent'.

Pros	Cons
Unique data visualisations such as gauges and maps.	Can be difficult to configure in a SharePoint farm. SQL 'Denali' will improve this by exposing SSRS as a SharePoint Service Application.
Doesn't require a SharePoint Enterprise license.	Do not provide an interactive, self-serve experience although sub-reports can be used to provide some drill down.
Can be exported to a wide variety of formats including PDF, Excel, HTML)	
Supports full printing capability.	
Manage the report authoring, approval and publishing process right in SharePoint using document management capabilities.	
Report Parts and Shared Data Sets allow reports to be built from standard building blocks.	

Summary

It has been a challenge to cover this topic in a single chapter – and I haven't even covered Visio Services that offers the ability to visualise data in ways only limited by the library of shapes on offer!

The wide variety of products can often be confusing for report authors when deciding the best tool for the job. I hope that this chapter has helped summarise each tool and list some of the pros and cons of each gained from my personal experiences. Microsoft have recently released a superb document on TechNet which goes into much more detail on this decision making and is a great resource:
http://download.microsoft.com/download/A/B/2/AB2 7C2C1-EA88-40D5-B183-D4AD6E858E86/Microsoft_BI_Tool_Choices.docx

About the Authors

Paul Beck

Paul Beck is a SharePoint solutions architect who currently focuses on designing solutions for a major global healthcare group as the technical lead in their SharePoint Centre of Excellence (CoE) based in London.

Paul has consulted on multiple SharePoint projects since 2004 guiding many developers, administrations and architects in successful SharePoint projects.

Paul is a frequent blogger and speaker on SharePoint.

Blog   : http://blog.sharepointsite.co.uk
Twitter : @paulbeck1
Email   : paul.beck@sharepointsite.co.uk

Veronique Palmer

Veronique Palmer runs her own company in South Africa called Lets Collaborate. It focuses on issues of SharePoint adoption, governance and end user training. She is one of only five SharePoint business MVP's in the world and has spoken at conferences globally.

Veronique is a team lead at Information Worker, SharePoint Business Workshops, SharePoint Experts on LinkedIn; and runs SharePoint Saturday Johannesburg.

You can find her blogging and tweeting all things business to get people thinking differently.

Blog   : http://veroniquepalmer.wordpress.com
Web   : http://www.letscollaborate.co.za
Twitter : @veroniquepalmer
Email   : Veronique@letscollaborate.co.za

Jasper Oosterveld

Jasper Oosterveld lives in Amsterdam and works for Wortell in Lijnden. Wortell is based in a renovated church where the New World of Work is implemented. Wortell has won multiple Microsoft awards and got chosen partner of the year in 2010.

Jasper has been working with SharePoint since 2008. His main focus is implementing out-of-the-box SharePoint functionalities, InfoPath, SharePoint Designer and Nintex Workflow. Jasper also assists sales managers during sales meetings with prospects and customers. He also enjoys training end-users in their first encounter with the SharePoint world.

Blog   : http://www.jasperoosterveld.com
Web   : http://www.wortell.nl
Twitter : @JasITConsultant
Email   : Jasper.Oosterveld@wortell.nl

Symon Garfield

Symon is a leader, technologist and management consultant.

He helps organisations to define and understand their challenges; to create a vision; and to design and successfully implement innovative solutions which deliver measurable benefits. His focus areas include Microsoft SharePoint, Knowledge Management, and Information Worker Productivity, and Cloud Computing.

Over the past five years Symon has worked with medium and enterprise clients in the UK in a wide variety of sectors including retail; public; financial; media and communications; energy; and professional services.

Blog   : http://www.symongarfield.me.uk
Twitter : @symon_garfield

Giles Hamson

Giles Hamson has been working with collaboration technologies since 2001 and has been implementing SharePoint solutions from 2004; starting with SharePoint Portal Server 2003 whilst working in the Microsoft Dynamics division.

Giles has worked in multiple roles throughout his career working as a business analyst, moving into system analysis and development roles.

After gaining experience across Linux, Solaris and Microsoft disciplines, Giles moved into consultancy within the education market creating learning platform solutions based on SharePoint and integration with 3rd party vendors. After several successful implementations Giles moved into consultancy in SharePoint and Project Server across multiple industry verticals.

Blog   : http://ghamson.wordpress.com
Web   : http://ghamson.sharepoint.com
Twitter : @ghamson
Email   : ghamson@hotmail.co.uk

Suzanne George

Suzanne George, MCTS has developed, administered, and architected online web site applications since 1995 and has worked with many Technology Top 100 companies such as Netscape, AOL, Sun Microsystems, and Verio.

With a focus on custom applications and SharePoint integration with applications such as ESRI, Deltek Accounting Software, and SAP; she has often been asked to speak at conferences around the country.

Currently, Suzanne sits on the MSL IT Manager Advisory Council, was a contributing author for SharePoint 2010 Administrators companion, and is a Senior Technical Architect for Perficient (formerly SpeakTech).

Twitter   : @spgenie
Email   : suz_george@hotmail.com

Rene Modery

Rene Modery is living and working in Singapore, and is currently doing his second Asia Pacific wide SharePoint implementation.

Over the past 4 years, he has been involved in and responsible for a whole range of projects and activities in multiple countries, such as developing solutions and workflows, providing support and guidance for IT and users alike, training end users, and planning and supporting the upgrade to SharePoint 2010.

Blog   : http://www.modery.net
Twitter   : @modery
Email   : rene@modery.net

Conrad Grobler

Conrad Grobler is a technical consultant, developer and architect working in the UK.

Conrad has more than 15 years experience working with Microsoft technologies and has focussed almost exclusively on SharePoint and related technologies for the last 5 years.

Ashraf Islam

Ashraf Islam is an independent SharePoint consultant based in London, United Kingdom. During the last eight years he has been heavily involved in a number of large scale SharePoint implementations using various Microsoft tools and technologies for world leading organizations. His main area of interests is System Architecture and Development.

Ashraf is an active contributor to various community projects, user groups and MSDN SharePoint forums.

Blog   : http://auislam.wordpress.com/
Twitter   : @AshrafSP
Email   : ashraf.islam@gmail.com

John Stover

John Stover is the CEO and Principal Consultant at Invenio.

He has been working with SharePoint for more than a decade and helps organizations leverage SharePoint as a business productivity platform. John uses his expertise and experience to help organizations use SharePoint for WCM, e-commerce, social networking, content and infrastructure governance, BI, information architecture, search and project management.

John is an active participant in the SharePoint community and has presented at more than a dozen SharePoint Saturday events and dozens of SharePoint conferences, user groups, and webinars, including SPTechCon, SharePoint Best Practices Conference, DCSUG Conference, and a keynote at SharePointConference.org.

Blog   : http://stovereffect.com
Web   : http://www.invenio-partners.com
Twitter : @StoverEffect
Email   : StoverEffect@live.com

Justin Meadows

Justin Meadows is a Systems Engineer for Mission Health System in Asheville, North Carolina. Among many other enterprise duties, Justin's team recently rolled out a small SharePoint farm for enterprise-wide use based on a request-fulfillment model.

Focused on collaboration and productivity, Justin previously developed a knowledge and workflow platform using an open source wiki and bug tracking software for an inpatient pharmacy department. As a recent Information Technology graduate and newcomer to SharePoint, Justin brings a fresh perspective to the SharePoint deployment experience and its role in enhancing collaboration and productivity.

Web   : http://justinmeadows.squarespace.com
Email   : justin.meadows@msj.org

Mark Macrae

Mark Macrae has worked with SharePoint Technologies since 2003 and now specialises in Business Intelligence solutions.

He lives in the UK where he co-directs Intelligent Decisioning Ltd - a SharePoint technologies solutions company based in the UK and Australia.

Mark is also heavily involved in the UK SharePoint community where he co-organises and speaks at SharePoint User Group UK and SharePoint Saturday UK events.

Blog   : http://macraem.wordpress.com
Web   : http://www.id-live.com
Twitter : @m_macrae
Email   : mark@id-live.com

John Timney

John is a thirteen year Microsoft "Most Valued Professional" award holder and a former MSDN "Regional Director".

A co-author of "Professional Microsoft .NET Windows Forms", "Professional .NET for Java Developers Using C#", "Professional JSP" and "Beginning JSP Web Development".

A prolific speaker on SharePoint and an Administrator of the SharePoint UK User Group, John has over 20 years of hard-core IT experience. Past roles include Assurance and Strategy Lead for the "2010 e-Government excellence" award winning flagship UK Government Information Workplace SharePoint programme at the Department for Education.

His current role is Enterprise Assurance and Strategy Lead Architect for E-CLOUD.

Blog   : http://www.johntimney.com
Twitter : @jtimney
Email   : john_timney@yahoo.com

Indexed Table of Contents

448 Indexed Table of Contents

www.ingramcontent.com/pod-product-compliance
Lightning Source LLC
Chambersburg PA
CBHW071543080326
40689CB00061B/1667